Calgary, Alta.
252-4990

INTRODUCTION TO MANAGEMENT INFORMATION SYSTEMS

ROBERT G. MURDICK

Florida Atlantic University

JOEL E. ROSS

Florida Atlantic University

Prentice-Hall, Inc., Englewood Cliffs, New Jersey   07632

Library of Congress Cataloging in Publication Data

MURDICK, ROBERT G
    Introduction to management information systems.

    Bibliography: p.
    Includes index.
    1. Management information systems. I. Ross, Joel E.,
joint author. II. Title.
T58.6.M87   658.4'5   76–28399
ISBN 0–13–486233–3

Printed in the United States of America

10 9 8 7 6 5 4 3 2 1

Prentice-Hall International, Inc., London
Prentice-Hall of Australia Pty. Limited, Sydney
Prentice-Hall of Canada, Ltd., Toronto
Prentice-Hall of India Private Limited, New Delhi
Prentice-Hall of Japan, Inc., Tokyo
Prentice-Hall of Southeast Asia Pte. Ltd., Singapore
Whitehall Books Limited, Wellington, New Zealand

Contents

iii

Preface

It is now generally recognized that future significant gains in productivity in business will have to come from new ways of managing people. The electronic computer and new organizational forms will play important roles in the new managerial styles. The most apparent change that will be observed, however, will be the new managers trained to "think systems."

Management systems will become the foundations for coordinated group effort. Individual contributors and new managers will share increased responsibilities based upon their technical competences. For individuals, increased information means greater control over their jobs. For managers, competency in conceptualization of systems and strategies will replace political skills as the basis for holding a position.

The development of management information systems has continued and spread inexorably despite a flood of articles denying the present existence or future possibility of the MIS. The purpose of this text is (a) to relate the systems approach and information systems to the functions of managing, and (b) to demonstrate the process of designing an MIS. It is intended as a text in a first course in managing with MIS. Therefore, it is suitable for a general management program, computer science majors, accounting majors, or public administration majors. As an introductory text, it is a practical approach. A subsequent course would provide more theory and more case studies.

The authors wish to express their appreciation to the many companies that supplied exhibits and assistance to make this book more relevant. Mr. Paul M. Peterson, Vice-president of Administration, STP, Inc.; Mr. Paul A. Strassman, Xerox Corp.; Mr. James Roberts, Assistant Manager of MIS, Motorola, Inc.; and Dr. Robert E. Markland, U. of Missouri provided us with special assistance.

We are especially grateful for the complete reviews of the manuscript and many helpful suggestions provided by Karla L. Bassler, Specialist—Financial Training, General Electric Co.; Dr. D. R. Deutsch, National Bureau of Standards, and Professor Charles R. Necco, California State University, Sacramento.

Emily Murdick provided valuable editorial and secretarial assistance throughout.

Finally, we thank Ms. Judith L. Rothman for her careful management and editing of the manuscript from its inception.

R. G. Murdick

J. E. Ross

chapter one

The Meaning and Role of MIS

CHAPTER 1 explains basic terms for a management information system (MIS), shows simple examples, and outlines the general process of developing an MIS.

When you have finished studying

THE MEANING AND ROLE OF MIS

you should be able to

1. Explain the meaning of a *system* in your own words
2. Explain what is meant by an *operating system* within a company
3. Explain in your own words the meaning of *management information system*
4. List the principal steps in MIS development
5. Tell how the MIS organization fits within the company.

The manager of the 1980s will require more prompt and selective information than ever before to deal with complexity and change. Supplying such information is what the management information system is all about.

THE AGE OF SYSTEMS

INTERRELATEDNESS
OF COMPONENTS
OF SOCIETY

The Industrial Revolution, starting in the 1700s, brought about the mechanization of production in large-scale factories. Large business organizations arose. People, business, government, and national resources all became interdependent. Automation of information processing has paralleled automation of manufacturing. This present late 20th century period might well be called the Age of Systems.

We are concerned with systems that we can control for the good of humankind such as

National transportation system
National water system
World ecological system
National political system
World and national health systems
Organization systems (including business organizations)

WHAT IS A
SYSTEM?

A system is essentially a group of things that are interrelated to accomplish some purpose. The fact that businesses, in particular, have become so complex has required us to operate them as systems, not just by segments such as selling, accounting, manufacturing, etc. This book is directed toward the development of *management information systems* (MIS), which make it possible to manage all types of complex systems

2

such as businesses, government agencies, or service organizations such as hospitals.

WHAT IS
INFORMATION?

Since business systems are based on information flow, information must be defined at this point. If we consider reports that are stored in files, or technical symbols and reports that are meaningless to the reader, or reports whose contents have not been organized in a meaningful way, we are dealing with *data. Information* is differentiated from data because it is tables, text symbols, or inputs that are meaningful, is being used by a person, and *is affecting the behavior* of the user.

THE MANAGER OF TOMORROW

SAME RESOURCES

The business manager of tomorrow will be working with the same basic resources as the manager of today—people, money, materials, machines.

NEW
TECHNOLOGY

Changes in physical systems such as the factory production system, the physical distribution system, the data processing system, or the engineering development and test system are occurring rapidly with the accelerating progress in technology. The manager of tomorrow will live and work in a push-button world of color video surrounded by automatically controlled physical operations. He will be able to pick up the phone at home and ask questions of a distant computer.

GREATEST CHANGE
—THE SYSTEMS VIEW

The really great change in managing, however, will be the change in the way we look at all organization and physical operations. This change will be in the development of system concepts. That is, all aspects of the total business, including people, their activities, the physical parts of the business, suppliers, customers, government, and the public will be integrated by management far beyond today's primitive level.

Why will such great changes in the conceptual framework of busi-

---

Time was when the data processing manager ran a computer department which sometimes amounted to an extension of the accounting department. Payroll checks, financial statements and general ledger work were the order of the day.

But times have changed. Businessmen no longer look at the computer as a super-adding machine, spewing out just basic financial data. They look to it as an information tool for the entire company, providing tighter control over their assets.

Ted Garvey of IBM explains: "We stress the need for management involvement in the creation of an information system plan, which is also an integral part of the business plan."

Source: "The Changing Role of the DP Manager," International Business Machines Corp.

---

ness occur? How will managers be able to handle the increasing complexity of business? Why will the manager be able to make better decisions that will lead to better total business system results? The answer is that the information utilized by the manager will be of far better quality, more timely, more selective, and more available. The "better quality" means that the information will be more nearly complete, more reliable, and processed to be available in many arrangements. The manager will be able to think rapidly through many approaches and solutions to complex problems because of such information. Providing this information will be a system of scanning the environment, an internal data bank and model bank, and computers beyond the imagination of old-time managers.

A FURTHER EXPLANATION OF *SYSTEM*

MORE ABOUT
WHAT A
SYSTEM IS

Very simply, a system is a set of elements, such as people and things, that are related to achieve mutual goals. Systems that we deal with have inputs from the environment and send outputs into the environment. The system itself is a *processor* that changes inputs into outputs. Figure 1-1 summarizes this. What we cannot show in Figure 1-1 without making it unreadable is the network of communications among system elements, i.e., the information systems.

We may now show the essentials of the system for a number of managed institutions to make the meaning of *system* clearer. We have tabulated these essentials in Figure 1-2. In the case of a business firm, remember that goals vary from producing or selling products to generating consulting reports to training people for careers. We have given the example of a manufacturing firm in Figure 1-2.

Figure 1-1   The system as a processor.

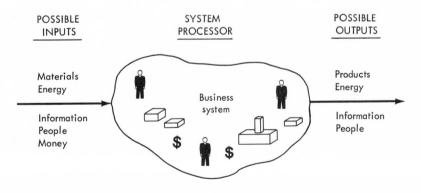

(Elements: People, machines, buildings, money)

System	Basic Goals	Elements	Inputs	Outputs
1. Department store	Provide the right goods at the right time	People, buildings, machines, money	Purchased goods, money, energy, information	Goods, services, information
2. Bank	Store money for customers, provide loans, trust services, checking services, and credit	People, buildings, machines, money	Money, information, energy	Money, services, information
3. Management consulting firm	Provide advice to customers	People, buildings, machines	Information, money, energy	Reports, services
4. University	Generate and disseminate information, develop leaders, provide community services	People, buildings, machines	People, money, information, energy	People, information, services
5. Electric utility	Provide energy in the form of electricity	People, buildings, machines	Energy, information	Energy in the form of electricity
6. Hospital	Provide health care, conduct research, teach doctors and nurses	People, buildings, machines	People, materials, energy, money, information	People, bodies, reports, services

Figure 1-2 Some systems and their basic characteristics.

OPERATING INFORMATION SYSTEMS

INFORMATION FOR OPERATIONS

For a system to accomplish its goals, there must be communication among its elements. In business, the communication systems that are developed to make the basic operations of the company possible are called *operating* information systems.

For example, in a manufacturing system, there must be an information system for planning and control of day-to-day production. In the order processing system, forms, communication channels, and procedures must be set up to accept orders for products that the company sells.

In Figure 1-3, we have shown a very simplified version of an order processing operation. We have described the system as a set of operations performed by people and the information system that relates to the operation. Let's see how this works:

Operation	*Input Flow of Information*	*Output Flow of Information*
1. Collect orders from all salesmen and put on standard forms	Order forms, telegrams, phone calls giving customer's orders	Customers' orders on standard form
2. Extend and calculate orders after checking discounts and availability of products	Discounts allowed per units available per inventory master file customers' orders	Prices, discounts, net prices, and units available and to be shipped for each order
3. Prepare and mail invoices	Prices, discounts, net prices, and units to be shipped to each customer shown on a standard form	Invoice to customer on a standard form to bill him for his order

Figure 1-3 Order processing and information flow.

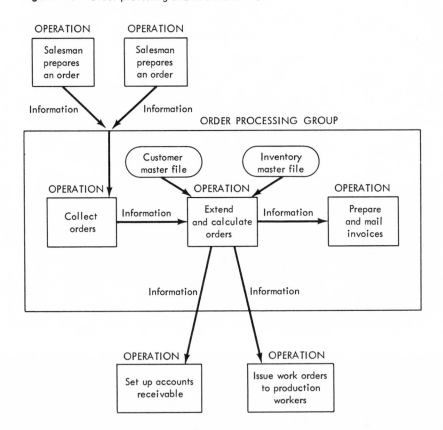

In Figure 1-3, we have shown a flow of information *into* the system (orders from salesmen) and a flow of information *out* of the system (billings for accounts receivable and items ordered and to be shipped). We can draw a box around the system to separate the system from operations outside the order processing system.

In summary, we have shown a set of related operations and the operating information system. In the next few paragraphs, we shall show how the *management* information system differs from the operating information system.

In Figure 1-4, we present a simple inspection control system for items purchased. The operations and information flows are listed.

THE MANAGEMENT INFORMATION SYSTEM (MIS)

MANAGERS PLAN, CONTROL, MAKE DECISIONS FOR THE LONG TERM

Managers have always had the responsibility for solving the larger and the unusual problems of the company. Managers are concerned with planning, controlling, and decision making on a broader scale than people engaged in elemental activities of the company. For example, plan-

Figure 1-4 Purchase inspection information system.

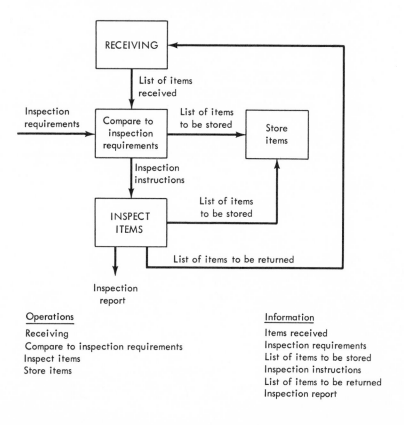

Operations	Information
Receiving	Items received
Compare to inspection requirements	Inspection requirements
Inspect items	List of items to be stored
Store items	Inspection instructions
	List of items to be returned
	Inspection report

ning for production resources for one year up to five years ahead is vastly different from planning the arrangement of materials and the operation of a lathe for the next four hours.

In the past, managers sought information from miscellaneous—haphazard—sources and processed the information on a personal basis. Too often they failed to ask for information concerning the impact of a decision in one area on other areas of the company.

Three changes are now occurring in progressive companies:

MIS: Managers
Need
Information
About the
Business System

1. *Management* has become system-oriented and more sophisticated in management techniques.
2. *Information* is planned for and made available to managers as needed.
3. A *system* of information ties planning and control by managers to operational systems of implementation.

The combined result of these concepts is the management information system (MIS). The purpose of an MIS is to raise the process of managing from the level of piecemeal spotty information, intuitive guesswork, and isolated problem solving to the level of systems insights, systems information, sophisticated data processing, and systems problem solving. Managers have always had "sources" of information; the MIS provides a *system* of information. It thus is a powerful method for aiding managers in solving problems and making decisions. In Figure 1-5 we have presented *the basic meaning of an MIS.*

As shown in Figure 1-5, the MIS has the purpose of assisting *managers* to make decisions. While all workers make decisions, managers' decisions are concerned with planning for, directing, and controlling work groups. They make decisions on longer-term and broader-scale issues than

Figure 1-5   The basic meaning of an MIS.

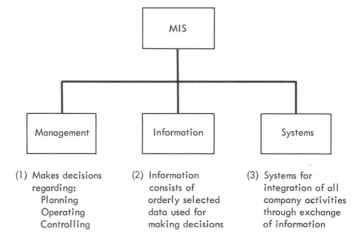

(1) Makes decisions regarding:
Planning
Operating
Controlling

(2) Information consists of orderly selected data used for making decisions

(3) Systems for integration of all company activities through exchange of information

the individual machine operator, clerk, technician, professional, or staff consultant.

The Three Components of MIS

Second, the MIS has the purpose of providing *selected* data, i.e., information, to managers at a time when they are useful in aiding the managers to make decisions. In fact, parts of the MIS may be designed to *provide* decisions for repetitive classes of problems.

Third, the MIS provides information to all managers so that all company activities may be tied together to operate the company as a *system*.

MIS: Managerial Part of the Total Business Information

How is the MIS related to operating information systems? The operating information systems are concerned with the transactions necessary to conduct the daily affairs of the business. The MIS is connected to the operating information system but does not monitor every transaction or detail. Rather, the MIS is *for managers*. It passes on summary (consolidated) information, selective reports for planning and control of operations, and exceptional circumstance reports for planning, controlling, and decision making appropriate to each level of management (Figure 1-6).

MIS: Selective Information for Managers

EXAMPLE OF AN MIS

The Ralston Purina Company produces pet foods and foods for people. The entire marketing, planning, and budgeting process at the Consumer Products Group of Ralston Purina takes place each year in the spring and summer. This group developed an MIS that processes raw *data* into reports containing meaningful *information*. With this information provided, managers at the division level and group level find out how different promotional budgets and product recipes will affect profits and cash flow.

Decision Information Flow at Ralston Purina

Inputs to the MIS consist of data on proposed new products and sales, which go into the brand accrual models shown in Figure 1-7.

The output of the brand accrual models consists of the monthly sales volume for each product and brand for the year ahead. Also costs and dollar sales are computed by the mathematical formulas of the model when it is stored in the computer. Next the computer consolidates the data for each brand into a projected earnings statement for product managers to evaluate.

The data on all the brands in a single division are combined, and selected information is prepared in the form of reports for the division manager.

Data Are Combined into Summary Information

Finally, the assumptions and consequences developed by all the division managers are brought together for the Consumer Products Group manager.

Even at this stage of our book, it is evident that managers may be greatly aided by a *system* of *information* that relates marketing, produc-

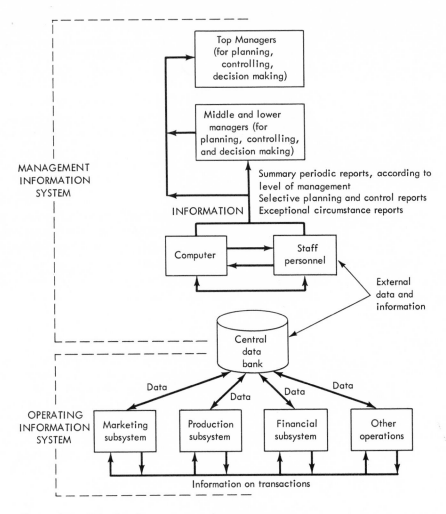

Figure 1-6 MIS related to operating information systems.

tion, and manufacturing information data by means of mathematical formulas (models), computer computations, and computer-developed reports. Such an MIS provides relevant information on alternative plans and permits managers to ask the question, "What will happen if I do this . . . or that?"

THE PROCESS OF MIS DEVELOPMENT

BASIC STEPS IN DEVELOPING THE MIS

This book consists of two major parts. One part is devoted to explaining the ideas related to an MIS. The other part is devoted to instructing you how to develop and implement an MIS. The basic steps in developing an MIS, as seen from the manager's viewpoint, are shown in the table on page 11.

Step	*Example*
1. Find out the *information needs* of all managers.	The marketing manager says that some of his needs are for monthly information about his company's sales and competitors' sales.
2. Write down the *objectives* of the MIS and anticipated benefits.	Financial reports for each month will be on the desks of each manager within 5 days after the end of the month.
3. Prepare a *plan* for the design of the MIS, including schedule and estimated costs.	The date for completion of the preliminary design is June 24, 1977. The estimated cost is $22,300.
4. Prepare a rough or *gross design* for the MIS that appears to be practical and that will likely achieve the objectives established.	A flow chart showing general information flowing to each manager and source of information.
5. Prepare the *detailed design*. This requires a refining and expansion of the gross design. Detailed description of management reports and detailed description of the flow of information are required. A data bank or list of all data to be kept in files must be prepared. A procedures manual must be prepared to tell how the MIS works and what people must do. The computer center must also be designed and *software* or programs made available.	One isolated item would be to say that the marketing manager receives a summary report on all competitors once a month. One file in the data bank would be a list of all competitors and their market share, up-dated monthly. (Obviously, the detailed design of an MIS is very lengthy to document.)
6. Put the new MIS into operation. Prior testing may be desirable to see that all parts work together. Imagine the problems that could arise in a company if the old system were abandoned and a computer program in the new system did not work.	Replace a small part of the old system with the new system and check out the new system.
7. Monitor and maintain the new system. That is, needed changes in procedures or the structure of the data files must be made from time to time. The MIS must be changed to meet changing inputs and changing managment needs.	A company changes its inventory accounting from FIFO to LIFO. This requires a change in procedure, computer program, and management reports.

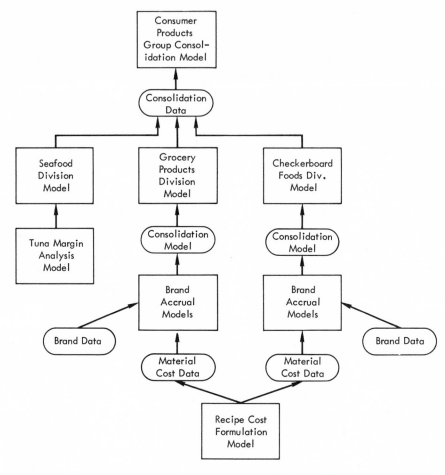

Figure 1-7 Consumer products on-line decision system for the Ralston Purina Company. Courtesy of the Ralston Purina Company.

MIS ORGANIZATION WITHIN THE COMPANY

TO WHOM SHOULD THE HEAD OF THE MIS DESIGN GROUP REPORT?

The design of the MIS and the measurement and redesign of the MIS should be made the responsibility of an MIS organization. The question is, "Where should this MIS organization be located within the company?" Further, how should the MIS group itself be organized?

The MIS Organization Within the Company

Two Good Places for the MIS Group and One Poor Place

In both large and small companies, the person with the general responsibility for the MIS within the company generally reports to the president or top management. For example, Northwest Industries, Inc. has a small staff organization that oversees the information and data processing in the operating companies that make up Northwest Industries. The head of this staff, Mr. Jay P. Thomas, Vice President—Management Information Services, is assisted by the Director of Systems Development and the Director of EDP Facilities Management [Figure 1-8(a)]. This provides the MIS function with good access to top management.

Another alternative is to have a vice president (VP) of the MIS on

Figure 1-8 Placement of the MIS function within the company.

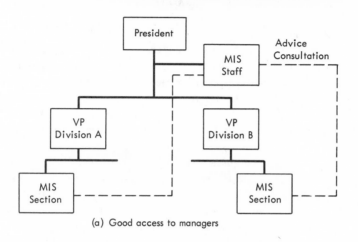

(a) Good access to managers

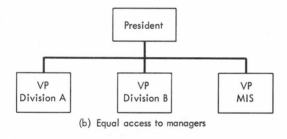

(b) Equal access to managers

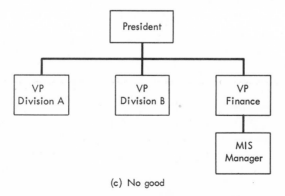

(c) No good

the same level as other VPs reporting to the president [Figure 1-8(b)].

A third situation found in some businesses is to have the MIS group or EDP (electronic data processing) group reporting to the VP—Finance. In such a situation, the group is apt to do data processing with emphasis on financial *data* and not companywide *information for managers* [Figure 1-8(c)].

Organization Within the MIS Function

Organizing the Specialists Within the MIS Activity

For a major first-time MIS effort, a company steering committee consisting of the MIS manager, the sales manager, the production manager, the finance manager, and the engineering manager may guide the systems effort. A special project team composed of representatives from each of the functional areas plus the technical systems people would carry out the design effort with heavy managerial involvement. Once the first MIS has been installed, there must be an organization that monitors it, keeps it running smoothly, and redesigns it from time to time.

The permanent MIS organization usually includes systems analysts (designers), computer and data communications specialists, and, sometimes, management scientists. The last develop mathematical relationships for processing raw data into useful information such as sales forecasts, inventory reorder levels, and capital expenditure evaluations.

Two examples of the MIS organization in actual companies, Kraftco and Xerox, are shown in Figures 1-9 and 1-10. Note that in Kraftco, systems development and data processing are at the same level of the organization but brought together under the Director—Systems Services.

Skills of the MIS Manager

MIS Manager— Generalist or Technician?

What are the most important skills for the MIS manager to possess? Surprisingly to some, general business skills are more important than knowledge of technical aspects. Figure 1-11 shows how both general management executives and MIS managers rank the skills required.

SUMMARY

In this chapter we have presented an overall view of the meaning of management information systems. We did this by defining terms and giving simplified diagrams, an outline of the process of MIS design, and MIS organizational relationships. We have assumed that the reader has

Figure 1-9 MIS organization at Kraftco Corporation. Courtesy of Kraftco Corporation.

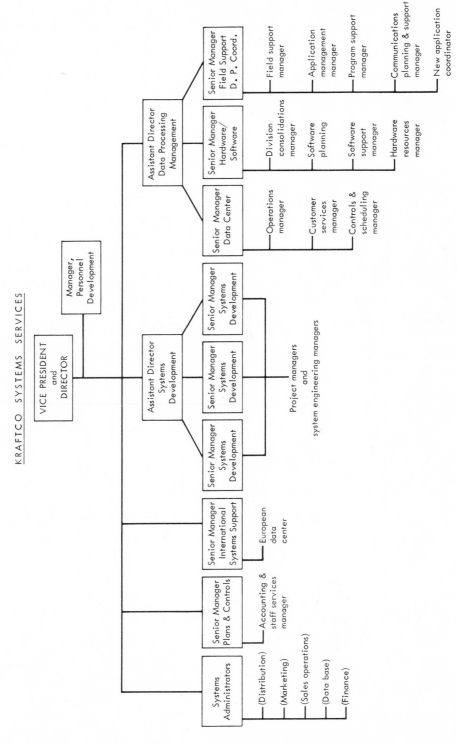

KRAFTCO SYSTEMS SERVICES

Figure 1-10   Placement of MIS organization in Xerox Corporation. Courtesy of Xerox Corporation.

an overall understanding of business such as may be obtained from a basic accounting course, a basic production course, a basic marketing course, and a principles of management course or comparable business experience. This is because the MIS cuts across all areas of business and is directed toward integrating them.

Figure 1-11 Skills of the MIS manager.

Skill	*Ranked by MIS Executives*	*Ranked by General Management Executives*
Knowledge of total company and its objectives	2	1
Ability to communicate effectively, orally and in writing	6	2
Relationships with heads of other business departments that utilize the system's functions	1	3
Ability to manage projects	4	4
Relationships with top management	3	5
Relationships with subordinates	5	6
Knowledge of information processing and data communications technology	8	7
Ability to design and judge the design of systems	6	8

Reprinted with special permission from *Infosystems*, Jan. 1973 issue, copyright 1973 by Hitchcock Publishing Co., Wheaton, Ill. 60187, all rights reserved.

QUESTIONS AND PROBLEMS

1. To define a particular system, we must identify, define, or describe the items in the left-hand column below. Define the meaning of an MIS by completing the right-hand column, except item (4).

     System Definitions
     Define or Identify

   (1) Objectives   (1)
   (2) Elements   (2)
   (3) Processes performed   (3)
   (4) Structure or interrelationships of elements   (4) (Varies for every MIS)
   (5) Inputs   (5)
   (6) Outputs   (6)

2. Set up a table with headings across the top as shown in Figure 1-2. Complete the table for the following systems:

   a. A manufacturing company

   b. marketing system within a manufacturing company

   c. The order processing system of Figure 1-3

   d. The purchase inspection system of Figure 1-4

3. By placing the appropriate letters opposite the numbers below, indicate the sequence of the basic MIS development steps:

a. Write the objectives   1. ___a___

b. Prepare a detailed design   2. ___5___

c. Find information needs of managers   3. ___1___

d. Monitor and maintain the new system   4. ___7___

e. Implement the new MIS   5. ___6___

f. Prepare the gross design   6. ___4___

g. Prepare a plan for the MIS development   7. ___3___

4. Draw a portion of a company's total organization that relates the following positions in a way that you think is appropropriate:

a. President

b. Vice President of Services

c. Manager—Corporate Accounting

d. Manager—Data Processing

e. Manager—Management Information Systems

chapter two

Management, Information, and the Systems Approach (Part 1)

CHAPTER 2   and the next chapter explain how the management functions of planning, organizing, and controlling are carried out by means of information flow and the systems approach.

When you have finished studying

MANAGEMENT, INFORMATION, AND THE SYSTEMS APPROACH (Part 1)

you should be able to

1. Describe in your own words the meaning of the systems view of managing
2. Explain the meaning of management systems and give an example
3. Explain the steps in the systems approach
4. Describe the meaning, need, and dimensions of plans
5. Given the list of planning steps, relate them to an actual company as an example
6. Describe information needs for long- and short-range planning.

A managed organization consists of two systems:
1. A structured behavioral system of individuals.
2. An information processing system for problem solving and decision making.

Managed organizations come in many styles today. Not just businesses, but hospitals, government agencies, community services, consumer movement groups (such as Common Cause), and philanthropic foundations are familiar to most of us. The widespread recognition that all organizations require professional management makes the subject of management so important.

INFORMATION SYSTEMS SUPPORT THE EFFORTS OF PEOPLE IN THE ORGANIZATION

The basic job of managers is to create a system that will be most effective for achieving the purposes of the business, agency, or institution. Since businesses are run by people, this means that managers must create an environment that will both *motivate* people to do their best and *facilitate* their doing their best. The second idea means simply that managers must design the business system to support the efforts of the people in it.

SYSTEMS VIEW OF MANAGING

At the operational level in a business, people carry out technical and functional activities such as operating machines, cleaning offices, selling, designing products, accounting for transactions, training employees, etc. In essence, they are implementing plans and procedures.

MANAGERS PERFORM SPECIAL ACTIVITIES

The work of the manager consists not of technical or functional activities but rather of acting upon company resources by

Setting objectives
Planning
Organizing human and physical resources

20

Initiating action to be taken by other people

Controlling the processes of the business system

Communicating and providing communications channels throughout the organization

Decision making and Communications Are Managerial Activities that Integrate All Parts of the Organizational System

These activities are called the *processes* of managing. One very general activity required to carry out these processes is *decision making*. Decision making is so important that some people believe that it is the only managerial function. They believe that operational people and staff specialists *propose* while managers *dispose*. We feel that decision making is central to all the specific processes that we have listed above but that it is only a part of each process. Like the communications process, decision making is an integrating activity that keeps the parts of the business functioning as a *system*. That is, when all parts of the system (company) are working cooperatively to obtain the best results for the system as a whole, we say that the parts are integrated.

Interaction of Managerial Functions

In Figure 2-1, you can see the systems view of the managerial process. Each process interacts with every other process. Thus when we plan, we plan objectives, we plan the organization of resources, we plan the means and timing of initiating action on plans, we plan our control methods, and we plan our communication process.

Follow each input in the first column of Figure 2-1 across to see how it is related to each of the other managerial processes.

THE MANAGEMENT SYSTEM

A MANAGEMENT SYSTEM IS A DESIGN FOR ACTION

Many organizations and managers make the basic mistake of believing that a management *information* system can be designed or made operational without the backup of an adequate *management* system. An adequate management system includes organizational arrangements, structure and procedures for adequate planning and control, clear establishment of objectives, and all the other manifestations of good organization and management. Given this management structure, this framework of good management practices, an information system can be designed upon its foundation. Only then can the information system provide the manager with the information he needs in the form, place, and time that he needs it in order to perform his job according to the specifications of the *management* system.

The purpose of the management system is to develop plans for achieving objectives, to organize for implementing plans, and to control performance so that plans and actions occur on schedule. The place of information in performing these three basic processes is shown in Figure 2-2. The first step, recognition of a problem or an opportunity, is usually

Figure 2-1 The systems view of the managerial process. © R.G. Murdick 1974.

	SET OBJECTIVES	PLAN	ORGANIZE RESOURCES	INITIATE	CONTROL	COMMUNICATE
SET OBJECTIVES	D	Set objectives for the company	Match objectives to available resources	Develop objectives at the level of management	Develop key objectives for control	Set objectives for communication at each level of the organization
PLAN	Plan around basic objectives	E	Plan the company organization and allocation of resources	Plan the sequence and schedule of the organization of resources	Plan for standards and procedures for control	Plan procedures for communications throughout the organization
ORGANIZE RESOURCES	Organize the hierarchy of objectives	Organize for planning	C	Organize the system for action	Organize a control system	Organize resources to provide for communication
INITIATE	Take action to establish objectives	Initiate the planning process	Start the organization of human and other resources for conduct of the business	I	Start the control of objectives, plans, action, standards, and communication	Keep communications flowing freely at all stages and for all processes
CONTROL	Control the setting of objectives to suit the nature of the organization	Control the setting of plans to ensure plans are properly prepared on time	Control the mix of resources to achieve a balance	Control the process of directing action	D	Control the communication of standards. Control the communication performance for corrective action
COMMUNICATE	Communicate objectives to attain a unified sense of direction	Communicate plans in the proper detail to each person in the company	Communicate through organization charts, manuals, and reports: the distribution of resources	Communicate to initiate action at the proper time	Communicate standards of performance. Communicate performance to responsible individuals for corrective action	E

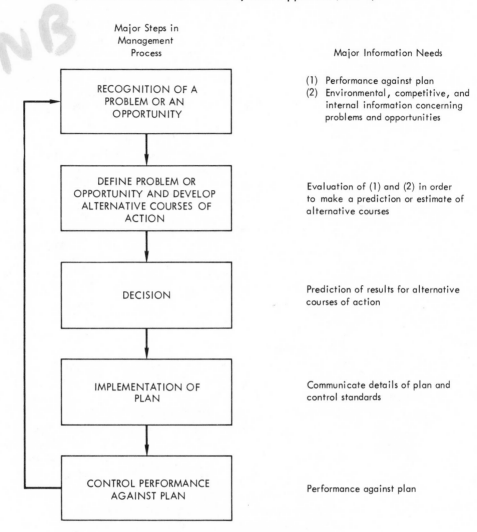

Figure 2-2   The management process and information needs.

prompted by information from the control process concerning a deviation from standard or by search and evaluation of those systems (environmental, competitive, internal) affecting the planning process. Definition of the problem, determination and evaluation of alternative courses of action, and selection of a course of action are fundamentally steps in the planning and decision-making process. Information needs for this process are those indicated in Figure 2-2. Finally, once a decision is made or a plan developed, it is necessary to *implement* and *control* the solution. Implementation becomes a matter of organizing the necessary resources and directing them in the performance and correction of deviations. The process starts

---

**"They Don't Laugh When I Sit Down
at the Terminal"**

Anyone who doubts that vice presidents can be persuaded to use terminal-based computer "infosystems" to solve their problems should take a look at what American Airlines has done. They've also proved that management infosystems capable of producing "bottom-line" profits can be developed on time and within budget.

American Airlines (the same people whose technical competence and flair for the unusual brought you SABRE, the first successful on-line reservation system, and the in-flight piano bar) has developed an infosystem to be admired. It's called AAIMS, An Analytical Information Management System.

AAIMS can be used for information retrieval, but its primary use is as an analytical tool that easily and rapidly generates reports and/or plots. The AAIMS user need not know anything about programming. He converses with the time-sharing computer using English language commands to describe what is to be accomplished.

Source: "AAIMS: American Airlines Answers the What Ifs," *Infosystems*, Feb. 1973, p. 40

---

over again either by a recognition of the need for planning or by the appearance of a new problem arising from the control process.

THREE MAJOR MANAGERIAL PROCESSES IN THE SYSTEMS APPROACH

In the rest of this chapter, we shall study three aspects of the major managerial processes: planning, organizing, and controlling. First, a definition and description of the process will be given so that you will understand how the process is performed. Second, we shall show how the *systems approach* to the managerial process differs from the traditional approach. Finally, because *managing* requires its own special information system, we shall set the stage for an MIS. We do this by describing how planning, organizing, and controlling are made possible by obtaining, processing, communicating, and presenting selected *information*.

Since the systems approach needs to be explained, let us first say a few words about this. See Figure 2-3.

SYSTEMS APPROACH

SYSTEMS APPROACH TO DESIGN AND PROBLEM SOLVING

The *systems approach* consists both of a way we look at a group of operations such as the total business and a method for designing, evaluating, or studying a system.

The systems view is that a system is a processor. It has objectives. It is made up of components or subsystems. Objectives of components or subsystems must be modified so that the *total* system works best.

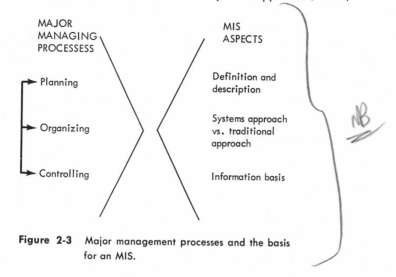

Figure 2-3   Major management processes and the basis for an MIS.

The systems approach to designing, evaluating, or studying a set of operations consists of

1. Identification of needs of users of the system.
2. Identification of overall objectives, i.e., objectives of the *whole*, not just the parts of the system.
3. Specification of major interaction among components.
4. Evaluation of available resources for the system.
5. Evaluation of alternative designs of the system.
6. Continuous information feedback about operation of the system for control.

If we were to try to summarize all this in two simple sentences, we would say that the systems approach

1. Concentrates on the process as a whole rather than on the parts.
2. Relates the parts to each other to achieve the total system goals.

Now we are in a position to relate the systems approach to the three major managerial processes.

PLANNING

The first and most basic management function is planning. All managers at all levels plan, and the successful performance of the other management functions depends on this activity. Planning is deciding in advance what has to be done, who has to do it, when it has to be done, and how it is to be done. It bridges the gap from where we are to where we want to go. Managers plan for the allocation of resources and the work of other people, in contrast to the nonmanager, who plans only his own activities.

NEED FOR PLANNING

The past decade has witnessed a tremendous upsurge in formal planning by all types of organizations, both government and industrial. Various causes have been advanced to explain this phenomenon. Steiner attributes the growth in planning to six basic factors:

1. A changing philosophy, which insists that an organization can initiate trends and set its own course rather than sail on the tide of market conditions and business changes.
2. The rapid rate of technological change.
3. Increased complexity of management, owing to the growth in size and diversity of business.
4. Growing competition, resulting partly from product obsolescence and growth of new industries.
5. The increasingly complex environment of business.
6. The lengthening span of time for which commitments must be made and the resultant need to forecast for longer periods of time in making today's decisions.[1]

Dimensions of Plans

PLANS INTEGRATE THE BUSINESS ACTIVITIES

Plans occur throughout the company. They must be consistent, related to each other, and directed toward the objectives of the company as a whole (systems approach). Table 2-1 shows the classification of plans by key characteristic.

Percent of Surveyed Corporations Preparing Annual Corporate Plan 1965 Versus 1973

Revenue ($)	Number of Corporations	1965	1973
10–50 million	7	14%	71%
50–150 million	7	0	71
150–350 million	6	33	83
350–1 billion	7	29	100
1–20 billion	7	57	100

Source: William E. Lucado, "Corporate Planning—A Current Status Report," *Managerial Planning*, Nov./Dec. 1974, p. 27.

[1]George Steiner, *Top Management Planning*, Toronto: Collier-Macmillan Canada, Ltd., 1969, pp. 14–16.

Table 2-1 Characteristics of plans.

Characteristic	Illustration		
Time	Long range (5–25 years)	Medium range (2–4 years)	Short range (1 week—1 year)
Level	Corporate	Divisional	Operational
Function	General management	Research and development	Advertising
Purpose	Strategy	Project or program	Task
Scope	Companywide	Division or product line	Quality control department

Table 2-1 shows how plans are integrated by characteristics. If we read across for time, we recognize that long-range plans shape or constrain intermediate plans and that intermediate plans shape short-range plans. A similar nesting or hierarchical arrangement exists for each of the other characteristics.

Integration Occurs for Each Characteristic

If we read down a column, we find that characteristics for a single column provide an integrated description of a particular type of plan. The type of planning illustrated in the first column is so important from an integrating systems view that we shall next focus on this type.

The Strategic Planning Process

The strategic planning process consists of two steps: (1) developing the *strategy* and (2) formulating the steps, timing, and costs required to achieve the strategy. The expression of these steps, timing, and costs is called the strategic plan (or, often, the long-range plan).

STRATEGY— THE FUTURE "SHAPE" OF THE FIRM

Strategy is the desired configuration of the firm *at a future specified date*. This configuration, identity, or posture of the firm may be described in terms of

1. Scope: products, customers, markets, price/quality relationships of products, and product characteristics.
2. Competitive edge: special market position or supply position, unique product advantages, special financial strength or credit lines, unique management or technical talents, or capacity for rapid response to competitive moves.
3. Specifications of targets: quantitative statements of acceptable and desired goals such as size of the company, market share, profitability, return on investment, assets, and trade-off between risk and reward.
4. Assignment of resources: allocation of long-term capital, investment

and disinvestment, emphasis on particular activities such as marketing, engineering, production, management development, geographic regions, market segments, etc.[2]

The strategic planning process consists of the following steps, shown schematically in Figure 2-4:

EIGHT STEPS TO DEVELOPING A STRATEGY

1. *Analyze the environment*.[3] Identify those existing and future conditions in the environment that have an influence on the company. The objectives in performing this step are to identify *new opportunities* for existing and new products and services and to identify major future *risks* to market position and profit margins. Conditions of primary interest would include economic, competitive, technological, governmental, and market.

2. *Identify company strengths, weaknesses.* After an analysis of the conditions in step 1 and an orderly review of products, markets, processes, personnel, and facilities, certain strengths and weaknesses will emerge. Such resource analysis will not only serve to highlight possible competitive advantages available to the company but will also tend to focus on opportunities and risks.

3. *Consider personal values of top management.* The aesthetic, social, religious, and personal values of top management and influential stockholders exert a significant influence on strategy. Additionally, the emerging constraints of social responsibility and consumerism are factors to consider. Personal values represent both guides and constraints upon the direction of the business.

4. *Identify opportunities and risks.* The company should, at this point, be able to identify opportunities in the environment for it to fill a unique niche. These opportunities occur when there are specific needs for products (or services) which the firm is uniquely able to supply because of its resources.

5. *Define product/market scope.* This involves the explicit definition of the future scope of the company's activities. The main idea is to concentrate on a very limited number of carefully defined product/market segments. These depend on the analysis resulting from steps 1 to 4 above. Careful identification of the product/market scope is advantageous because it (a) reduces the time and complexity of decisions regarding acquisitions, new investments, and other elements of the development plan, (b) promotes integration of divisions and other organizational entities by providing a basis for their plans, (c) allows the company to focus on decisions and actions that take advantage of their competitive edge.

[2] Robert L. Katz, *Management of the Total Enterprise*, Englewood Cliffs, N.J.: Prentice-Hall, Inc., 1970. See also J. Thomas Cannon, *Business Strategy and Policy,* New York: Harcourt Brace Jovanovich, Inc., 1968.

[3] For a comprehensive treatment of this step in the strategic planning process, see Francis J. Aguilar, *Scanning the Business Environment,* New York: The Macmillan Company, 1967.

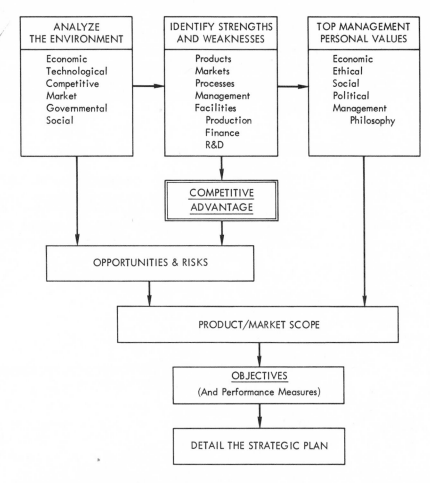

Figure 2-4 The strategic planning process.

6. *Define the competitive edge.* This requires a careful evaluation of unique company skills, position, market advantages, and other competitive factors.

7. *Establish objectives and measures of performance.* Quantitative specifications are required to describe many characteristics of the firm and to provide a clear definition of strategy. Quantitative goals may be established for such parameters as annual rate of growth of sales, profits, return on investment; market share; number of employees; value of assets; debt; standing in the industry; and so on.[4]

8. *Determine deployment of resources.* Should resources be applied

[4] See, for example, Robert L. Katz, *Management of the Total Enterprise*, Englewood Cliffs, N.J.: Prentice-Hall, Inc., 1970; see also Edward P. Learned, C. R. Christensen, and K. R. Andrews, *Business Policy*, Homewood, Ill.: Richard D. Irwin, Inc., 1972; and Steiner, *op. cit.*

to growth from within or to acquisitions? Upon what areas should the company focus its resources? Readjustment of application of resources is thus established in a manner similar to the grand-scale shifts of men and materiel in military conflicts. Conversion from one type of resource to another such as changing from labor-intensive to capital-intensive manufacturing is also a part of such deployment.

Short-Range Planning

Short-range planning (frequently called operational or annual planning) is almost always heavily financial in nature; it states objectives and standards of performance in terms of financial results. The basic objective is to decentralize responsibility to *profit centers* or *cost centers*, where sales, cost of sales, gross profits, or expenses may be established. These in turn are broken down into measurable and controllable elements such as investment (fixed assets, inventory, accounts receivable, cash, etc.) and cost of sales (direct labor, overhead, selling, transportation, and administration).

In the traditional approach, financial planning is the integrating process. Its major failure is that emphasis is put on dollars instead of the work to be done.

On the basis of short-range plans, specific objectives may be established for each individual in the organization. The individual and his manager negotiate the objectives, their cost, their schedule, and the level of desired quality of performance. Formal systems for feeding back information on actual performance are included in the MIS to detect problem areas. The individual and his manager meet regularly once a month or once a quarter to review progress and add new objectives. This focus on objectives by an individual worker is known as MBO (management by objectives).

Short-Range Plans Must Fit Strategic Plans

MBO as an Aspect of Managing

The Systems Approach to Planning

The *systems approach to planning* starts with the strategic plan as the framework. The strategic plan is specific but not detailed, because although specific goals may be established for the distant future, detailed methods for achieving these goals must be related to current environmental (including competitive) conditions. The distant-time goals of the strategic plan provide the constraints for setting intermediate- and short-term goals. Therefore, as shown in Figure 2-5, the strategic plan ties together the development plan (short-range plan). The development plan focuses on the growth of the company through internal or external expansion. The operations plan is the one-year plan which links together in full detail the functional plans with project or program plans.

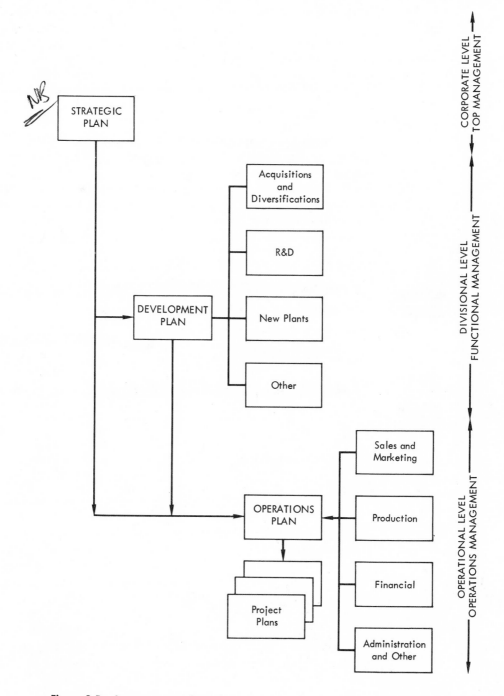

Figure 2-5 Systems approach to planning.

Information and Planning

MIS Aids Planning

It is evident that the first four steps in the planning process depend heavily on the availability and utilization of critical information. It is hard to imagine the manager trying to develop any of the three major types of plans without first gathering the necessary planning premises that permit adequate evaluation of alternative courses of action to achieve the plan.

The planning information needs of an organization can be classified into three broad types: (1) environmental, (2) competitive, and (3) internal. Because these are so important in the planning process and in the design of an information system for planning, it is desirable that each category be considered in some detail. Conceptually, planning premises can be viewed as shown in Figure 2-6.

ENVIRONMENTAL INFORMATION

Look Outside the Company

Each company will have to determine specific information about the environment that is important to it. In addition, a system for "scanning" the environment or just trying to identify future threats and opportunities should be established. Some general areas that companies should consider are

Political and governmental considerations. Some information on political stability, at whatever level of government, is important for forecasting plans. Additionally, the nature and extent of govern-

Figure 2-6 Planning premises.

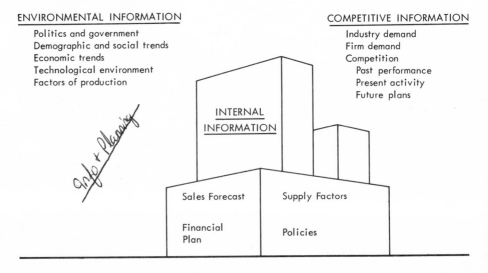

ENVIRONMENTAL INFORMATION
Politics and government
Demographic and social trends
Economic trends
Technological environment
Factors of production

COMPETITIVE INFORMATION
Industry demand
Firm demand
Competition
    Past performance
    Present activity
    Future plans

INTERNAL INFORMATION

Sales Forecast

Financial Plan

Supply Factors

Policies

ment controls and their effect on the organization must be taken into account. A third factor is the important role played by government financial and tax policies; they have a very significant effect on many planning decisions.

Demographic and social trends. The products, services, or outputs of most firms and organizations are affected by the totals, composition, or location of the population. Social trends and consumer buying behavior are important. It is necessary therefore to forecast trends for both the short and long run in this critical area.

Economic trends. Included herein would be (1) the GNP level and trend and consumer disposable income, which are significant for almost all organizations; (2) employment, productivity, capital investment, and numerous other economic indicators that provide valuable planning information for those firms whose output is a function of these important variables; and (3) price and wage levels, whose effects are vital to almost all organizations regardless of product or service.

Technological environment. Because of accelerating technical changes and their effect on new products and processes, it becomes necessary or desirable for many firms to forecast the technological changes in their industry and the probable effect on the firm. Firms like TRW, Inc. forecast key technological advances in all fields for a period of 20 years.

Factors of production. These include source, cost, location, availability, accessibility, and productivity of the major production factors of (1) labor, (2) materials and parts, and (3) capital.

COMPETITIVE INFORMATION

The MIS should provide a formal approach to obtaining information about the industry as a whole and major competitors in particular.

Industry Structure Since the company is bound so closely to the industry it is in, it should monitor the structure of the industry and trends that will affect the entire industry. Then, more specifically, forecasts and trends of sales for the industry should be monitored. The reason is that the company's sales will fluctuate with industry sales. In addition, total market potential for the industry should be estimated.

Other industry information of value would concern financial resources, profitability, pricing, promotional methods, new tactics, new products, and new channels of distribution.

Competitive Information When there are relatively few firms in the industry or a few dominant leaders, detailed information on these firms should be gathered continuously. Information on past performance, return on investment, share of the market, and breadth of product lines helps to identify threats posed by competition. Such information also provides yardsticks for measuring a company's performance.

INTERNAL INFORMATION

Because internal premises affect the planning decisions of so many levels in the organization, in some respects they are more important than the external information. Though the premises about the business environment and competition are very important, these categories of information are utilized by relatively few managers in a firm, mainly top managers and marketing managers.

As they relate to the total planning process, internal data are aimed at an identification of the organization's strengths and weaknesses. It is useful to think of internal premises as being of the following types:

1. *Sales forecast*. This is perhaps the single most important planning document in the organization, because the allocation of the entire company's resources is a function of the sales plan. It sets the framework on which most other internal plans are constructed and can therefore be regarded as the dominant planning premise internal to the firm.

2. *The financial plan*. This plan, frequently called the budget, is second only to the sales forecast in importance. In many ways, the financial plan preempts the sales forecast because it represents a quantitative and time commitment of the allocation of the *total resources* of the company (manpower, plant, capital, materials, overhead, and general and administrative expenses). Properly constructed, the financial plan involves the entire organization and, when completed, provides subsidiary planning information for a variety of subplans throughout the company. It is a system that links all activities of the company together.

3. *Supply factors*. Manpower, capital, plant and equipment, organization, and other supply factors are vital planning premises that provide constraints or boundaries within which planning takes place. These factors are controllable to a large extent by the firm, but their availability and limitations must be taken into account in developing the financial plan and subsidiary plans for achieving objectives.

4. *Policies*. Basic policies are relatively fixed for long-run purposes. To the extent that product, marketing, financial, personnel, and other basic policies are unchangeable in the short run, they provide constraints to planning in much the same way as do supply factors.

SUMMARY

Managing consists of a set of activities or processes that are different from the technical processes carried out by individual contributors. The three major processes are planning, organizing, and controlling.

All the processes are interrelated to form a system. Decision making and information flow (communications) are integrating processes for this system.

Every company must have a management system for conducting the management processes. Only then can the MIS be developed.

This systems approach to the study of management differs from the traditional approach. We show why this is so in this chapter and the following one.

The systems approach to the study of management basically means setting objectives and focusing on the system as a whole.

The process of planning has been described with particular emphasis on strategic planning. Then the systems approach to planning and the role of information in planning have been covered briefly.

QUESTIONS AND PROBLEMS

1. Complete the following table:

A Item in the Strategic Plan	B Item in the Short-Range Plan	C Some Item Information Required
Eliminate 261 company-owned retail outlets by 1979	Develop franchise program for current and future franchised outlets	Sales and profit information on each store
Competitive edge will be satisfaction or immediate refund to customers		
Automate all assembly lines for production of footwear by 1980		
Develop shop-at-home by CRT (Cathode Ray Tube) display and telephone by 1985		
Increase risk of new strategic objectives to a 20% failure rate but a 25 ROI rate		

2. What form of information is the following?

Code: (a) environmental, (b) competitive, (c) internal.

_____C____ (1) Classification of competitors by sales volume.

_____C____ (2) Sales of our company by month and by product.

_____C____ (3) Real estate owned by our company.

_____B____ (4) Development of new laser application by an English firm.

     A   (5) Decline in the economic index for the United States.

     B   (6) A new company gains 20% of the market for a product similar to ours.

     C   (7) Our inventory rose by $300,000 at the end of the year.

3. Using a firm of your own choice, describe how developments of the past 10 to 15 years have caused an increase in the need for planning.

4. Distinguish between external and internal information and the ease with which obtaining each is facilitated by an information system.

chapter three

Management,
Information,
and the Systems Approach
(Part 2)

CHAPTER 3   continues to relate managing, information, and the systems
approach by focusing on organization of the business and
control of system activities.

When you have finished studying

**MANAGEMENT, INFORMATION, AND THE SYSTEMS APPROACH
(Part 2)**

you should be able to

1. Describe the classical bases for organizing departmentation, span of
   management, and authority relationships
2. Describe the nature and impact of systems concepts on the process of
   organizing human resources
3. Show how the organization provides the framework for information
   systems
4. Describe the systems control process in terms of standards, performance, feedback of information, and correction of deviations
5. Differentiate among the type of information and reports issued for
   different levels of management.

We continue our study of the major management processes. We shall describe the processes of organizing and control. Then we shall relate these processes to information and the systems approach.

ORGANIZING

ORGANIZE PEOPLE
ACCORDING TO
THE TASKS TO
BE DONE

Organizing human resources by managers is the method by which effective group action is obtained. A structure of roles must be designed and maintained in order for people to work together in carrying out plans and accomplishing objectives. This is the task of organizing. It involves the grouping of tasks necessary to accomplish plans, the assignment of work to departments, and the delegation of authority to obtain coordination. The structure provided by the function of organizing facilitates the operation of the organization as a system. This concept is shown in Figure 3-1.

The Classical Organization Structure

Subdivision of
Work Leads to
Hierarchy of
Organization

The classical (bureaucratic or pyramidal) hierarchical organization structure is the most common form of the modern corporation. It provides the foundation upon which adaptations and modifications are constructed.

The key words are *structure* and *formal*. The basic tenets are specialization of work (departmentation), span of management (supervision of a limited number of subordinates), chain of command (authority delegation), and unity of command (no subordinate has more than one superior). Because the classical format is so prevalent, we shall examine the basic tenets of this form of organization.

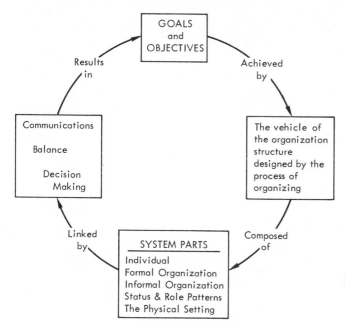

Figure 3-1 lettering (inside diagram):

GOALS
and
OBJECTIVES

Results
in

Achieved
by

Communications

Balance

Decision
Making

The vehicle of
the organization
structure
designed by the
process of
organizing

Linked
by

Composed
of

SYSTEM PARTS
Individual
Formal Organization
Informal Organization
Status & Role Patterns
The Physical Setting

Figure 3-1   Integration of the organizational system through the organizing process.

DEPARTMENTATION

Departmentation Means Grouping People on Some Logical Basis

Departmentation deals with the formation of organizational units. At the lowest level homogeneous activities are grouped together. The activities form departments. Methods of departmentation that have proved logical and useful are the following: by function, by product, by territory, by customer, by process, and by project. An example of each of these methods of departmentation is illustrated in Figure 3-2. For example, departmentation by *function* is shown at the top level by the common functions of marketing, personnel, operations, R&D, and finance. The breakdown of operations into the furniture division, the metal products division, and the floor covering division is an example of product organization. The sales department is organized into eastern and western districts to establish a *territory* departmentation, and these territories are further departmented by the *customer* breakdown of retail, government, institutions, and manufacturer's representatives. The manufacturing operation in the metal products division depicts both *process* (assembly, welding, stamping) and *function* (maintenance, power, shipping). Finally, a special *project* team, organized for new-product development, reports to the president.

Bases for Departmentation

Functional departmentation is by far the oldest and most widely used form of grouping activities. In almost every organization there are three fundamental activities of producing, selling, and financing to be performed. These are the basic functions. As organizations grow, addi-

Figure 3-2 Methods of departmentation.

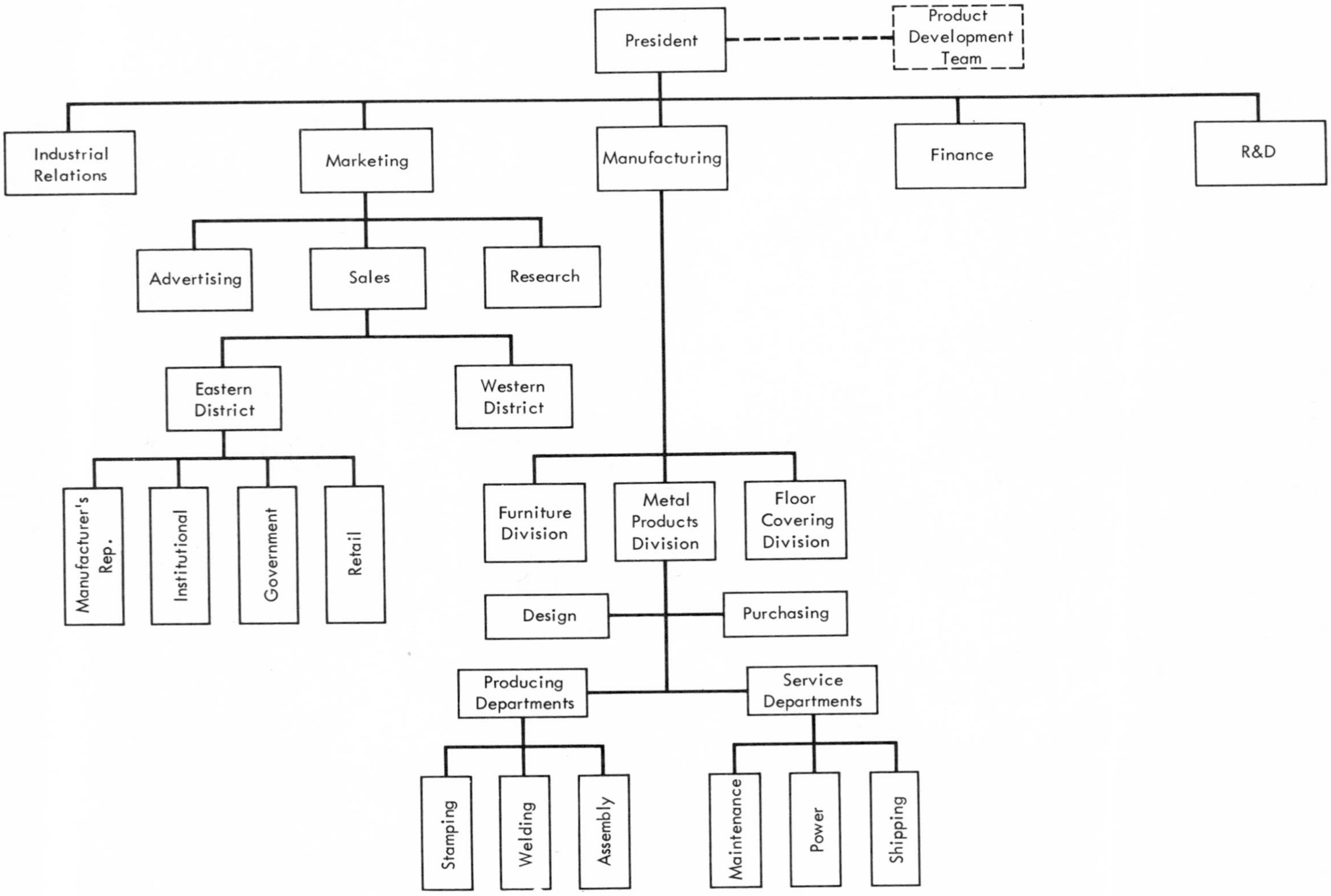

tional staff or service functions are added. Almost all organizations show some functional division of labor.

Product departmentation is common for enterprises with several products or services. The method is easily understood and takes advantage of specialized knowledge. Common examples are department stores (e.g., appliances, furniture, cosmetics) and banks (commercial, personnel).

Territory departmentation is frequently used by organizations that are physically dispersed. The rationale is that activities in a given area should be grouped and assigned to a manager. Such an approach takes advantage of economies of localized operation. The most frequent use of this method is in the sales force, where division by geographical region favors recruitment and training. Manufacturing and distribution may be organized by territory for similar reasons.

Customer departmentation may be used when the major emphasis is upon service to the customer or where it permits taking advantage of specialized knowledge. Sex, age, and income are common yardsticks for identifying customers. Examples of this type of organization include banks (loans to retailers, wholesalers, manufacturers), department stores (men's shop, teen shop, bridal salon), and aircraft manufacturers (government, foreign, domestic).

Process departmentation, most frequently used in manufacturing enterprises and at the lowest level of organization, is a logical method whereby maximum use can be obtained from equipment and special skills. Frequently the process matches an occupational classification, such as welding, painting, or plumbing.

Project departmentation, sometimes referred to as team or task force, is relatively new and growing in importance. This approach has gained much favor in defense-related industries because the work involved in research and development lends itself to identification in natural blocks or events. A major advantage of the project organization is the feeling of identification it gives its members.[1]

SPAN OF MANAGEMENT

HOW MANY PEOPLE SHOULD REPORT TO EACH MANAGER

If it were not necessary to coordinate the activities of an organization, departmentation would permit its expansion to an indefinite degree. However, this coordinative need requires a structure composed of levels of supervision, a structure achieved by establishing these levels of supervision within the confines of the span of management—the number of subordinates that a manager can supervise. The importance of this factor

[1] See *Project Manager's Handbook*, New York: Booz, Allen & Hamilton, 1967, Chap. 2, "Organization"; see also D. W. Karger and R. G. Murdick, *Managing Engineering and Research*, 2nd ed., New York: Industrial Press, Inc., 1969, Chap. 9, "Project Management."

can be appreciated if we consider that were it not for a supervisory limit, there would be no need to organize, since everyone in the organization would report to the president. Hence, one reason for organizing is to overcome the limitations of both human ability and time.

The basic question surrounding the span of management—stated two ways—is (1) How many subordinates should be assigned to a superior and (2) Should the organization structure be "wide" or "narrow"? Figure 3-3 depicts the types of organizational structures involved in each instance, and Figure 3-4 gives examples.

Generally speaking, the effort to identify a specific number or range of subordinates has not been productive. In practice the number varies widely. For example, former President Eisenhower was noted for his span of management of one—his chief of staff. To take another extreme, 750 Roman Catholic bishops report directly to the Pope.

Factors that
Determine the
Best Span for
a Manager

The span of management appears to depend on the manager's ability to reduce the time and frequency of subordinate relationships. These factors, in turn, are determined by (1) how well the subordinate is trained to do his job, (2) the extent of planning involved in the activ-

Figure 3-3   Two approaches to span of management.

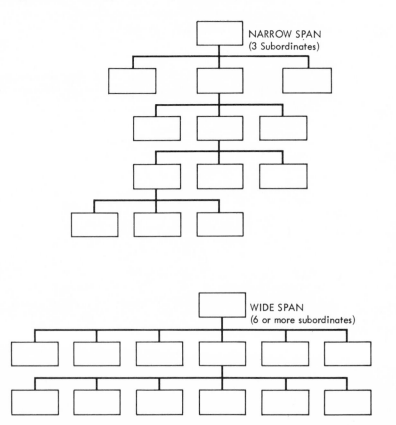

Kaiser Aluminum's new 'flat' management

C.C. Maier
President and Chief Executive Officer

10 operating managers	9 staff specialists

Its old 'pyramid' structure

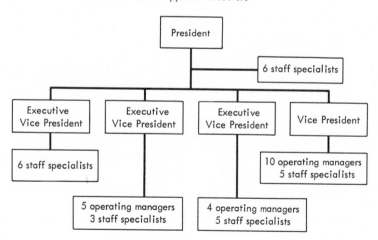

Figure 3-4

Source: "Kaiser Aluminum Flattens Its Layers of Brass," reprinted from the February 23, 1973 issue of *Business Week* by special permission. © 1973 by McGraw-Hill, Inc.

ity, (3) the degree to which authority is delegated and understood, (4) whether standards of performance have been set, (5) the environment for good communications, and (6) the nature of the job and the rate at which it changes.

AUTHORITY RELATIONSHIPS

AUTHORITY:
THE RIGHT TO
SET OBJECTIVES
AND GET
ORGANIZATIONAL
WORK DONE

Without delegation of authority the formal organization would cease to exist; there would be only one department because the chief executive would be the only manager. It does no good to set up a structure of activities unless authority is delegated to the units within the structure to accomplish particular assignments.

The major determinant of a manager's ability to delegate authority is his temperament and personality, but other determinants are beyond his control. Some of these are (1) cost—the more costly the decision, the more likely it is to be centralized; (2) uniformity of policy—the more uniform and centralized a policy (price, personnel), the less need there is to delegate authority surrounding it; (3) the established formal organization structure; (4) custom of the business—frequently the delegation philosophy and character of top management determine authority delegation; and (5) environment for good management—the availability in the company of managers and good management practices (including control techniques) that would encourage delegation.

Among the tools and techniques for communicating the delegation of authority and organization structure are the organization manual, organization charts, position descriptions, activity charts, and procedural flow charts. Others are plans, policies, programs, budgets, and procedures.

CLASSICAL STRUCTURE—SUMMARY

·There is little doubt that dissatisfaction with the classical hierarchical organization structure is growing. Both researchers and businessmen are saying that it does not meet the complexity of today's pressures in business. Nor does it provide the systems approach we are seeking. As one corporate president said, "Under the classical structure, marketing is selling something that engineering can't design, that production can't manufacture, and to customers for which finance won't approve credit."

The advantages and disadvantages can be summarized:

Disadvantages	*Advantages*
It is too mechanistic and ignores major facets of human nature	It has widespread acceptance by businessmen
It is too structured to adapt to change	It is not cast in bronze—it can accommodate change when the need arises
Communications are hindered by formal directives and procedures	It is easily understood and applied
It inhibits innovation	It works
It pays the job and not the man	
It relys on coercion to maintain control	

Disadvantages
It is "job-defensive" and encourages "make work" practices
Its goals are incompatible with those of its members
It is simply out of date with the needs of the 1970s

No Substitute for a Basic Hierarchy?

Despite the shortcomings of the classical structure, it will probably be around for a long time to come. A recent survey of the Fellows of the Academy of Management attempted to forecast the shape of the organization of the future.[2] The results of the survey indicated a 75% probability prediction that the dominant organizational structure in 1985 would be the pyramid (classical).

Organizing and Systems Concepts

CAN WE ORGANIZE AROUND SYSTEMS?

By its very nature, the systems philosophy of organizing creates several basic and valuable by-products. The first of these is integration of the many subsystems making up the total organization. We have seen how planning tends to put managers in the frame of mind for thinking of the organization as a system. This approach to organizing will accomplish similar results. Further, people will begin to understand how their jobs interact with others in the company. A second benefit is the enhancement of decentralization. Advantages of decentralization include greater economies of supervision, improved morale, better development of managers, and in general more awareness of the contribution that decentralized units make to the whole. The systems approach and computer-based information systems give us many new and different capabilities for organization and management of a business, especially more centralized and more automated control of major portions of operations.[3] It is this *centralized control* that permits *decentralized operations*.

Systems Concepts Overlay the Basic Hierarchy

The greatest impact will come in the organization structure itself. Traditional organizational practice and theory have emphasized structure and authority. Under the systems approach the concept of the organization is changing from one of structure to one of process.

Advanced technology, the information explosion, increasing complexity—these require an organization structure that will accommodate change. We are fitting increasingly sophisticated techniques to a primitive

[2] Robert M. Fulmer, "Profiles of the Future," *Business Horizons*, Aug. 1972, pp. 5–14.
[3] Victor Z. Brink, "Top Management Looks at the Computer," *Columbia Journal of World Business*, Jan.–Feb. 1969, p. 78.

In Times of Change, We Changed

For half a century and more, the operating forces of the Bell Telephone companies have been deployed in keeping with their three main functions: traffic, plant, and commercial. The endurance of this organizational structure is testimony to its strengths. What now leads to change it is the prospect that interdepartmental coordination, once safely assumed on the basis of long experience, can no longer be taken for granted in the face of the volume and variety of customer service needs we confront today. Accordingly in recent years, AT&T and the telephone companies, each according to its needs, have been moving in the direction of a form of organization that places the *entire* responsibility for customer service and for coordination of all three of our operating disciplines at a lower level in the organization. The aim: to establish *total* responsibility for service as close to our customers as possible.

Source: American Telephone and Telegraph Company, *1974 Annual Report,* p. 18.

---

vehicle, the bureaucratic structure. By adopting the systems approach to organizing, we emphasize integration of the parts as well as design of an organization that will accommodate accelerating change.

Focus on Systems, Not Task or Skill Specialties

Equally important is the emphasis that the systems approach places upon the *systems* as opposed to the *functions* of organizations. The typical business has been organized along functional lines (sales, finance, production) at the top and by other methods (customer, process, territory, etc.) at lower hierarchical levels. This emphasis on organization structure has frequently overlooked the interrelationship of the parts and the programs, projects, and processes that the parts were designed to produce.

Emerging Concepts: The Team Approach

HOW TO PUT SYSTEMS CONCEPTS OF ORGANIZATION INTO PRACTICE

If we are to take the systems approach to organizing, the tasks involve integrating the subsystems of the organization and accommodating to change. There is a growing recognition that some form of task force or team approach can achieve these goals. Warren Bennis sees the key word describing the systems approach as "temporary." He says, "There will be adaptive, rapidly changing *temporary* systems. These will be task forces organized around problems to be solved."[4]

MATRIX PROJECT MANAGEMENT

Crossing Organization Lines

This form of task force gets its name from the fact that several project managers exert planning, scheduling, and cost control supervision

---

[4] Warren F. Bennis, "The Coming Death of Bureaucracy," in David I. Cleland and William R. King, eds., *Systems, Organizations, Analysis, Management: A Book of Readings,* New York: McGraw-Hill Book Company, 1969, p. 11.

over people who have been assigned to their projects while the functional managers exert line control. Thus there is shared responsibility for the worker, and he must please two superiors. The organization of a typical project in a major aerospace firm is shown in Figure 3-5. The program manager is essentially a "contractor" who hires his personnel from the line or functional organization.

LINE PROJECT MANAGEMENT

Organizing for
Total System
Objectives

In this form of project management organization, each employee has only one home: the project to which he is assigned (or to an auxiliary service group). Usually a number of projects are active in different stages of their life cycles. As new projects begin and build up, people are transferred from other projects that are approaching completion.

The line project manager has complete responsibility for resources of both money and men. He contracts for auxiliary services. He is held accountable for meeting planned time, cost, and technical performance goals. A typical organization chart is shown in Figure 3-6.

VENTURE TEAMS

More and more multinational, multidivisional, multiproduct companies are beginning to realize that the traditional *functional* organizational structure cannot accommodate risk, innovation, and new ventures or products. They are turning to the venture team, a recent organizational innovation that resulted from the need to meet the demand for a breakthrough in product marketing.

The venture team resembles the project-manager-type approach in that its resources and personnel are obtained from the functional departments. Other similarities include organizational separation of team members, multidisciplinary composition of personnel, and the goal-directed effort of a single project—in this case the development and introduction of a new product.

Information and Organizing

Using Information
Systems To Get
a Systems
Approach to
Organization and
Management

Organization structure and information needs are inextricably interwoven. In an analogy between an organization and the human body, the organization *structure* can be compared to the human anatomy and the *information* to the nervous system.

The systems view of the organization takes into account the integrative nature of information flows. This concept is demonstrated in Figure 3-7, where each organizational entity is seen as an information system with the components of input, processor, and output. Each is connected

Figure 3-5 Typical program manager in aerospace industry.

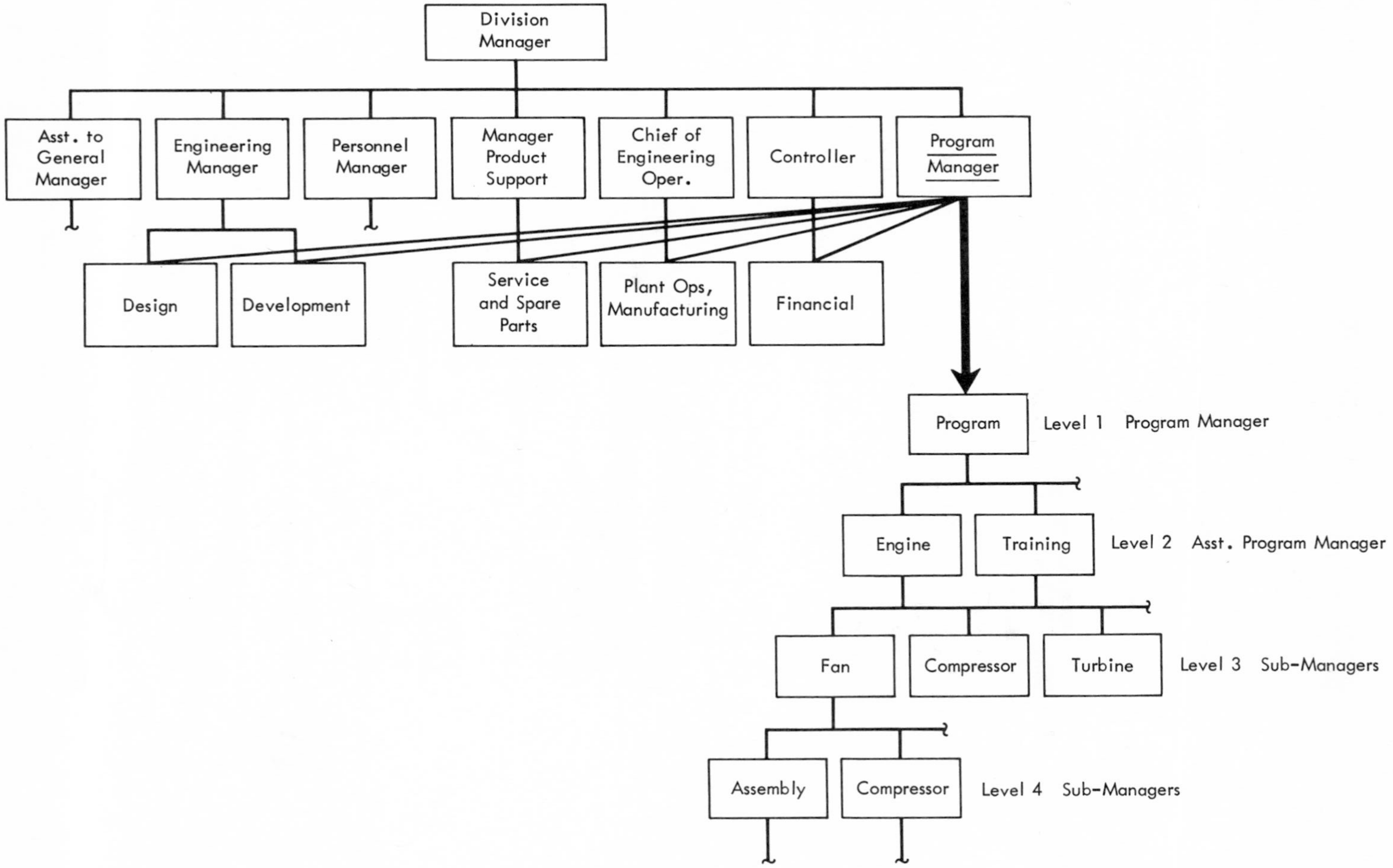

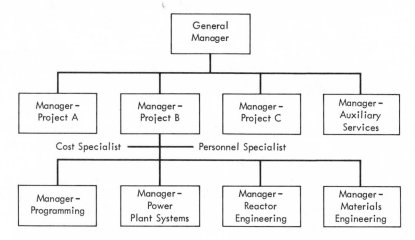

Figure 3-6 Line project management.

to the others through information and communication channels, and each organizational entity becomes a decision point.

Information also affects organizing by the manner in which information systems are designed. These should conform to the organizational

Figure 3-7 The organization as an information system.

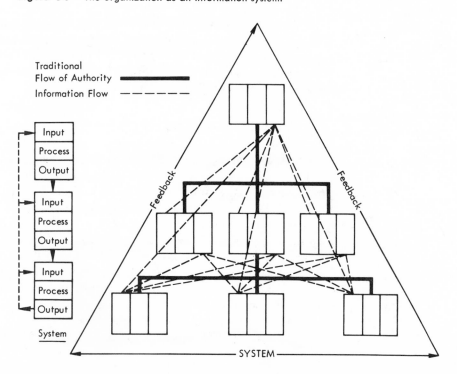

structure and the delegation of authority within the company. Only then can each organizational unit's objective be established and its contribution to companywide goals be measured. This means that organizations must be designed around information flow and those factors of information chosen to plan and control performance. Frequently organizational structure and performance reporting do not coincide. In these cases information systems cannot truly reflect plans and results of operations.

Another major cause of organizational and information mismatch is the lag between organizational changes and information systems to facilitate them. As needs, structure, and managers change, the information system should be changed to support them. Rarely does one find a change in informational systems matching a change in organizational responsibilities and the needs of managers. The result is often an "information lag."

Controlling

CONTROL THE
PARTS AND THE
PROCESS TO MEET
SYSTEM
OBJECTIVES

If the manager could depend on the flawless execution of plans by a perfectly balanced organization, there would be no need for control because results would invariably be as expected. However, plans and operations rarely remain on course, and control is needed to obtain desired results. The real test of a manager's ability is the result he achieves.

Control is a basic process and remains essentially the same regardless of the activity involved or the area of the organization. The fundamental process consists of three steps: (1) setting standards of performance, (2) measuring performance against these standards, and (3) correcting deviations from standards and plans.

STANDARDS OF PERFORMANCE

Standards Are
the Bases for
Measuring
Performance

Setting standards of performance involves defining for personnel in all levels of the organization what is expected of them in terms of job performance. Hence, standards are criteria against which results can be measured. These criteria can be quantitative (e.g., 10% increase in sales) or qualitative (e.g., maintain high level of morale). A frequently used definition of standards of performance is *a statement of conditions existing when a job is performed satisfactorily.*

A discussion of standards can be better understood when related to actual examples. Table 3-1 illustrates the basic components of a very important operation plan—the financial plan. Note that a standard of performance is indicated for each of these major items.

The usual standards of performance for an activity are related to

Table 3-1 Standards of performance for controlling the financial plan.

Financial Plan	COST	TIME	QUANTITY	QUALITY	Illustration of Standard
Sales	x	x	x		Sales quota during time period at standard cost
Cost of goods sold					
Raw materials	x		x		Unit usage rate at standard cost
Direct labor			x		Hours per unit of output
Manufacturing expense	x	x	x		Maintenance cost per machine-hour
Total					
Gross margin on sales	x		x		Percent of sales
Less:					
Distribution expense	x				Percent of sales
Administrative expense	x	x	x		Budgeted amount
Total					
Operating income	x		x		Percent of sales
Federal income tax					
Net income	x		x		Return on investment

cost, time, quantity, and quality. For example, in Table 3-1 the *cost* of raw materials for manufacturing a product can be controlled in terms of cost per unit, and this standard would apply in the purchasing operation. *Time* is a standard for the sales force when performance is measured in terms of meeting sales quotas during established time periods (e.g., weeks, months). In manufacturing, the direct labor-hours per unit of output in a process operation is a common *quantity* measure. *Quality* is a common measure in judging the acceptability of such factors as product specification, grades of products sold, and reject rates in quality control.

The foregoing are yardsticks, not areas of activity to be measured. Ideally, everyone in the organization should have some standard so that he understands what is expected of him.

Important Types of Standards

Types of critical standards have been identified:[5]

[5] Adapted from Harold Koontz and Cyril O'Donnell, *Management*, 6th ed. New York: McGraw-Hill Book Company, 1976, pp. 657–58.

1. *Physical.* The fundamental nonmonetary measurements so common at the operating level. They may reflect quantitative performance (units per man-hour, raw material usage rate) or quality (color, hardness).

2. *Cost.* Monetary measurements that attach value to the cost of operations. These are usually cost ratios such as, for example, overhead cost per unit of output.

3. *Revenue.* Monetary values that are attached to sales, expressed in ratios such as average sales per customer.

4. *Program.* Unlike ongoing operations, programs are one-time processes, and performance is measured in terms of time to complete events, meeting program specifications, or cost.

5. *Intangible.* These are standards that are not ordinarily expressed in quantitative terms because they are hard to measure. Examples are advertising, employee morale, industrial relations, and public relations.

Total System Standards

In addition to operating standards, there are critical areas of overall company performance that are the concern of top management. Is the company achieving its objectives? Are its strategies paying off? Indeed, by appraising overall company performance in these areas, the company evaluates its progress toward its basic purposes and objectives. These areas include

1. Profitability
2. Market standing
3. Productivity
4. Innovation and product leadership
5. Employee and managerial attitudes and development
6. Public responsibility
7. Use of resources
8. Balance between short-range and long-range objectives

MEASURING PERFORMANCE

How To Measure System Performance

Once standards have been established, it is necessary to measure performance against the expectation of the standards. The statement of measurement, and of any differences, is usually in the form of a personal observation or some type of report—oral or written.

The oldest and most prevalent means of measuring performance is by personal observation. The shop supervisor is on the scene and can personally check the time, cost, and quality of product. Sales managers visit sales offices or make calls with their salesmen to observe performance personally. Advantages include the benefits of immediacy, personal direct contact, and firsthand observation of intangibles such as morale, personnel development, or customer reaction. Disadvantages are those associated with the time-consuming nature of the method and the lack of precision in measurement.

Oral reports of performance may take the form of interviews, informal reports, or group and committee meetings. Measuring performance in this way has many of the advantages and drawbacks of the personal observation method. Additionally, oral reporting usually does not result in any permanent record of performance.

Increasingly, control and performance reporting is in written form, owing in part to the accelerating use of computer-based information systems and related reporting. The written report has the advantage of providing a permanent record, subject to periodic review by the manager and subordinates. This method of measuring performance may take a variety of forms. Among the most common is the statistical report, which presents statistical analysis of performance versus standard, either in tabular or chart form. Special or one-time reports are frequently made in problem areas as they arise. A significant portion of written reports is operational in nature and concerns performance against standards for the financial plan.

CORRECTING DEVIATIONS

Using Managerial Processes for Correcting Out-of-Line Performance

It does little good to set standards of performance and measure deviations from standard unless corrections are made to get the plan back on course to achieve the objective. Methods and techniques for correcting deviations can be described in terms of the functions of management:

Plan: Recycle the management process: review the plan, modify the goal, or change the standard.

Organize: Examine the organization structure to determine whether it is reflected in standards, make sure that duties are well understood, reassign people if necessary.

Staff: Improve selection of subordinates, improve training, reassign duties.

Direct: Provide better leadership, improve motivation, explain the job better, manage by objectives, make sure that there is manager-subordinate agreement on standard.

Control: Provide an organizational structure that channels the flow of information on performance to managers and others who have the responsibility for taking corrective action.

Control and Systems Concepts

The concept of control lies at the very heart of the systems approach. Indeed, no system could exist for very long without control. Unlike our classical notion of control as a process of coercion, or "compelling events to conform to plan," control in a cybernetic sense or systems sense views the organization as a self-regulating system. The key idea underlying control is *feedback*.

An example of feedback is the heating system. A thermostat maintains the temperature at a predetermined level by making or breaking an electrical circuit that starts or stops the heating system. Another example is the case of raw materials inventory. When inventory exceeds the accepted standard, a reduction in orders occurs until the inventory level is within standard. These examples illustrate the major characteristics of cybernetic systems: (1) a predetermined equilibrium to be maintained; (2) a feedback of changes in environment to the system, causing changes in the state of the system; (3) a transfer of information from the external environment to within the system; and (4) a device that prompts corrective action when the output of the system oscillates beyond desired limits.

The objective of control is to maintain the output that will satisfy the system requirements. This necessitates the building of control into the system. In the case of information systems, control is a major consideration of systems design and may take the form of a programmed decision rule. The steady state of the system (organization) is maintained by feedback of information concerning the functioning of the system within allowable limits.

Information and Control

Control systems depend on information systems, because the rapidity and appropriateness of corrective action—the end result of the control process—depends on the kind of information received.

Information required to perform control is different in both type and characteristic from information needed for planning. Planning places greater emphasis on structuring the future; control is based more on the immediate past, present, and specific trends.

To control the business organization, we may divide the business into five groups of subsystems and control each of these subsystems. The first set consists of the management-level subsystems. The top-management level is concerned with strategy, and its performance as a whole should be kept in line with measures established by the board of directors. Middle management, as a system of managers concerned with short-range planning and operations, must be subject to control in terms of productivity and efficiency. Similarly, first-line management represents the system for conducting day-to-day transactions. This system must also contain information feedback and be subject to control.

Resource Subsystem

A second set of subsystems that make up the business is the resources set. Human resources, capital assets, materials, liquid assets, and credit line subsystems must be kept within control limits established by the responsible managers.

Functional Subsystems

Another set of subsystems over which all companies seek to maintain control is the functional subsystems. Control information required in this instance, more specifically, is

> *Marketing information* concerning the progress of the sales plan: quotas, territories, pricing, and the like. In other words, market information is basically that required to measure performance against the sales forecast. In addition, control information may be obtained in other areas of the marketing plan, such as product acceptance, advertising, market research, and distribution costs.
>
> *Manufacturing information* concerning quantity and quality of direct labor, materials, overhead, and inventories. Control is also concerned greatly with the time aspect in the production system.
>
> *Personnel information* concerning profiles and performance of personnel, recruiting reports, staffing reports, training reports, etc.
>
> *Financial information* such as the financial master plan, financial reports, variances, cash flow forecasts, etc.
>
> *Research, development, and engineering information* giving performance, cost, and time for projects and periodic reports of variances from project plans.

Product Subsystems

Another set of subsystems for which control information is required is the product set. Each product line must be controlled by supplying information to product managers or product division managers. Such information as sales, profitability, trends, competition, and marketing/manufacturing/financial information for product planning and control is required.

Operating Phase Subsystems

Finally, the operating phase subsystems must be controlled by providing information to managers and key people. These operating phase subsystems are forecasting, financing, designing, material handling and processing, costing, and selling.

The different characteristics of planning and control data reflect the difference in the nature of the two functions—time, futurity, comprehensiveness, and so on.

INFORMATION AND CONTROL— THE SYSTEMS APPROACH

The traditional approach to control has several shortcomings:

Old Approach to Control

1. *Performance standards* were usually related to short-run financial

Capitol Aggregates, Inc. Relates Control to Planning by Information Appropriate to Organizational Level. (Copyright © 1974 by the American Institute of Certified Public Accountants, Inc.)

Plant Level Reports

COST DETAIL, PLANT NO. 14 NEW AUSTIN GRAVEL PLANT

	Period 1	Period 2	Period 3	Period 4	Period 5
FIXED COSTS:					
DIRECT LABOR	0	137280			
DEPRECIATION	0	221286			
TOT FXD COST	0	358566			
VAR COSTS:					
OPER SUPPLIES	0	1847			
KILN BRICK	0	9233			
ELEC POWER	0	23294			
REPAIRS	0	33237			
ROYALTY	0	51702			
SHOP CHARGES	0	7386			
GRAVEL PURCH	0	80876			
MISC EXP	0	7386			
TOT VAR COST	0	214961			
TOTAL COST	0	573527			

PLANT INCOME, PLANT NO. 14 NEW AUSTIN GRAVEL PLANT

	Period 1	Period 2	Period 3	Period 4	Period 5
SALES:					
SAND	0	167918	176415	185341	194720
GRAVEL	0	204422	214767	225633	237049
FILL MATRL	0	58559	61522	64635	67906
TYPE I SACK	0	91260	95878	100729	105826
I C GRAVEL	0	199555	209653	220261	231406
TOTAL SALES	0	721714	758235	796599	836907
DEDUCTIONS	0	0	0	0	0
NET SALES	0	721714	758235	796599	836907
FIXED COSTS	0	358566	334573	314700	298487
VRBLE COSTS	0	214961	226862	239454	252771
TOTAL COST	0	573527	561435	554154	551258
OPRTG INCM	0	148187	196800	242445	285649

Area Level Summary Report

OPERATING SUMMARY, AREA 01 AUSTIN

	Period 1	Period 2	Period 3	Period 4	Period 5
PLANT 01	280211	251442	266468	280805	294453
PLANT 03	30657	32730	35611	41317	43245
PLANT 04	201112	0	0	0	0
PLANT 06	117611	134145	149651	162477	171631
PLANT 10	16606	17144	19173	22299	22793
PLANT 12	0	0	0	0	0
PLANT 14	0	148187	196800	242445	285649
TOT OPR INC	646197	583648	667703	749343	817771
AR SPRT COST					
ADMIN+SALES	228161	233655	240433	250649	261595
TOT AD+SL EX	228161	233655	240433	250649	261595
TOT AR INC	418036	349993	427270	498694	556176
OPR RATIOS					
INC/SALES	17	14	16	17	17
PLANT ASSETS	3569915	3419370	3297306	3220333	3174439
OVHD ASSETS	62471	62934	66620	70265	73164
TOT ASSETS	3632386	3482304	3363926	3290598	3247603
AVG ASSETS	2533934	3557345	3423115	3327262	3269101
PERCH R O A	16.5	9.8	12.5	15.0	17.0

planning and frequently overlooked the measurement of progress toward overall company objectives.

2. The *control process* took on a restrictive meaning, and the process became the overriding concern instead of the work that was to be controlled.

Corporate Level Reports

CAPITOL AGGREGATES CORPORATE OPERATING SUMMARY

	Period 1	Period 2	Period 3	Period 4	Period 5
OPERATING INCOME:					
...AREA .01 ...	418036				
...AREA .02 ...	1947960				
...AREA .03 ...	97451				
TOTAL	2463447				
GEN+ADMN ..	238989				
EXPLORATION ..	14207				
OTHR INC+EXP	(37015)				
PRFT SHRING ...	264334				
TOT ADMN EXP .	480515				
OPER INC	1982932				
INTEREST	485042				
INC BEF FIT	1497890				
FED INC TAX ..	718987				
INVEST CRT	(331722)				
NET INC	1110625				
PERCENTAGES:					
NT INC/SALES ..	11				
PERC R O A I ..	17				
NET INC/EQTY ..	18				
EQTY/T ASSET .	47				
AVG ASSETS ...	12013204				

CAPITOL AGGREGATES CORPORATE CASH FLOW SUMMARY

	Period 1	Period 2	Period 3	Period 4	Period 5
NET INCOME	1110625				
DEPRECIATION ..	948047				
SHT TRM DEBT	0				
DEPLETION	6080				
NEW L T DEBT ...	3354000				
TOTAL AVLBLE ...	5418752				
ASSET REPLMT ..	448890				
PRPSED ASSET	4290000				
SHT DEBT RTR	300000				
SCH DEBT RTR	1087846				
REC REQRMNTS ..	477280				
INV REQRMNTS ...	(97734)				
LAND INVESTM ...	0				
OTHER ASSETS ...	0				
ACCTS PAYBLE ...	335271				
TAX LIABLTS	0				
TOTAL RQRMNT ...	6841553				
NET CASH FLW ..	(1422801)				
DEBT/ASSETS	.53				
TOTAL DEBT	6960254				
POLICY DEBT	6717607				
AVAILABLE	(242647)				

CAPITOL AGGREGATES CORPORATE BALANCE SHEET

	Period 1	Period 2	Period 3	Period 4	Period 5
CASH	(1122801)				
RECEIVABLES ...	1566772				
INVENTORIES ...	420477				
CURR ASSETS ..	864448				
PLT+EQUP	13637602				
ACUM DPRCTN .	3941461				
NET PLT+EQUP .	9696141				
LAND	2016370				
OTHER ASSETS .	593920				
TOTAL ASSETS .	13170879				
SHT TERM DEBT .	0				
CRR PORT LTD ..	1168440				
ACCTS PAYBLE ..	664729				
FIT PAYBLE	0				
CURR LIABLTS ..	1833169				
LNG TRM DEBT ..	5127085				
TOTL LIABLTS ...	6960254				
OWNERS EQTY ..	6210625				
LIABLTS+EQTY ..	13170879				
CURRENT RATIO ...	.5				
	.47				

CAPITOL AGGREGATES CORPORATE OVERVIEW REPORT

	Period 1	Period 2	Period 3	Period 4	Period 5
CURRENT RATIO ...	.5	.9	1.5	1.9	2.4
EQTY/ASSETS	.47	.30	.35	.38	.45
TOTAL ASSETS	13170879	25191364	25247775	28770269	28953701
NT CASH FLOW	(1422801)	819801	476423	1129449	1329290
AREA 01 P/L	418036	349993	427268	498695	556177
PERC R O A I	17	10	13	15	17
AREA 02 P/L	1947960	1550535	3495365	3978810	4356416
PERC R O A I	25	11	17	19	20
AREA 03 P/L	97451	106518	112772	116939	116016
PERC R O A I	242	148	190	219	227
NET INCOME BEF INT+TAXS ..	1982932	1664312	3438134	3904374	4262708
R O A I BEF INT+TAXS	17	9	14	14	15
NET INCOME	1110625	1205395	1114257	1603144	1552675

Source: Robert E. Engberg and Roger L. Moore, "A Corporate Planning Model for a Construction Materials Producer," *Management Adviser,* Jan.–Feb. 1974, p. 51.

3. *Control reports* were viewed as a tool of subordinate measurement, not as a tool to improve operations.

4. *Lateness* was a characteristic of variance reporting. The lapse of time between a deviation and its discovery precluded corrective action until it was too late.

To overcome these objections and to achieve a greater degree of integration in the organization, a modern control system should be constructed around four central ideas:

Systems Approach to Control Is Integrative, Decision-Oriented, and Forward-Looking

1. *Integrate planning and control.* The central idea of information, planning, and control is that each level of plans provides the standards of performance (objectives) for the next lower level of operations.

2. *Relate the control system to the organization structure.* The information system has usually been built around a financial chart of accounts, not decision centers. Moreover, the organization has not achieved synergism because the parts (functions or organizational elements) have not been related to a whole unified set of objectives or to the other parts.

3. *Design the system for decision making*, not after-the-fact reporting. The manager-user must define systems in terms of information demands for decision making.

4. *Timely information is essential*. The ideal control system is one that provides information in sufficient time to correct a deviation *before* it occurs.

Feedback Control Has a Time Lag

A basic requirement of any control system is feedback. For the most part, existing control systems rely on feedback *after* deviation from desired performance, and managers are being frustrated by discovering too late that actual accomplishments are missing the desired objectives. They have been dependent on accounting data and information systems that are historical in nature.

Feed-forward Control Works on Inputs and Predicted Outputs

A modern business control system will utilize *feed-forward* control. It will anticipate the lags in feedback systems by monitoring inputs and predicting their effects on outcome variables. In so doing, action can be taken to change the input and thereby bring the system output into equilibrium with desired results *before* the measurement of the output discloses a historical deviation from standard.

SUMMARY

Although we have attempted to examine information as it affects each of the major management functions of planning, organizing, and controlling, these functions cannot be separated; they are linked both functionally and by a common system of information. These systems characteristics of integration and linkage are shown in Figure 3-8. It can be seen that although the inputs of planning and of control information are basically different, the planning that results affects subsequent control, and the action and information processing resulting from control provide, in turn, a feedback that affects the planning process.

Figure 3-9 represents the three subsystems of planning, operating, and controlling integrated into the system of management. Shown also is the basic flow of information for operation of the integrated system. The planning system receives as input the planning premises and objectives, from which we get the output of management plans. These plans in turn provide the input to the operating system, which utilizes them as premises for the organization that attempts to achieve the plans. A basic output of the operating system is performance against plan, and information concerning this performance is in turn provided as input to the control system.

Feedback on performance is obtained through the control system, which monitors the operating system and furnishes feedback information to it as well as to the planning system. Decisions are made within each

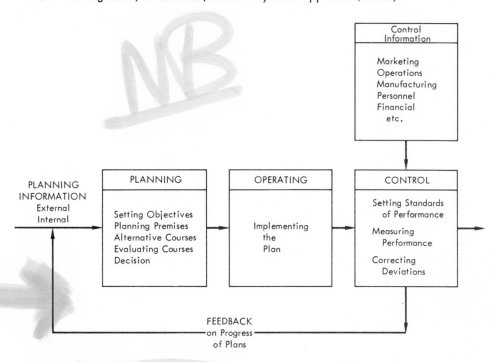

Figure 3-8 Information and management.

system based on information, and within each system there is a flow of information to implement changes and correct deviations based on feedback from other systems. It is evident that the key to success in planning, organizing, and controlling lies in the information-decision system. It follows that success in achieving the objectives of the organization lies similarly in performing these managerial functions through the aid of properly designed management information systems.

The concept of how a management information system operates in the context of a "total system" of the organization is depicted in Figure 3-10. *Notice that the information flow for the information system is integrated with the four other resource flows (money, manpower, materials, and machines and facilities) to provide a system of planning and control for the entire organization.* Both the planning information and the data for the specific system provide inputs that are transformed by the processor into an output whose objective is to provide information for planning and control.

Sensors must be developed to measure the attributes of the output as well as the attributes of the transformation process. We shall call these sensors *control*. A part of the control component contains management reports that track the status of the output relative to a predetermined standard of performance for the transformation process.

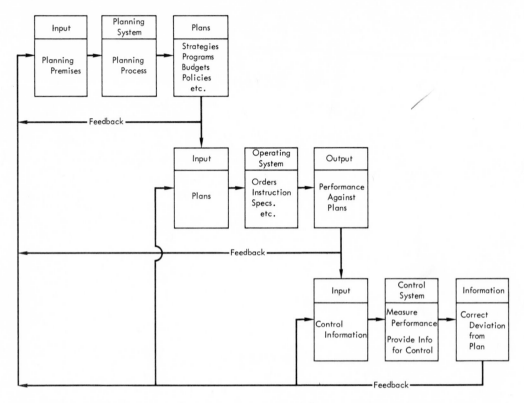

Figure 3-9 Information flow in the management process (planning system, operating system, control system).

If the results being achieved in the organizational system (as opposed to the information system) do not conform to standard, this information is fed to the *planning analysis and control* component, which makes decisions regarding one or both of two actions: (1) Alternative resource allocations are made as system input changes, or (2) modifications are made in the transformation process. Either or both of these decisions may be taken, based on decision rules or data stored in the central data base.

If an inventory accounting system were represented by the system of Figure 3-10, its operation could be outlined as follows:

1. The *objectives* of the system are as follows: (a) Inventory levels should not vary from established limits, and (b) sufficient inventory should be on hand to meet customer demand.
2. The *planning information* of the system includes inventory policies, levels, and procedures for the design and operation of the system.
3. The *input* to the system is information regarding the transactions that take place.

Figure 3-10 A management information system for planning and control.

Information Flow
Physical Flow

SENSOR

Control Through Management Reports

Information for Planning and Control

Product or Service

Other Subsystems

Customer

Management Information System

The Organization as a Transformation Processor

DATA BANK

DECISIONS

Planning Analysis and Control Group

Planning Information Data for Resource System

Resource Systems
Manpower
Money
Materials
Machines & Facilities

61

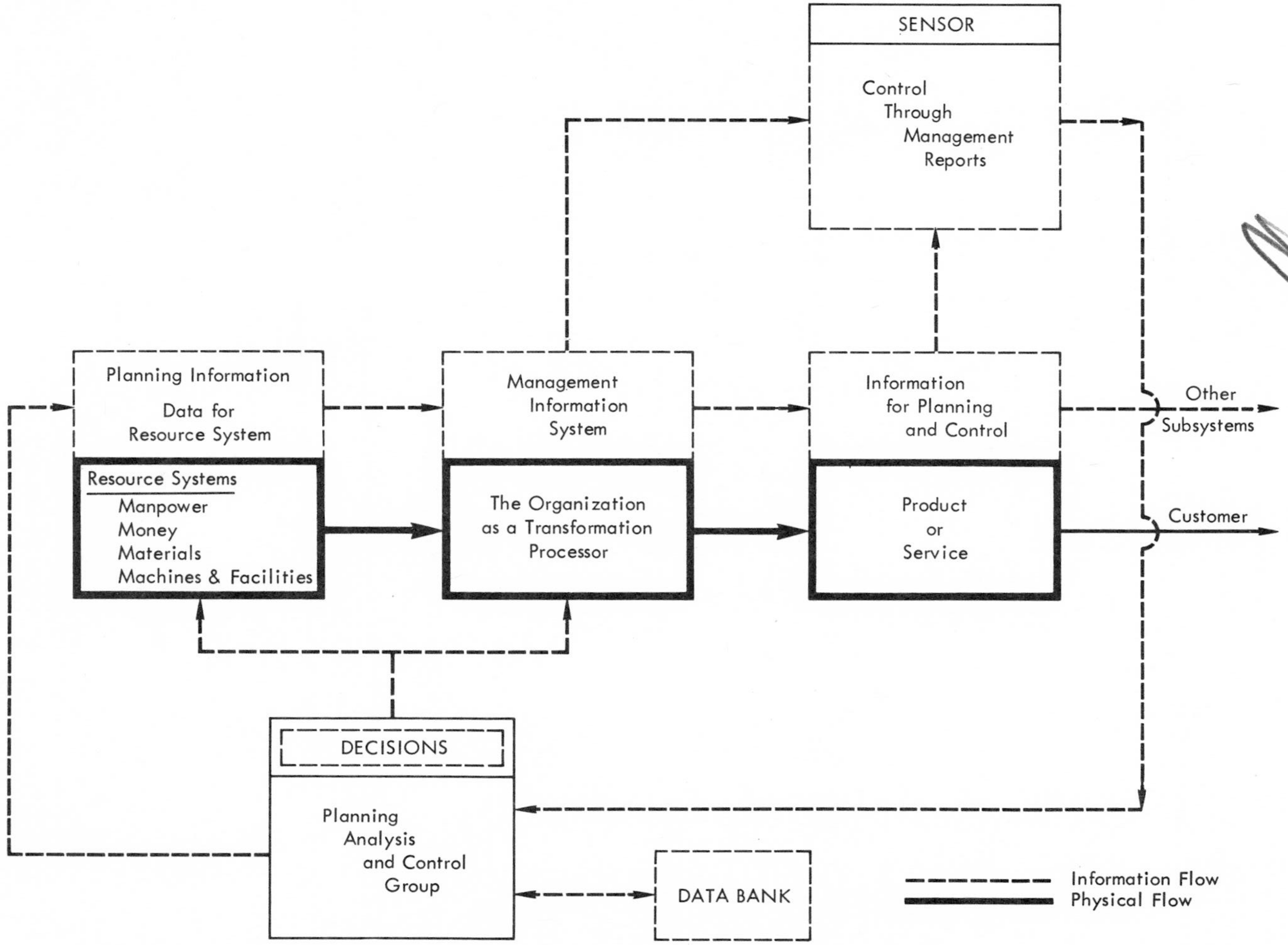

4. *System design* includes the organization of people, equipment, money, and procedures to process the information.

5. The *processing* of the system involves the processing of the transactions with programs and procedures.

6. *Control* consists of measuring inventory levels as reported by the *output* of inventory status reports against the *standards* of inventory policies and predetermined decision rules regarding inventory levels. Note that under this system as presently designed there is no output of the information system that provides a measure of performance against the objective of meeting customer demand.

7. Information concerning deviations from standards that are outside control limits is provided to the planning analysis and control component through *feedback*—an essential element of the *control* component.

QUESTIONS AND PROBLEMS

1. Match the items in the right column to those in the left column by placing the correct letter opposite the number:

_____ C___ (1) Departmentation

_____ C___ (2) Span of management

_____ E___ (3) Authority relationship

_____ A___ (4) Classical organizational structure

_____ B___ (5) Systems approach to organizing

_____ D___ (6) Project management

_____ B___ (7) Information system

a. Structured, formal, pyramidal

b. Formal integrating communication system for the organization

c. Number of people reporting to a manager

d. Organization based on unique large jobs with a definite termination date

e. Delegation of the "right to command"

2. Complete the following table in a manner similar to the first row shown:

Illustration of Criteria

Item Controlled	Cost	Time	Quantity	Quality
Salesman	Travel expense	Minutes on each customer per call	Number of calls per day	Sales per call
(1) Shop machine operator				
(2) Product line of items sold by the company				

    (3) Training
       program

    (4) Engineering
       work

3. Place the correct letters next to the five items listed below:

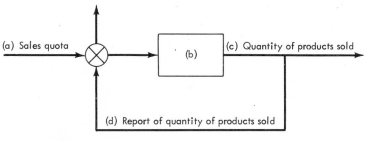

(a) Sales quota

(b)

(c) Quantity of products sold

(d) Report of quantity of products sold

(e) Report on difference

    D (1) Feedback

    B (2) System processor

    C (3) Output

    E (4) Input to manager as part of the MIS

    A (5) Input

4. Contrast the traditional approach to control of business operations with the systems approach to control:

Traditional Approach		**Systems Approach**	
Characteristics	*Shortcomings*	*Characteristics*	*Shortcomings*
(1) Performance	short-run fin plan, instead → go object measure'nt not tools to improve operat'ns lapse between disc a deviat'n + corrective act'n	1 Integ, p+ con 2 Relate control + orgam sys	set standards for next lower level of operat'ns - info and FA data not decis'n centers - has not related to whole unified set of objectives
(2) Control Places			
(3) Control Report		3 Design system for decis'n making	- after the fact reporting
(4) Lateness		4 Timely info	- info sufficient time to correct befor deviat'n occurs

chapter four

Information Systems for Functional Operations

CHAPTER 4 explains information systems as underlying management information systems. Major functional systems and their associated information systems are described with the aid of schematic systems diagrams.

When you have finished studying

INFORMATION SYSTEMS FOR FUNCTIONAL OPERATIONS

you should be able to

1. Identify at least five major operating systems common to manufacturing companies
2. Identify objectives of financial systems, production systems, marketing systems, and human resource systems
3. Identify major inputs and outputs of the preceding four systems
4. Given a schematic of each of the above four systems, explain the information flows and the principal activities of each.

> Information systems should be designed as an integral part of the business and not superimposed upon it. Too often computer systems have been built to replace manual and card systems, and justified on the basis of projected clerical or machine savings which almost never materialize.
>
> Harry A. Stern
> General Foods Corporation

INFORMATION
SYSTEMS
AND MIS

All information that management receives from within the company is derived from the day-to-day operations and transactions of operating personnel. Each operating system has its own information system. Selected items from these systems are of interest to managers and are picked out to be reported. Figure 4-1 attempts to relate operating systems and their information systems with management functions and management information systems.

EVOLUTION OF AN INFORMATION SYSTEM

By examining the basic information needs of a company (large or small) and what constitutes a satisfactory management information system, we can gain a better understanding of how information needs become more complex as organization operations expand. We learn also how information systems may be improved through modification of a manual system or design of a computer-based system.

MR. OWNER AS
MANAGER OF A
SMALL BUSINESS

Figure 4-2 portrays a small company (Owner and Sons) not so many years ago. Mr. Owner is president, proprietor, chief executive, and chairman of the board. Mr. Owner, Jr., is vice president of sales, director of market research, controller, treasurer, and director of research and development. Their entire work force consists of two helpers.

Figure 4-2 also demonstrates Mr. Owner's complete information

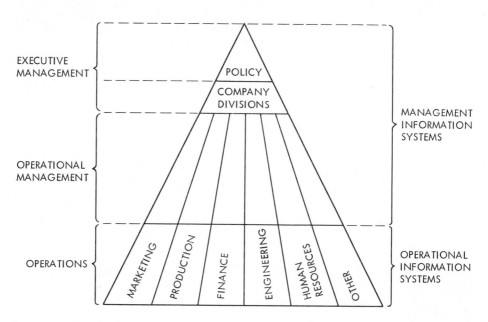

Figure 4-1 Up the information system.

processing system. His transaction tickets are skewered on the spindle as the transactions occur. Historical information is contained in storage books on top of Mr. Owner's desk. With this system, upper management has on-line entry into the basic resource records of the company and immediate access to its entire data bank. Cash flow and balance information are within sight in the safe in the corner of the office. There is even an advanced system of exception reporting on the blackboard on the washroom door. What Mr. Owner has developed is a *real-time* information system—all information required to run the business is within reaching distance of the president and is available within seconds.[1]

MR. OWNER AS MANAGER OF A LARGE BUSINESS

Times change, however, and Mr. Owner's business has grown into the larger company depicted in Figure 4-3. The functions have remained basically the same, but the volume and complexity of information needs have increased enormously. As with all growing companies, new products are developed, sales volume grows, the number of employees increases, factors outside the company become increasingly important, and generally the complexities of the operation expand more rapidly than company size.

[1] As opposed to batch processing, a real-time information system provides response to information inquiries in a time frame short enough to permit the user to shape an ongoing situation or make an immediate decision. The best known illustrations are telephone systems (communications), aerospace systems (command and control), and airline reservation systems (logistics).

More Activity
and More
Information
Needs

This increase in company size results in an increase in information collecting, processing, and distribution. It now becomes necessary to handle many customer accounts and many production records with many more interrelationships. In addition to the increased records, information needs, and associated difficulties, there are now the problems connected with delegation of authority and responsibility. It is now necessary to assign people to supervise other people, and this development expands communication lines and compounds these problems.

Beginning of
Automation of
Data
Processing

As the need for information grows, additional people and equipment must be added to handle the information. Typewriters and calculators are purchased, and additional clerks are hired. The next step may be to use a computer service company. Next, a minicomputer and supporting hardware may be purchased. Finally, a large electronic computer system may be leased or purchased in order to take advantage of the latest information processing technology.

Meanwhile, what has happened to management? Like the other

Figure 4-2   Owner and sons information system.

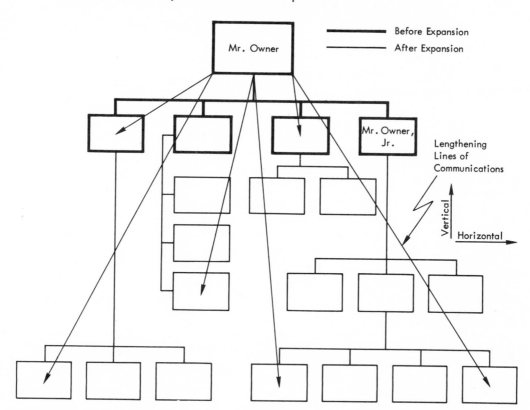

Figure 4-3   Complexities of growth (communication, delegation, information).

Management
Functions
Remain the
Same

basic functions of the company (production, sales, finance, etc.) management functions have not changed and will not. Basic information needs remain the same, as shown in Figure 4-4. Management still plans, organizes, staffs, directs, and controls. However, the communication network for information has increased greatly. A succession of delegations of duties and authority has lengthened the lines of communications and increased the complexity of the communication network of Mr. Owner's business a 1000-fold.

Need for a
Better MIS

Despite these complexities, the management of the now-larger company would like to be able to operate in the same fashion and with the same information requirements that old Mr. Owner enjoyed. The objective of developing or improving a management information system can be explained largely in terms of the new Mr. Owner's problems: (1) to provide the type of information environment that will integrate the basic operating functions, and (2) to provide management with access to information relative to complex activities in decentralized organizations. Both (1) and (2) need to be done with approximately the same ease that

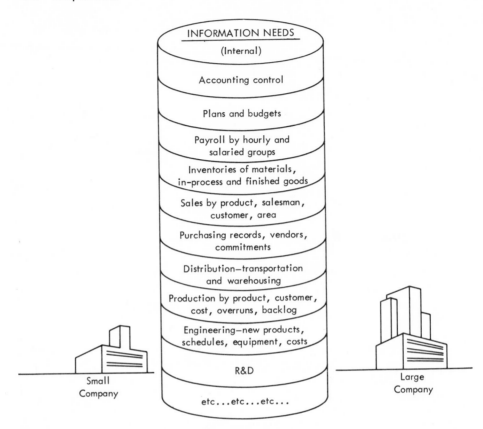

Figure 4-4   Internal information needs—large or small company.

Mr. Owner enjoyed in his small operation with four persons and the information system contained in his rolltop desk.

It is apparent that change will continue to take place in management and in the operation of organizations. To handle the changes properly, the manager of the 1970s must learn what to do with information in order to deal with the resultant increased complexity. In other words, *the manager must be prepared to take an active part in the design and installation of management information systems.*

BASIC INFORMATION SYSTEMS

BASIC
INFORMATION
SYSTEMS
SUPPORTING
THE MIS

Over time, the typical company develops a *formal* information system as part of each operating system. During the same period, it is likely that a *formal* MIS is installed so that the manager of each operation can plan, organize, and control operations better.

The major operating systems are

1. Engineering
2. Manufacturing operations
3. Marketing (including order processing and physical distribution)
4. Finance
5. Human resource services
6. Administration, such as building maintenance, plant security, mail distribution, utility services
7. Public and stockholder relations
8. Technical service units of various kinds (research laboratories, test centers, audio and visual aids group, EDP center)

Central Data Base Integrates All Systems   The information system for each of these operations is, in large modern computerized companies, tied to all others through a central data base. Since all retrieve data from the same source (such as magnetic tapes), it is possible to avoid duplication and considerable cost. In Figure 4-5 we show the nature of a typical set of basic information systems and the data required by each.

Financial Information

All companies have some kind of financial information system. The basis of the system is the flow of expenses, expenditures, and revenues. If the system is designed correctly, it assists in providing measurement and control of organizational units of the company (Figure 4-6).

Financial Information Systems Cut Across All Operations   Financial information systems bring together and organize large amounts of historical data. These data are then transformed into reports on expenses and variances from plans for corrective action by managers. Besides historical information, financial information systems project budgets and *pro forma* earnings statements, balance sheets, cash flow, and capital expenditure budget breakdowns. Thus they deal both with the past for measurement and the future for planning.

By and large, the conversion of a *manual* financial system to a *computer-based* system is subject to less improvement as a managerial device than are other types of information systems. From a data handling and cost point of view, financial systems are usually the first candidates for conversion. There is less opportunity to improve the quality of this information system because of the nature of its operations, which are usually concerned primarily with budgetary control. Improvement is obtained in promptness and accuracy of reporting.

Periodically, management approves some type of financial plan (the master budget) that assigns responsibility for maintaining incomes, in-

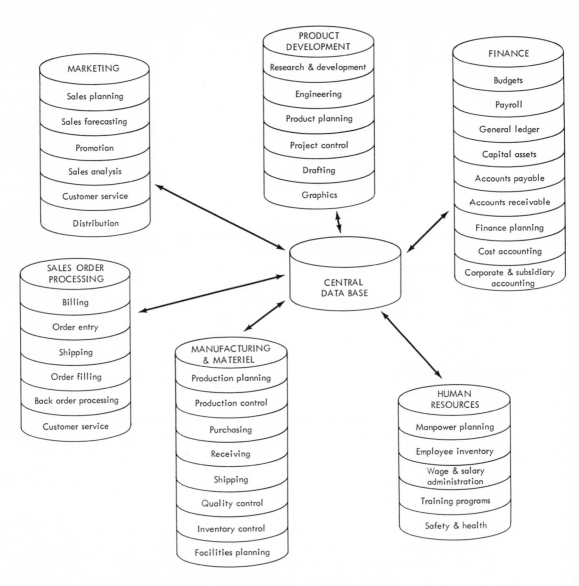

Figure 4-5 Basic information systems.

vestments, and costs within standard limits. This plan then becomes the basis for periodic reports on performance against plan, and these reports become the device by which control is exercised. Major problems in such a system involve (1) determining equitable standards for control, (2) determining when action is required, and (3) obtaining rapid, up-to-date information on variances.

Figure 4-6 Integration of operating systems with accounting and financial information systems.

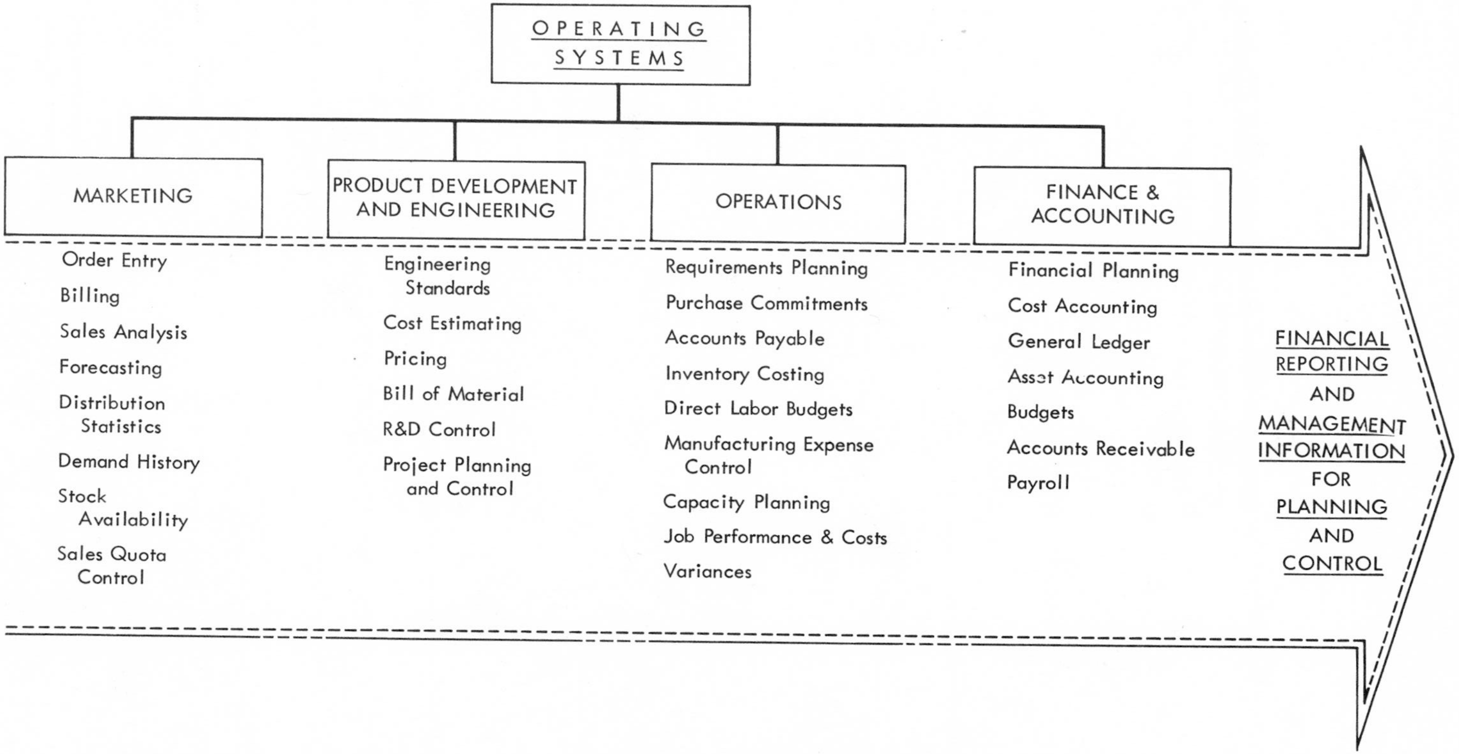

OPERATING SYSTEMS

MARKETING

Order Entry
Billing
Sales Analysis
Forecasting
Distribution
Statistics
Demand History
Stock
Availability
Sales Quota
Control

PRODUCT DEVELOPMENT AND ENGINEERING

Engineering
Standards
Cost Estimating
Pricing
Bill of Material
R&D Control
Project Planning
and Control

OPERATIONS

Requirements Planning
Purchase Commitments
Accounts Payable
Inventory Costing
Direct Labor Budgets
Manufacturing Expense
Control
Capacity Planning
Job Performance & Costs
Variances

FINANCE & ACCOUNTING

Financial Planning
Cost Accounting
General Ledger
Asset Accounting
Budgets
Accounts Receivable
Payroll

FINANCIAL REPORTING AND MANAGEMENT INFORMATION FOR PLANNING AND CONTROL

EXAMPLE—BILLING

Billing is perhaps the most widely used data processing application. Despite the fact that the preparation of invoices is often viewed as a somewhat casual clerical function, the speed and accuracy of the operation can have a significant impact upon cash flow as well as customer goodwill. Additional advantages include clerical savings, more timely processing, the release of high-salaried employees for other functions, and the flexibility to absorb additional work load during times of increased growth.

A customer's invoice, the output of the typical billing system, is illustrated in Figure 4-7. Notice that in addition to the managerial objectives indicated, the customer's invoice also can provide the input for additional vital subsystems. Here we see an excellent example of how an otherwise routine clerical operation can be upgraded for managerial decision making.

Figure 4-7   Customer's invoice.

Courtesy of IBM Corporation.

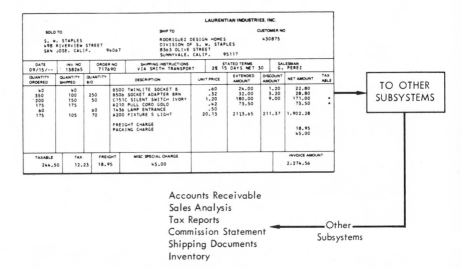

BILLING

Objectives: Provide Input to Other Subsystems
Improve Cash Flow
Maintain Customer Good Will
Timely Invoice Processing
Keep Salesmen Informed

Accounts Receivable
Sales Analysis
Tax Reports
Commission Statement
Shipping Documents
Inventory

Production/Operations

The production/operations system is concerned with information about the physical flow of goods or the production of goods and services. It covers such activities as production planning and control, inventory control and management, purchasing distribution, and transportation.

Production Information System Keeps Production on Target

Because the quantities of data are so large and the timing of information so essential, the production/operations system is the most adaptable to automation and yields the largest benefits in terms of immediate solution of critical and costly problems. That is, as daily orders for varied products reach manufacturing, the sequence of orders, the assignment of machines to produce the products, and the assignment of men to machines must be made. Idle machines, idle men, and back-up work are all bad news. The computer makes possible very quickly fairly good scheduling involving all these variables.

The production problems of planning and scheduling have all the characteristics for computerized solutions: many variables, reasonably accurate values of input variables, need for speed, repetitive situations, and large amounts of information involved in the problem structure.

Production Is Central to All Other Systems

The production operating and information systems in a manufacturing company interact with all other major systems. Marketing information provides inputs to production planning. Cost of production involves labor and materials payments as tracked by the accounting information system. The personnel information system must utilize data about production system employees. Figure 4-8 demonstrates how the production information subsystem interacts with these other subsystems.

Although other applications (e.g., decision making, total system simulation) may offer greater potential, this functional area usually offers immediate payoffs.

Dearden and McFarlan have identified six characteristics of the type of information that lends itself best to computer use:

Production Information Is Especially Suited to Automation

1. *A number of interacting variables.* The computer has the ability to solve rapidly problems with multiinteracting variables, and hence its value is high in this type of usage.

2. *Reasonably accurate values.* Coefficients of equations should have reasonably accurate values, and equations should express accurately the relationships among the variables. The computer has an infinite capacity for compounding errors of inaccurate values and relationships.

3. *Speed an important factor.* The value of a computer in an information system is a function of the requirement of speed in processing data.

Figure 4-8 Integration of subsystems through the information flow in the production/operations system.

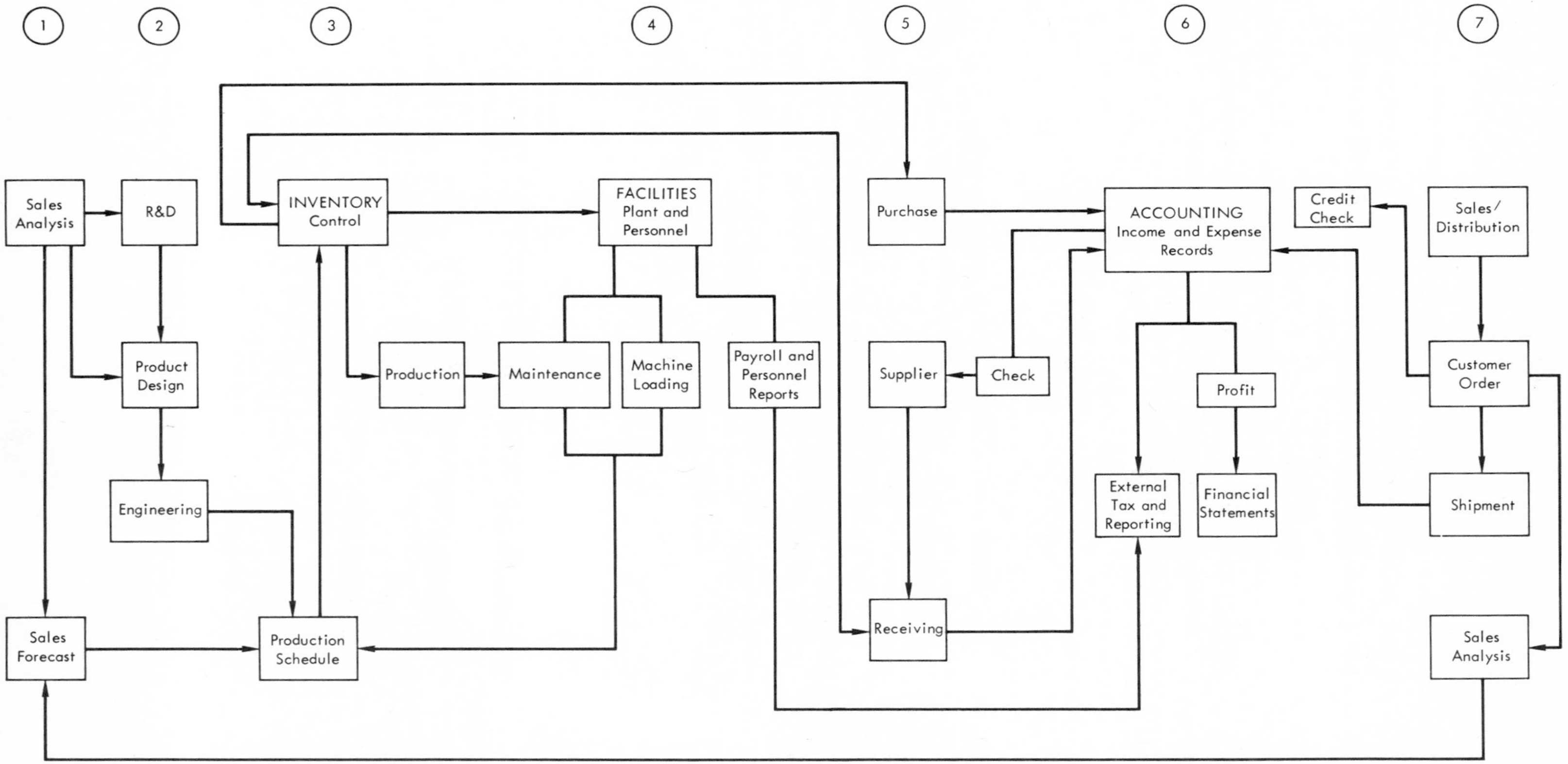

1   Sales Analysis
2   Engineering
3   Inventory Control and Production Scheduling
4   Production/Operations Facilities

5   Purchasing
6   Financial
7   Sales and Distribution

4. *Repetitive operations.* Operations of this type offer the most profitable area of applications.
5. *Accuracy as a requirement.* The greater degree of accuracy required in the output, the more likely it is that a computer will be helpful.
6. *Large amounts of information.* Because computers can handle large amounts of data quickly, applications with this attribute offer profitable employment.[2]

Because the information needed for effective management of production/operations has all these characteristics, these systems are probably the most adaptable to automation of any in the company. Moreover, because of the requirement for timeliness in handling large quantities of data, the greatest advances in improvements and economy are likely to be made in the production/operations area.

The production/operations system, particularly in a manufacturing company, is unquestionably the most important from an operating standpoint. It crosses all subsystem boundaries and has an effect throughout the company. Yet despite this importance, the production/operations system has had less management involvement and consequently less development than the financial system. This is unfortunate, because in most companies this area offers more opportunity for development, cost saving, and management improvement than any other. Indeed, much of the *total systems* activity in recent years has begun because of problems in the production/operations area and because, once begun, an examination of this area leads to the design of related and integrated subsystems throughout the company. This attribute and the importance of the production/operations system and its impact on systems elsewhere in the organization can be seen in Figure 4-8, which demonstrates how the production subsystem interacts with all major functions of a manufacturing company. Note that the critical input to this system is the customer order.

EXAMPLES—PURCHASING, MATERIALS PLANNING, OPERATIONS SCHEDULING

Some of the operations involved in this major system can be understood by examining three of the most widespread information subsystems. Critical objectives and information needs are

Purchasing Objectives

Determine economic order quantity to buy.

Reduce clerical costs.

Monitor buyer performance.

---

2 John Dearden and F. Warren McFarlan, *Management Information Systems*, Homewood, Ill.: Richard D. Irwin, Inc., 1966, pp. 10–11.

Identify high-volume vendors in order to negotiate higher discounts. Determine supplier performance by identifying late deliveries and poor quality.

(*See Figure 4–9*)

Materials Planning Objectives

Plan and control parts from a predetermined production schedule. Reduce the time and costs of determining and ordering material requirements.

Allow nondisruptive changes to the production schedule.

Forecast future needs for ordering material.

Forecast changes in material requirements resulting from a production schedule change.

(*See Figure 4–10*)

Capacity Planning and Operation Scheduling Objectives

Identify work center loads for future time periods and those that are over- or underloaded.

Evaluate alternatives of subcontracting or overtime to meet delivery dates.

Identify orders to be rescheduled in order to level the load.

Forecast the time and location of equipment and tooling needs.

Compute start dates for shop orders in order to meet delivery dates.

Forecast skills and trades required.

Forecast order release dates.

(*See Figure 4–11*)

Marketing Information

Marketing Information Systems Are the Most Complex

The basic areas of the marketing function that lend themselves to improvement through information systems include (1) forecasting/sales planning, (2) market research, (3) advertising, and (4) operating and control information required to manage the marketing function. Examples of the last include such information as sales reports and distribution cost reports.[3]

Marketing information is one of the most important information systems to most businesses, yet it is most often the one overlooked. Few

[3] In a survey of 122 marketing vice presidents, their top four choices for utilizing their company's computers were forecasting sales, customer services, predicting market for new products and services, and sales analysis and control. See "Reading the Crystal Ball," *Nation's Business*, Feb. 1969, p. 16.

| Buyer Price Analysis Report | | | | | | | | Date of report OCT 5 Buyer's name D Chambers For qtr. ending 9/30 | |

Material code	Product code	Part no.	Supplier name	Unit cost base period	Unit cost current period	Total costs base period	Total costs current period	Variance
877	36	2919067	MACILVAINE BROS.	1.27	1.27	4,216	4,216	450
877	40	4319108	DUNSMUIRE	8.10	7.60	13,110	12,660	82-
877	45	1437001	CARLSON	4.23	4.47	460	378	

Determine buyer performance by comparing actual purchase amounts with amount figured at base or standard prices.

| Vendor Delivery Performance Report | | | | | | | | 10/06 | |

Buyer	Vendor name	Vendor no.	Total value open orders	Open orders	Orders behind	Percent behind	YTD purchase percent behind	YTD orders behind
CA	GENERAL MFG. CO.	19080	792.00	16	4	25	15	27
CA	POWER DESIGN CO.	40001	2,103.75	2	1	50	25	8
CA	CENTRAL TOOL CO.	56012	301.20	10	1	10	2	50
	BUYER TOTAL		3,196.95	28	6	21	7	85
TK	ORIN FORGE CO.	49045	3,115.00	30	6	20	20	50
TK	LAKE MILLING	73111	603.00	23	0	0	4	30
	BUYER TOTAL		3,718.00	53	6	11	12	80
	DEPT. TOTAL		6,914.95	81	12	15	9	165

Highlights trend of vendor delivery performance by comparison of current and year-to-date (YTD) figures.

| Open Purchase Order Status | | | | | | | | Date 02/03 | | By P/O ☐ By Supplier ☒ By Part ☐ | |

Purchase order no.	Part no.	Mat. code	Supplier no.	Supplier name	Qty. on order	Qty. rec'd	Balance date	Delivery date	Value outstanding $	Action
140562	201610	924	0021	BAILY & CO.	220	110	110	03/06	200	
144250	222521	924	0021	BAILY & CO.	25		25	04/05	47	
146402	368065	924	0021	BAILY & CO.	200		200	04/03	634	
									881	
136781	179923	801	0027	ACTION INC.	4,000	3,500	500	01/03	774	EXP.
144548	474149	801	0027	ACTION INC.	800		800	03/06	175	

All orders placed with suppliers can be listed in a variety of categories (e.g., supplier, part number, order number).

Courtesy of IBM Corporation.

Figure 4-9 Output, reports from purchasing subsystem.

marketing executives use information effectively on their jobs; most of them rely on intuition as a basis for decisions.[4] The vast majority of firms tend to maintain information only about sales records or orders

[4] Richard D. Buzzell, Donald F. Cos., and Rex V. Brown, *Marketing Research and Information Systems*, New York: McGraw-Hill Book Company, 1969.

Figure 4-10 Materials planning reports.

Courtesy of IBM Corporation.

End product requirements							
		Six month projection					
Stock no.	Description	1	2	3	4	5	6
1016H	ENGINE	100	0	100	50	100	100
6094HD	ENGINE	50	0	50	50	0	75
4377L	POWER UNIT	60	60	0	120	60	0
3355LD	ENGINE	0	50	0	25	0	25
3355B	ENGINE	0	25	25	25	25	25
9774AB	POWER UNIT	125	75	125	0	50	100

Summary of demand for end items and/or service assemblies that can be exploded to determine parts requirements.

Requirements planning report								
Item no.	Description	Stock	10/08	10/22	11/05	11/19	12/03	12/17
A300-9965	FILTER	50						
	GROSS REQ.		337	196	231	175	372	563
	NET REQ.		287	196	231	175	372	563
	PLANNED ORDERS				700			700
	LEADTIME OFFSET			700			700	
A403-4773	GAUGE	150						
	GROSS REQ.			600		300	265	
	NET REQ.			450		300	265	
	PLANNED ORDERS			500		250	250	
	LEADTIME OFFSET		500		250	250		500

Consolidated gross requirements by time period, and orders necessary to meet requirements.

Requirements planning exception report					
Item no.	Item description	Exception code	Req. date	Req. qty.	Comments
A320-4447	FILTER	01	10/08	254	ORDER SIZE EXCEEDS MAX. ALLOWABLE
A340-6674	BRACE UNIT	05	9/08	20	OPEN ORDER DOES NOT COVER REQ.
A449-3754	REGULATOR	10	12/08	187	NOT PROCESSED—OUTSIDE OF HORIZON
C203-8883	CONNECTOR	01	10/08	144	ORDER SIZE EXCEEDS MAX. ALLOWABLE
C493-7655	ASSEMBLY UNIT	05	9/08	20	OPEN ORDER DOES NOT COVER REQ.
E212-3993	VALVE SWITCH	10	12/08	163	NOT PROCESSED—OUTSIDE OF HORIZON
E222-7063	PUMP METER B	18	10/08	15	OPEN ORDER DUE—NO REQ.

Exception report that highlights areas that require special handling.

Work center load summary								07/15		Machine shop A
Dept. no.	GRP no.	Description	No. of mach.	Wk.	Capacity	Load	Available capacity	Overload		
1	01	BENCH MILLS	5	1	136.0	130.0	6.0			
				2	170.0	150.0	20.0			
				3	170.0	165.5	4.5			
				4	170.0	179.0		9.0		
				5	170.0	162.3	7.7			
				6	170.0	185.1		15.1		

Summary of labor operations required for shop orders by time period and machine group.

Shop load schedule										07/15
Mach./ GRP	Hrs./day	Scheduled		Part no.	Job	Oper.	Priority code	Order qty.	Claimed qty.	
		Day	Hr.							
1609-01	7.50	622	.0	461235	3422	020	1	2,100	210	
		622	4.50	461747	6343	035	5	1,988		
		623	5.50	461396	4211	020	5	113		
1207-01	15.00	622	.0	537141	3762	055	2	2,759	500	
		622	6.25	537593	4727	030	3	457		
		623	13.40	537547	3249	040	5	637		

Utilized for scheduling jobs and improving use of men and machines.

Tooling list									Date 07/15
Part no.	Job	Oper.	Dept.	Mach./ GRP	Scheduled		Tool no.	Tool code	Description
					Day	Hr.			
131634	1700	0040	018	1610-01	624	11.1	31665	B	FIXTURE
							1021545	B	CUTTER
133195	1800	0045	005	1609-02	622	.0	1000555	B	VISE JAWS
133694	6601	0090	011	1400-01	622	8.7	153310	D	INDEX GAUGE
							151347	D	COMP. CHART
							95601	B	COMP. FIXT.

Allows prepacking of tools by listing those required by each operation.

Courtesy of IBM Corporation.

Figure 4-11   Operations scheduling reports.

and shipments. What is needed is a system that will give marketing managers information to help them make better decisions about pricing, advertising, product promotion policy, sales force effort, and other vital marketing matter. Such a system should also take into account the necessity elsewhere in the organization for information concerning marketing that affects decisions in other subsystems of the company.

Marketing Interacts with the Environment   The effectiveness of marketing information systems depends to a large extent on feedback from the marketplace to the firm, so that the firm can judge the adequacy of its past performance as well as appraise the opportunities for new activity. Despite this feedback need, many firms consider their marketing information system to be some type of *sales analysis* activity that has been superimposed onto an accounting system. Yet there is no reason this vital area of management activity should not take an approach similar to that of other areas of the firm whose information needs are designed around the managerial functions of planning, operating, and controlling.

Table 4-1 summarizes some of the more important types of informa-

Table 4-1 Selected applications and outputs of a marketing information system.

Application	Output
Market planning	
Forecasting	Parts requirements and production schedule based on demand for industrial goods
Purchasing	Automatic optimization of purchasing function and inventory control based on decision rules
Credit management	Automatic computer processing of credit decisions
Market research	
Pricing policy	Policy based on historical analysis of past
Advertising strategy	Strategy based on sales analysis of a variety of market segment breakdowns
Advertising expenditure	Correlation by numerous market segments of sales and advertising expenditures
Marketing control	
Marketing costs	Current reports of deviation from standard and undesirable trends
Sales performance	A variety of data to help discover reasons for sales performance and correct deviations
Territorial control of sales, distribution, costs, etc.	Timely reports of performance on territorial basis to permit reallocation of resources to substandard areas

tion systems applications in the marketing area and indicates selected outputs that are useful for market planning, market research, and marketing control. These three types of marketing systems are summarized:

1. *Control systems.* Provide monitoring and review of performance against plan. Also provide information concerning trends, problems, and possible marketing opportunities.
2. *Planning systems.* Provide information needed for planning the marketing and sales program. A good system furnishes information to permit the marketing manager to weigh the effects of alternative plans in trade promotion, pricing, and other variables in the forecasting equation.
3. *Market research systems.* Used to develop, test, and predict the effects of actions taken or planned in the basic subsystems of marketing (pricing, advertising, design, etc.)

The sales/marketing function has historically been serviced with information contained in month-end sales reports. Generally, these reports have suffered from two shortcomings; they were clerical in nature and therefore did not contain decision-making information, and they arrived too late for remedial action.

These shortcomings can be overcome with a general marketing system somewhat along the lines depicted in Figure 4-12. Characteristic of this type of system is an inquiry capability located in field, branch, district, and headquarters offices. These terminals are connected via tele-processing facilities to a computer, and the system can provide a broad inquiry coverage relating to sales activity updated on a daily basis.

The systems designer and marketing manager who uses the system can design his own inquiry formats to fit his particular needs. The four formats depicted in Figure 4-12 can be described thus:

Figure 4-12   The general marketing information system.

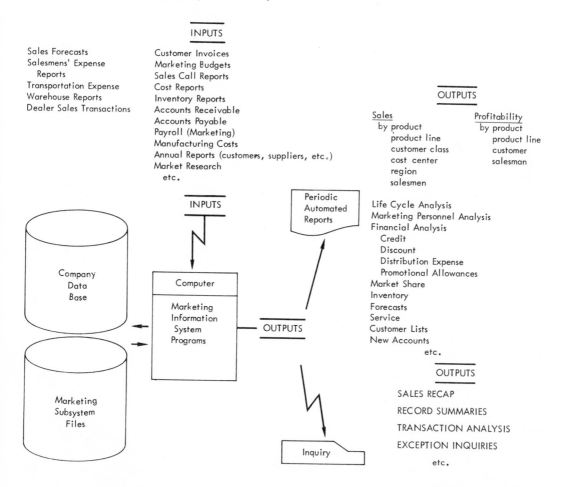

1. *Sales recap.* An overall performance summary to date, compared with previous periods, budgets, or other standards. This recap can be programmed to trigger successive levels of detailed reports when the analysis indicates substandard performance. Major areas of performance analysis might include total sales by product, sales expense, new accounts, replacement sales, cancellation rates, and a variety of profitability analyses.

2. *Record Summaries.* Optional levels of detail that permit in-depth analysis of deviations spotted by the sales recap. Ideally, this format should be programmed so that the user can structure his own reporting needs. These might include such items as sales by model, by sales plan, by industry and by customer type and sales to major and national accounts. Additionally, a variety of ratios, such as sales units to travel expenses, should be available if desired.

3. *Transaction analysis.* This format might be called the *significant* transaction analysis because its purpose is to provide a "management by exception" approach to transactions that are so out of the ordinary that they require special treatment. Such transactions might be defined in terms of dollar volume, number of sales, or other significant measures that exceed control limits.

4. *Exception inquiries.* This is the highest level of systems sophistication in that it gives a true inquiry capability to the user. This can be understood by such questions as "Which sales offices have achieved a level of 50% of their sales in the manufacturing industry but are less than 80% sales quota in the retail industry?" It is easy to see how this inquiry capability is a vital tool to any marketing/ sales manager.

EXAMPLE—INVENTORY MANAGEMENT

Inventory Is Related to Forecasts of Demand

A marketing-related system of immense importance to profitability is inventory management. Too little inventory means lost sales and costly rush orders. Too much inventory means carrying costs, interest costs, warehousing costs, and the chance of obsolescence. Two typical inventory management reports are shown in Figure 4-13. They are

1. *Distribution-by-value report.* Items are shown in sequence by sales dollars, so that the item with the largest annual sales comes first and the item with the smallest annual sales comes last. Percentages are also shown. From Figure 4-13 it can be seen that the top 1% of items accounts for almost 18% of sales—six items accounting for nearly one-fifth of sales. The top 20% of items accounts for 70% of sales.

2. *Distribution-by-value with item movement.* This report permits (1) life cycle analysis, (2) segmentation of inventory to allow concentration on high investment items, (3) establishment of order quantities and order points, and (4) cycle review of vendor lines.

Distribution-by-Value Report

Item No	Cumulative Count		Annual Units	Unit Cost	Annual $ Sales	Cumulative Sales	
	Rank by $ Sales	%				$	%
411045	1	.2	104,578	.966	101,023	101,023	3.8
411118	2	.4	375,959	.246	92,486	193,509	7.3
411063	3	.5	40,602	2.012	81,693	275,202	10.4
411075	4	.7	69,570	1.123	78,128	353,330	13.3
411176	5	.9	133,534	.490	65,432	418,762	15.8
411381	6	1.1	106,651	.510	54,392	473,154	17.8
411368	110	20.0	90,191	.073	6,584	1,886,385	71.0
411425	111	20.2	7,513	.800	6,011	1,892,396	71.2
411263	112	20.4	1,820	3.286	5,983	1,898,379	71.4
411503	113	20.5	10,611	.553	5,868	1,904,247	71.6
411444	545	99.2	813	.145	118	2,657,997	100.0
411465	546	99.4	4,227	.022	93	2,658,090	100.0
411243	547	99.6	90	.715	65	2,658,155	100.0
411516	548	99.8	4	2.916	12	2,658,167	100.0
411541	549	100.0	0	0	0	2,658,167	100.0

Distribution-by-Value with Item Movement Activity

LAURENTIAN INDUSTRIES, INC. **ANALYSIS OF INVENTORY ACTIVITY**											
12 **MONTH PERIOD ENDING** 7/1/--											
STOCK LOCATION	STOCK NUMBER	DESCRIPTION	UNIT	DATE OF LAST ACTIVITY	NET ISSUES FOR PERIOD			BALANCE ON HAND			
					NUMBER OF TRANS.	QUANTITY	AVERAGE PER MONTH	QUANTITY	MONTHS' SUPPLY	VALUE	
2715-237	127205	LIGHT RECEPTACLE	EA	7/--	2	4	.3	16	53.3	$ 4.32	
2715-420	247389	SOLENOID, HEATER	EA	7/--	1	1	.1	7	70.0	4.48	
2715-267	111462	SWITCH, STARTER	EA	8/--	1	4	.3	4	13.3	8.64	
2715-601	896124	PINION STUD	EA	9/--	4	16	1.3	84	64.6	9.24	
2716-234	59827	GASKET, MANIFOLD	EA	11/--	2	12	1.0	16	16.0	7.52	
2716-320	614	WASHER, RUBBER	DZ	12/--	1	3	.2	14	70.0	2.52	
2717-086	6213	BOLT, CARRIAGE	DZ	12/--	1	2	.2	27	135.0	32.40	
2717-742	1032	BEARING, CLUTCH	EA	1/--	1	1	.1	9	90.0	34.83	
2717-748	148722	AXLE	EA	3/--	1	1	.1	3	30.0	24.60	
2719-147	2642	BRUSH, GENERATOR	EA	3/--	3	9	.7	42	60.0	7.14	
2719-382	222649	REGULATOR	EA	3/--	4	4	.3	3	10.0	3.78	

Courtesy of IBM Corporation.

Figure 4-13   Inventory management reports.

Personnel Information

The personnel information system deals with the flow of information about people working in the organization as well as future personnel needs. In most organizations, the system is concerned primarily with the five basic subsystems of the personnel function: recruiting, placement, training, compensation, and maintenance.

Personnel
Information
Systems
Should Be
Designed for
Managerial
Planning

It is likely that many personnel managers are concerned only with personnel records for their own sake. Human resource management, as opposed to the traditional view of the personnel function, should be considered a total system that interacts with the other major systems of the organization—marketing, production, finance—as well as the external environment. Indeed, the primary purpose of the human resource management program is to service these major systems. Forecasting and planning the manpower needs of the organization, maintaining an adequate and satisfactory work force, and controlling the personnel policies and programs of the company are the major responsibilities of human resource management.

To achieve the foregoing, a *manpower system* is necessary. Like any system, it consists of a number of inputs and outputs and a number of related subsystems, processes, and activities, all operating through the medium of information. Such a system is shown in Figure 4-14. Note that the output from the manpower subsystems goes to personnel staff specialists as well as to line operating managers. Many personnel managers mistakenly conceive of their information systems as a tool of the personnel function alone rather than as the real reason for a manpower system—organizational effectiveness. A systems-oriented approach to manpower management interrelates and integrates the functions of the personnel manager with the duties of the operating personnel, who benefit most from a manpower information system.

Briefly, the six major subsystems of the manpower management system designed to accomplish these objectives are

Figure 4-14   Manpower information systems.

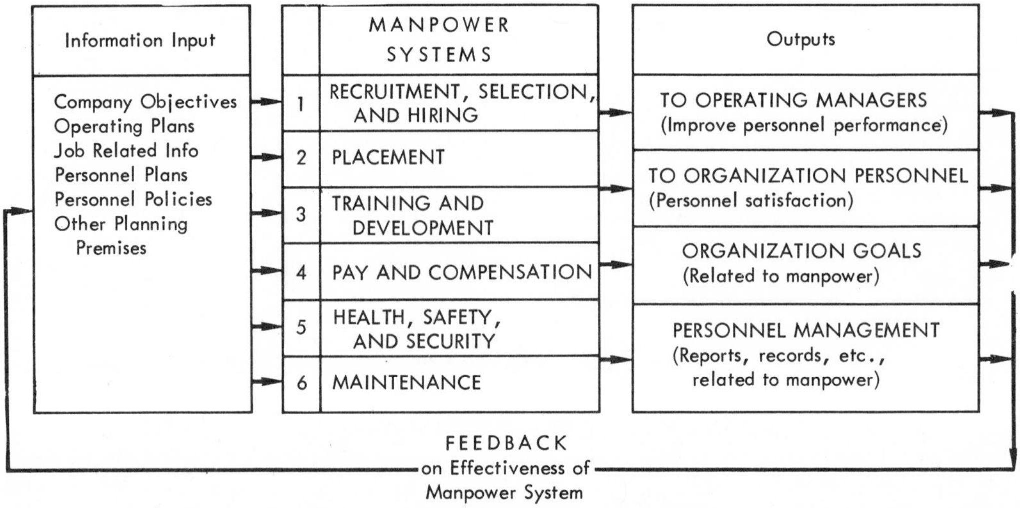

1. *Recruitment.* Properly managed, the recruitment system forecasts personnel needs and skills and recruits the personnel at the proper time to meet organizational needs. A properly designed information system will furnish information concerning (a) skills required for company programs and processes and (b) inventory of skills available in the organization. Manning tables, job specifications, and other personnel data are also useful in this subsystem.

2. *Placement.* This system is perhaps the most vital of all personnel functions because it matches available personnel with requirements, and hence the effective use of manpower as a resource takes place within this system. A properly designed placement information system takes into account the latest behavioral tools and techniques to ensure that the capabilities of people are identified and placed with properly organized work requirements.

3. *Training and development.* As technological changes and demands for new skills accelerate, many companies find that they must necessarily develop much of their talent requirements from internal sources. In addition, a large part of the work force must constantly be updated in new techniques and developments. This task is the function of the training and development system. Basic information requirements include a continuing skills inventory of company personnel matched against a forecast of current and estimated needs for improved skills.

4. *Compensation.* The pay and other values (fringe benefits, for example) for the satisfaction of individual wants and needs and for compliance with government, union, and other requirements is the basic function of the compensation system. Information included in or required by this system is largely that associated with the traditional payroll and other financial records.

5. *Maintenance.* This system, largely for the benefit of operating managers, should be designed to ensure that personnel policies and procedures are achieved. It may extend to the operation of systems to control work standards, those required to measure performance against the financial plan or other programs, and the many subsidiary records normally associated with the collection, maintenance, and dissemination of personnel data.

6. *Health, safety, and plant security.* As the name implies, this system is concerned with the health of personnel and the safety of job practices and related operations. Plant security includes actions necessary to prevent theft, damage, or compromise of classified information.

"Skills Bank" for Planning Use of Human Resources

Recently, a good deal of attention has been focused on the design and utilization of skills inventory programs. These are sometimes called *skills banks* or *manpower assessment programs*. The objective of such programs is to identify and locate the talent resources of the organization in order to maximize their use. It is easy to see how such an objective could be essential in engineering, research, or other firms where talent is the most costly and valuable resource.

Figure 4-15 depicts the conceptual operation of a skills inventory program. Notice that in addition to the regular reports generated by the program it may also include a computer-simulated model. It is a valuable tool for gaining information about different manpower approaches under varying assumptions.

SUMMARY

Management information systems ultimately derive their inputs from operating information systems.

Information systems may be manual or computerized. The computerized information systems are becoming increasingly widespread as business complexity increases. The rapid rise of minicomputers and microcomputers, more suitable to small businesses, is hastening the computerization of information systems.

Figure 4-15   Operation of a skills inventory program.

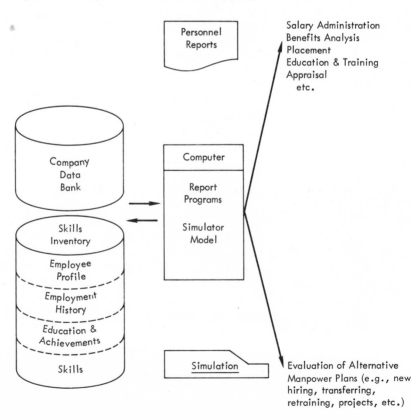

Each identifiable business subsystem requires its own information system. These information systems are linked to produce the basic informations, many of which we have listed in this chapter.

This chapter has outlined information flows for a number of basic operating systems. We have shown samples of outputs of these information systems. It is easy to see that such output must be processed further before it is suitable for use by managers, particularly higher-level managers.

QUESTIONS AND PROBLEMS

1. Major operating systems in a company are as checked:

_____ a. Order processing	_____ f. Human resource services
_____ b. Marketing	_____ g. Training and development
_____ c. Advertising	_____ h. Manufacturing
_____ d. Engineering	_____ i. Mail distribution
_____ e. Finance	_____ j. Capital budgeting

2. For the following systems, give the basic objective and a typical output report that goes to a manager in the company.

Operating System	Objective	Output Report to a Manager
a. Sales promotion		
b. Purchasing		
c. Billing		
d. Manpower planning		
e. Product planning		
f. Capital budgeting		
g. Quality control		
h. Production planning		
i. Cost accounting		
j. Personnel placement		

chapter five

What the Manager
Should Know
About MIS Hardware

CHAPTER 5   explains the components and functions of the computer and associated equipment for processing data.

When you have finished studying

WHAT THE MANAGER SHOULD KNOW ABOUT MIS HARDWARE

you should be able to

1. Explain the kinds of things that data processing equipment can do
2. Compare a manual information system with a computer system by matching inputs, outputs, processing, and data storage
3. List six parts of a data communications system
4. List five variables that must be specified when selecting a computer system
5. Explain the five basic steps in converting a manual information system to a computerized information system.

"Tell it to start saving all the money they promised me . . . "

Source: Infosystems, Nov., 1974, p. 30

Much of the promise of the MIS is lost in the swamp of computerized data processing. This chapter's purpose is to acquaint the manager with the nature, promise, and pitfalls of equipment that is changing the nature of our world. We shall not give a technical or in-depth treatment of hardware.

Not since the invention of writing in about 3000 B.C. has there been such an advance in information processing as that provided by electronic computer equipment. Jumps in technology of computer equipment are occurring faster than textbooks can come off the press. While minicomputers are still newcomers on the scene, *micro*computers, which also give promise of matching early giant computers, are appearing.

MIND-BOGGLING
HARDWARE

Today, computers separated by great distances talk with each other. Computer output microfilmers translate data into readable language and microfilms at a rate 100 times faster than paper printers. Paper printers are not exactly slow, either, printing over 1000 lines per minute. A computer may store over 1 billion characters internally. On-line storage capacity may be expanded to nearly ½ *trillion* characters. In comparison, the average human, living 70 years, stores information equivalent to 1 trillion *words*.

DATA PROCESSING AND THE COMPUTER

As previously suggested, there are several prerequisites for a modern, effective computer-based management information system. The *first* of these is a *management* system: the organizational arrangements, the structure, and the procedures for adequate planning and control. *Second*, there must exist data and information: information about the company's goals, resources, environment, policies, operations, plans, and performance against plans. These types of information represent knowledge about the company's managerial and operational processes. *Third*, to process these data, it is necessary to have equipment that will (1) provide the capability for economic, rapid access to large-scale storage of retrievable data; (2) process these data economically and at high speed; and (3) enter information into the system and retrieve and display it. These three activities are now often performed by special electronic communication devices and by today's computers and related hardware. *Fourth*, a final prerequisite to an effective computer-based management information system is an organization for designing, maintaining, and managing the required systems and procedures.

MANAGEMENT
SYSTEM,
INFORMATION,
AND HARDWARE

In this chapter we want to examine how information is stored, processed, transmitted and displayed, and retrieved by means of the electronic computer and related devices. The objective is to understand how the computer operates as the fundamental information processor and the essential element of a management information system.

COMPONENTS AND OPERATION OF A DATA PROCESSING SYSTEM

An information system is composed of five basic components, as shown in Figure 5-1. In a manual system, human beings perform the five basic functions; in a computer-based system, the functions are performed

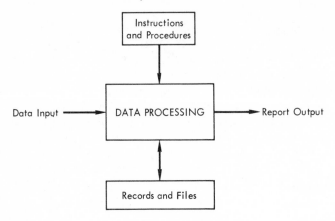

Figure 5-1 Basic components of an information system.

by equipment. In either type of system the basic functions are (1) entering data into the system; (2) processing the data (rearranging input data and processing files); (3) maintaining files and records; (4) developing procedures that tell what data are needed and when, where they are obtained, and how they are used, as well as providing instruction routines for the processor to follow; and (5) preparing report output.

BASIC SYSTEM ELEMENTS: INPUT, PROCESSOR, OUTPUT

Both manual and computer-based information systems have the elements and attributes of systems in general and can be described in terms of these elements: input, output, and processor. Our examination of computer systems in this chapter will proceed by analogy to make the transition from the easily understood manual system to a slightly more complex computer-based system. The transition and analogy will accomplish two purposes. First, we shall be able to see how a computer-based data processing system can become a vital adjunct to management planning and control. Second, by examining the system through its components (input, output, processor), we shall be better able to understand how these components of an information system provide the framework for MIS design.

OPERATION OF A MANUAL INFORMATION SYSTEM

Humans are the most numerous data processors. Yet the human remains an unreliable data processor. On the other hand, where judgment and creativity are required, the human mind is indispensable.

WHAT ARE THE FORMS OF THE BASIC ELEMENTS OF A MANUAL INFORMATION SYSTEM?

All information systems were manual before the computer arrived; many of them still are. We shall describe a manual inventory system first and then compare it with a computerized inventory system. In each case, as in any company information system, the basic components of a system —input, processor, and output—are present.

In Figure 5-2, we depict a manual inventory system. The components are described below.

Input

We see that the *input device* for the manual inventory processing system is the in-basket of the inventory clerk. This device receives the *input data* to the system, which may be in various forms and media and is related to information surrounding inventory receipts and issues. Inventory records are updated with receipts on the one hand and reduced with orders for the item on the other. Receipts and issues may be recorded in writing by a storekeeper, stamped on an invoice by a mechanical device, or punched into a card. The resulting cards, invoices, receipt documents, issue papers, shipping documents, and a variety of other *input* information affecting the inventory system are entered into the in-basket for processing and ultimate preparation of output.

Processor

The processor consists of the storage, the arithmetic and logic elements, and the control elements.

THE HUMAN BRAIN The storage is made up of the *internal* (primary) memory. It is represented by the clerk's brain and the records being worked on. The

Figure 5-2 Elements of data processing (inventory system)

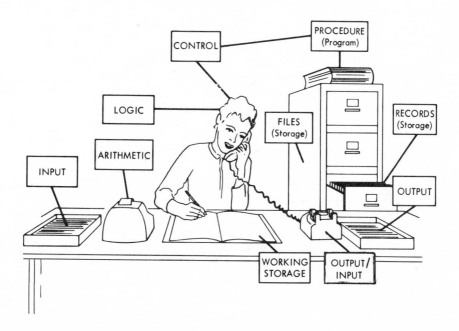

external storage is the *file* of individual *records* for an item of inventory. The organization and structuring of this external storage is very important in both manual and computer-based systems.

Internal Memory

The arithmetic and the logic elements are in the clerk's brain. The arithmetic unit adds, subtracts, multiplies, and divides. The logic unit compares two quantities to see if one is greater than, equal to, or less than the other in order to make a processing decision. Most people are surprised to learn that these five operations are all the manipulations that a computer can do.

Arithmetic and Logic

The control element tells the clerk what data to enter into primary storage and when to enter them. It tells the arithmetic/logic elements what operations to perform, where the data are to be found, and where to place results. It tells what files to enter. The control element in the manual system consists of the clerk's brain and the systems/procedures manual.

Control

The procedures manual may, for example, instruct the processor to "(1) multiply unit cost by units issued, (2) deduct units issued from balance on hand, and (3) deduct gross value of issue from dollar value of inventory." The clerk would then perform this processing on the input information, update the inventory balance (external storage), and prepare the required *output* report to go in the out-basket. Preparation of the *output* is the final step of the information processing system.

Output

Output may be (1) updated inventory records, (2) an inventory status report, and (3) other reports and documents related to inventory. The media are likely to be handwritten or typed reports. As we shall see, these limited media contrast greatly with the wide variety possible in computerized systems.

A schematic of the manual information system is shown in Figure 5-3.

COMPONENTS OF A COMPUTER SYSTEM

Although many managers are awed or confused by the computer, its operation simply parallels that of the manual system we have just described. If we wish to convert our manual inventory system to a computerized equivalent, the input data would be the same. Only the *form* of the input would be different. The computer *processes* the data—hence the name electronic data processing (EDP).

EDP

The manual inventory control system previously discussed, when converted to computer application, might appear schematically as in

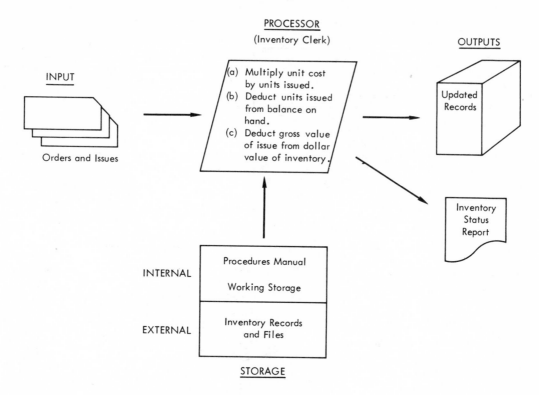

Figure 5-3 Manual inventory acounting system.

Figure 5-4, which illustrates the basic components of the computer system. Figure 5-5 shows the actual hardware components of modern-generation computer systems. A discussion of the components follows.

The function of entering data into the computer processor is performed by an input device. The input must be in a form acceptable to the computer as a machine. Normally this input form is a stack of punched cards, paper tape, magnetic tape, or electrical signal. An example of punched card input is shown in Figure 5-6. The punches in a column may indicate any one of 26 letters, 10 numerals, or 25 special characters.

The input devices (machines) read or sense coded input data. Typical computer input/output devices are shown in Figure 5-7.

The Central Processor

The central processor is the most significant component of the computer. As in the case of our inventory control clerk in the manual system, it consists of a *control* section, which coordinates the system components, and the *arithmetic/logic* unit, which performs the same functions (add,

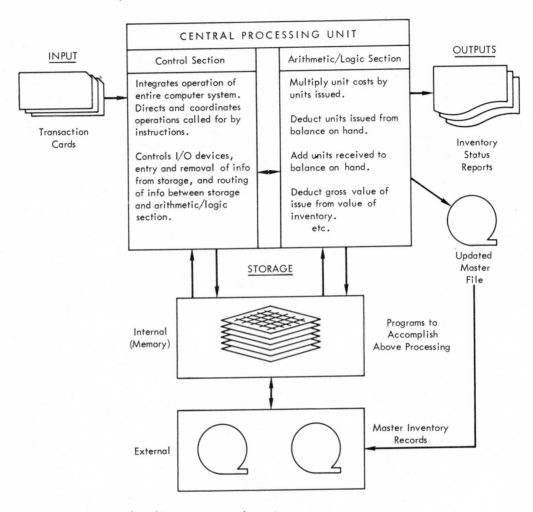

Figure 5-4 Computer-based inventory accounting system.

subtract, multiply, divide, compare, shift, move, store) as the clerk-calculator combination of the manual system. However, the CPU (central processing unit) of the computer accomplishes these tasks at fantastically increased speed and accuracy. This meager processing logic, accompanied by the five simple functions, accounts for the almost infinite variety of tasks the computer can perform. Figure 5-5 shows central processing units.

THE COMPUTER
BRAIN

The control section of the CPU directs and coordinates all operations called for by the instructions (programs) to the system. It controls the input/output units and the arithmetic/logic unit, transferring data to and from storage, and routing information between storage and the arithmetic/logic unit. It is by means of the control section that automatic, integrated operation of the entire computer system is achieved.

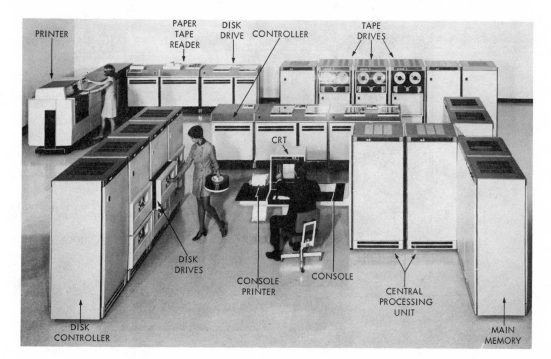

Courtesy of the NCR Corporation.

Figure 5-5(a) Components of a medium-to-large-scale computer system (NCR Century 300).

The arithmetic/logic section performs the arithmetic and logic operations. The former portion calculates, shifts numbers, sets the algebraic sign of results, rounds, compares, and performs the other tasks of calculation. The *logic section* carries out the *decision-making operations* to change the sequence of instruction execution, and it is capable of testing various conditions encountered during processing.

Storage

Storage within the computer is somewhat like a huge electronic filing cabinet completely indexed and accessible instantly to the computer. All data must be placed in storage before being processed by the computer. Storage consists of *internal*, which is a part of the processing component, and *external*.

Note the similarity between manual and computer systems. Internal storage, frequently referred to as *memory*, is the characteristic that permits the computer to store, in electronic form, data from input devices as well as long series of instructions called *programs* that tell the machine what to do. These programs are similar to the procedures manual of the

Computer Storage Is Like Human Memory

Figure 5-5(b)   Components of a small computer system (NCR Century 101).
Courtesy of the NCR Corporation.

Figure 5-5(c)   Components of a small computer system (IBM system 3).
Courtesy of IBM Corporation.

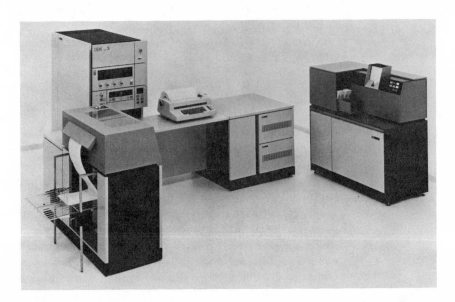

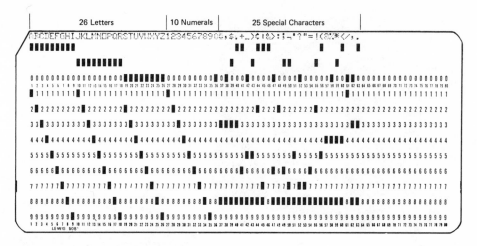

Figure 5-6 Business data input.

manual system. It is this memory facility that distinguishes the computer from devices such as calculators and bookkeeping machines, which, although they have input, output, and processing capabilities, cannot store programs internally within the processing unit. The program enables the computer to perform complex and lengthy calculations in order to process specific input data.

To understand how programs of instructions permit the computer to process data, we must examine the concept of *computer memory* to see how information and instructions can be stored within the computer. The information can be (1) instructions (programs) to direct the processing unit, (2) data (input, in-process, or output), and (3) reference data associated with processing (tables, code charts, constant factors, etc.).

Output

Computer memory is made up of a certain number of magnetic cores. We want to be able to represent in memory 10 decimal digits, 26 alphabetic characters, and 25 special symbols (comma, dollar sign, etc.) (see Figure 5-6). Binary schemes for representing these data vary, but all utilize a prearranged assignment of bits and groups of bits. This system of representation is important because of the need to arrange core storage and locate it by address.

From Computer Memory to Outputs We Can Read

Storage of computer memory is divided into locations, each with an assigned address. Each location holds a specific unit of data, which may be a character, a digit, an entire record, or a word. When a data item is desired, it is obtained from its known location in addressable storage units that are organized to provide data when wanted. There are several

IBM 1403 Printer

IBM 2540 Card Read Punch

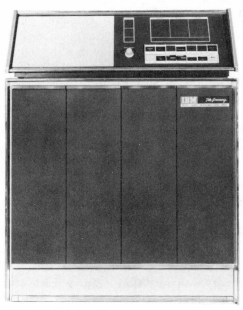

IBM 1009 Data Transmission Unit

Courtesy of IBM Corporation.

Figure 5-7(a) Input/output devices

Courtesy of Mohawk Data Sciences.

Figure 5-7b Mohawk data sciences terminal key station and tape drive.

Figure 5-7(c) Texas Instruments Silent 700 ASR terminal with magnetic tape casette off-line storage.

Courtesy of Texas Instruments.

schemes for using the processor to assist the programmer in keeping track of the storage locations. These schemes provide *data names*, such as "update inventory" or "calculate net pay," to automatically refer to sections in the program designed to perform these calculations. Notice the similarity between these programs and the procedures manual of the manual inventory system described previously.

External storage (consisting of records and files, reference data, and other programs) is of two types:

1. *Direct access.* Disc, magnetic drum, and data cell devices providing random-order mass data storage that can be accessed randomly, without having to read from the beginning of the file to find the desired data.
2. *Sequential.* Magnetic tape that is sequentially ordered and that must be read from the beginning in order to read or write a desired record.

Output devices produce the final results of the data processing. They *record* information from the computer on a variety of media, such as cards, paper tape, and magnetic tape. They *print* information on paper. Additionally, output devices may generate signals for transmission over teleprocessing networks, produce graphic displays, microfilm images, and take a variety of special forms. As indicated in Figure 5-4, the output from the inventory accounting system would be (1) a printout containing an inventory status report and (2) an updated inventory master file. Figure 5-7 shows some typical output devices that are linked directly to the computer system.

Many Forms of Output

Data Communications

No discussion of computer utilization would be complete without mention of data communications—the marriage of data processing and data transmission. The accelerating growth of this mode is reflected in the fact that in the period of time since the mid-1960s when only 1% of computers in use were linked to communication systems, it is expected that shortly over half of the existing computers will be so linked and that at least half of all communication transmitted over existing facilities will be nonlanguage, or data. To say it another way, the communications involved with computers "talking to each other" will exceed that of people talking to each other. Major users of data communications are listed in Table 5-1.

Long-Distance Computer Conversations

The data communications process generally requires at least six parts, tied together as shown in Figure 5-8:

1. A transmitter or source of information. This is usually some type of input/output device such as a typewriter, keyboard, or cathode ray tube (CRT) terminal. These were shown in Figures 5-5, 5-7, and 5-9.

Table 5-1 Major users of data communications.

Industry	Type Organization	Types of Applications
Transportation	Airlines, rail, truck, and bus	Reservation system, traffic control & dispatching, MIS, Maintenance systems
Utilities	Public utilities, common carriers	Communications facilities, MIS
Manufacturing	All manufacturing	Shipping, order processing, internal time sharing, MIS
Industrial	Natural resources, metals chemicals, machines, textiles, etc.	Warehouse control, shipping, process control, MIS
Retailing	All retailers	Point-of-sale systems, credit authorization, warehouse control, MIS
Service	Banks, financial, information services, warehousing, time sharing, insurance	Branch banking, money & securities transfers, time sharing, automated clerical operations, credit authorization, warehousing, quotation services
Government	Military & public administration	Communications, command & control, MIS, law enforcement, logistics, public health & education, postal automation

2. A modem on the transmitting end. These modems convert the digital signals of your data transmission into analog signals for transmission over the dial-up network. Until recently these converters were almost always supplied by *common carriers*, such as AT&T or Western Union. A recent court decision has opened up a proliferation of these products by a variety of manufacturers.

3. A transmission channel or carrier. Both the telephone companies and Western Union offer private-line teletypewriter-grade service at different speeds. TWX is the U.S. and Canadian exchange teletypewriter service, and TELEX is a worldwide exchange service offered by Western Union. Another illustration of line facilities is the WATS (Wide Area Telephone Service).

4. A modem on the receiving end. These modem convert the analog signal of the data link (transmission channel) back into a digital signal for computer use.

5. A receiver of transmitted information. This is the computer and a variety of input/output devices.

6. In addition, multiplexors or concentrators are often used to squeeze more input/output devices onto fewer communication channels, i.e., getting several messages through a channel at the same time. This is to reduce transmission costs.

The communications processor... why?

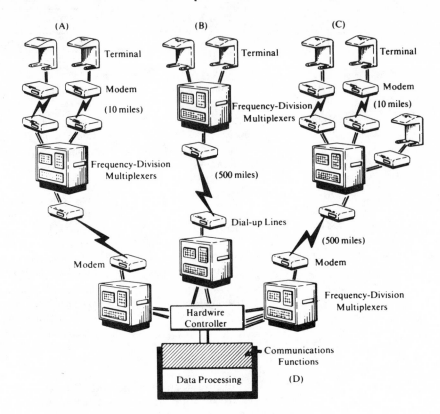

This system has been configured without communications processors—relying on hardware multiplexing devices to realize efficiencies in transmission line utilization. The inefficiencies of the system are that (1) line costs are not minimized (especially when messages are switched from one terminal group to another) and (2) a considerable portion of the host computer resources (central processing time and core memory utilization) is required to perform network control functions.

Source: Kenneth W. Ford, "About Communications Processors," *Infosystems*, Feb. 1973, p. 47.

Figure 5-8

Minicomputers

A NEW CHALLENGE
TO THE GIANTS

Minicomputers are "small" computers with all of the characteristics of large-scale computers but to a lesser degree. One authority defined them as central processors costing less than $23,000. However, the price keeps going down. Another definition is that a mini is small and inexpensive, with a primary storage of at least 4K words of from 8 to 24 bits.

Minis are very useful for small companies who neither need nor can afford a large computer. In Figure 5-9, a minicomputer is an integral part of a work station. This Data System 310 (Digital Equipment Corp.) has a core memory of 16K characters. Storage can be expanded to 1.34 million characters of disc storage. Warehouses, banks, insurance companies, and branch offices are typical users. A new trend is for companies to replace a large computer with a number of sophisticated minicomputers.

SYSTEM ALTERNATIVES

There is a very wide range of computer configurations available to the user today, ranging from the minicomputer to the huge data communications networks previously described.

Figure 5-9

Courtesy of Digital Equipment Corporation, Maynard, Massachusetts.

The first decision involves a selection among three alternatives: a card system, a tape system, and a direct access system. The general configuration of these systems is indicated in Figures 5-10 and 5-11 for two applications: inventory and accounts receivable.

The particular configuration of any computer system for a given organization is a function of a number of variables such as transactions, storage requirements, desired speed, ·cost constraints, and design sophistication. A *general* idea of computer needs can be gained by taking an approach somewhat like that shown in Figure 5-12. Here you can list frequent or planned applications, along with file medium, record size, processing frequency, and other *determinants* of computer needs. From this approach a general estimation of needs can be made.

Figure 5-10   Inventory and accounts receivable—punch card or tape.

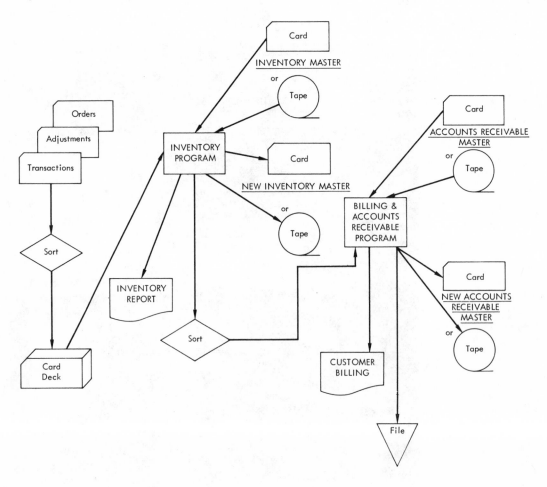

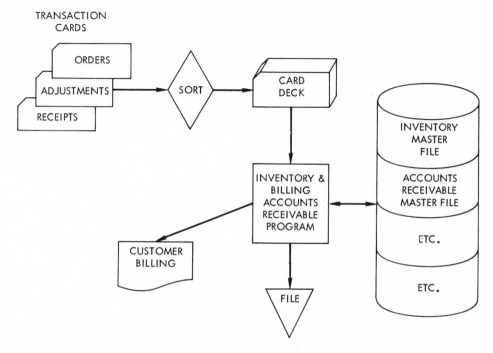

Figure 5-11   Inventory and accounts receivable—direct access.

THE PROCESS OF CONVERTING FROM A
MANUAL TO A COMPUTER-BASED SYSTEM

Basic Steps
from Manual
System to
Computerized
System

To increase our understanding of computer hardware it is helpful to provide an elementary description of the basic steps involved in making a simple one-for-one conversion from a manual to a computer system. In other words, we answer the question, "How do you get the system on the computer?"

The basic steps are

1. System description.
2. Input documents.
3. Output documents.
4. File design.
5. The program.

System Description

The system description is usually prepared after preliminary investigation and definition of the problem. The description is essentially a statement of the major inputs, outputs, processing operations, and files

Figure 5-12 Applications approach to computer configuration.

Application	Master File, Medium–Key	File Size, Records–Characters	Processing Frequency	Transactions Per Run	Average Run Time (hr)
Order entry	Disc–order no.	10,000–150	Daily	1,000	1
Sales analysis	Tape–cust. no.	2800–90	Weekly	7,000	1½
Inventory	Tape–prod. no.	2500–120	Daily	7,000	2
Distribution schedule	Network program	—	Daily	—	1
Production schedule	Linear program	—	Weekly	—	2
Payroll	Tape–employee no.	6000–400	Weekly	10,000	6
Accts receivable	Tape–cust. no.	3000–260	Daily	500	¾
Accts payable	Tape–vendor no.	3000–260	Daily	100	¼
Vendor analysis	Analysis program	—	Monthly	—	¼
General ledger	Tape–account	120–1000	Monthly	3,000	½
Purchasing	Disc–P.O. no.	600–200	Daily	600	½
(Other applications)					

How Do You Describe a System?

needed. The purpose is to show the logical flow of information and the logical operations necessary to carry out the particular design alternative chosen. Systems descriptions are in both *narrative* and *flow-chart* form.

The *narrative* description is an English language depiction of the operation of the system. It should describe inputs, outputs, files, and operations. It should be in that degree of detail that will allow users and computer technicians to understand the operation of the system and to utilize the narrative as a starting point for more detailed design. The narrative form of a simple inventory accounting system might take the following level of narration:

> The activity is concerned with an inventory control accounting system for finished goods inventory. Transactions (receipts and issues) are read from punched cards, the relevant magnetic tape master record is found and updated, and the new inventory status report is printed.

The *flow chart* puts in symbolic form what has been described in narrative form. It facilitates a quick analysis of the job being performed and provides a general symbolic overview of the entire operation. The flow chart for a typical order-entry system might appear as shown in Figure 5-13.

Input Documents

After the system description is completed, it is necessary to specify how the information will be put into a form that is acceptable to the computer. Volume of information, frequency, accuracy and verification

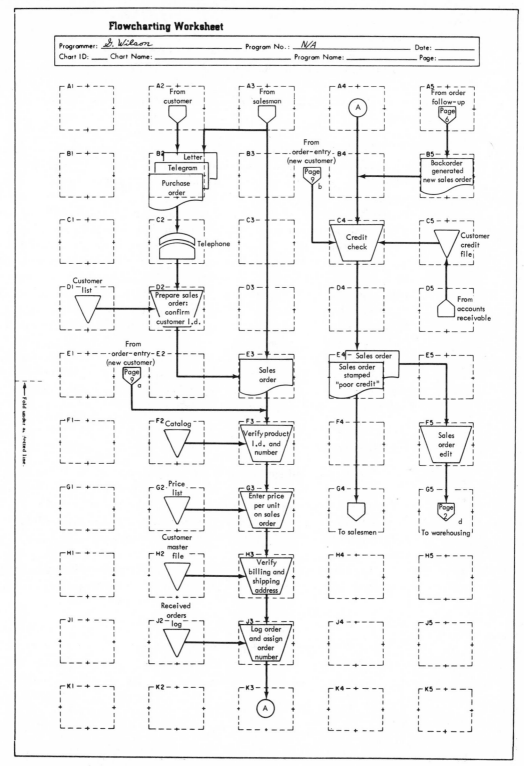

Figure 5-13 Order-entry flow chart.

Courtesy of IBM Corporation.

requirements, and the handling of the information are considerations in the selection of input format. Sometimes inputs have to be accepted in the form in which they are received from the outside. In this case, the task of conversion is merely one of preparing input to machine-usable form.

The exact layout of input documents is necessary because the computer program is an exact and precise sequence of steps that operates only when data are located in prescribed positions. In our example, the input format is determined to be punched cards. The holes in these cards are interpreted by the input device of the card reader, converted into computer-readable form, and stored in computer memory for processing.

The card input layout for our inventory accounting example is shown in Figure 5-14. The item number of inventory is represented by an eight-digit numeric field. A separate card is prepared for each transaction, with the quantity involved in the transaction represented by an eight-digit field and the nature of the transaction indicated by the last field on the card, which has an eight-digit code (this could be transaction by price, territory, customer, etc.).

Examination of the input document reveals that it provides all the relevant information contained in the system description. The typical *item description* normally associated with inventory is not contained in the input document because it is already filed in storage.

Output Documents

Outputs are subject to much the same considerations as input documents, but the output format should be treated with additional care because it represents the purpose or objective of the entire operation. It is the output document with which management is almost exclusively concerned, and because of its critical nature, care should be taken in its design.

The output layout of an inventory status report is shown in Figure 5-15. Although the computer is capable of printing much more complex

Figure 5-14   Layout for input transaction card.

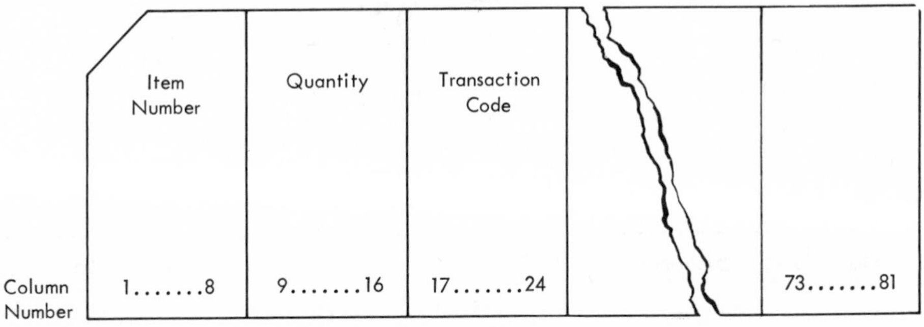

INVENTORY STATUS REPORT

ITEM NO.	DESCRIPTION	QUANTITY ON HAND	QUANTITY ON ORDER	TRANSACTION QUANTITY	QUANTITY B/O	AVERAGE UNIT COST	EXTENDED COST	LAST RECEIPT	LAST ISSUE	MIN. BAL.	MAX. BAL.
411116	8500 TWINLITE SOCKET BLUE	458	500			.35	160.30			800	1600
	ADJUSTMENT			42		.35	14.70				
	RECEIPT			500		.37	185.00				
	ISSUE			50-		.36	18.00-				
		950*				.36	342.00	2/11/--	2/14/--		
411122	8506 SOCKET ADAPTER BROWN	325				.19	61.75			300	800
	ISSUE			20-		.19	3.80-				
	ISSUE			38-		.19	7.22-				
	ISSUE			10-		.19	1.90-				
		257*				.19	48.83	12/19/--	2/11/--	UNDER	
411173	C151C SILENT SWITCH IVORY	50	150			1.16	58.00			100	200
	RECEIPT			150		1.20	180.00				
		200*				1.19	238.00	2/10/--	2/03/--		
411254	A210 PULL CORD GOLD	62	75			2.25	139.50			80	165
	ISSUE			16		2.25	36.00				
	ISSUE			30		2.25	67.50				
		16*	75			2.25	36.00	11/17/--	2/10/--		
	FINAL TOTALS	BEG. INV		48295.26							
		CHANGE		700.08							
		NEW VALUE		48995.34							

Figure 5-15 Inventory status report.

reports than our example, we show the minimum information required to meet the specifications of our system description and output requirements.

File Design

The logic required to control the flow of data through the system is a part of systems design, and the flow is in turn dependent on the design of data files. These two steps are closely associated and should be considered in conjunction with considerations of type of equipment, storage capacity, input and output media, and format.

The character-by-character contents of every record are specified by the file record layouts. Since magnetic tape files are already specified for our example, we are concerned with the tape input layout. This is shown in Figure 5-16.

Figure 5-16 Layout of magnetic tape records.

Frames	1.......8	9.......24	25.......32	
	Item Number	Item Description	Item Balance	End of Record Gap

The Program

Steps involved in providing system instructions to the computer are

1. Prepare the *program flow chart* to represent the detailed, logical sequence of *steps* for the computer to follow to accomplish a job.
2. Write the *translation instructions* in an *assembly language* or *compiler-level language* to be stored in the computer. The assembly language is one step above the binary (0, 1) language of the computer and uses a simple, easy-to-remember code for the numeric binary machine code. Compiler languages such as FORTRAN, COBOL, and PL/1 are higher-level languages that can incorporate several machine-level instructions into a single high-level instruction. Once a translation language is stored in the computer it is usually left there permanently.
3. Prepare the *computer program* by following the steps in the program flow chart to write computer instructions in the compiler language.
4. *Program storage* by the computer puts the program in the computer in binary form ready for processing data.
5. *Program operation* by the computer occurs when data are entered in the computer as called for by the program. The computer executes the instructions of the program in sequence until the program has been completed.

PITFALLS IN ACQUIRING COMPUTER HARDWARE

How to Avoid Mistakes When You Require a New Computer System

There are many kinds of mistakes possible in any expenditure of funds. There are, however, some very common and expensive mistakes associated with acquiring data processing hardware.

Pitfall 1: The Turnkey Operation

Some computer manufacturers and consultants may try to persuade you to buy a turnkey system. This is a hardware system designed, installed, and debugged ready for the buyer to push a button (turn a key) to start up.

The disadvantage is that you will have to spend a lot of time educating the seller or consultant in company operations. Second, installing the system without considerable orientation and training of your company's personnel is likely to result in chaos. Third, if you do not have a staff capable of designing your data processing systems, it is unlikely that the same staff can operate the turnkey system.

Borden, Inc. did some costly floundering around before developing some good computer systems. The vice president in charge concluded, "If you don't have an in-house staff doing the job of design and also available to maintain it, you are asking for trouble."

Summary: Systems are likely to be less expensive and to work better if you design them yourself.

Pitfall 2: Spending All Your Money on Hardware

A study showed that the average breakdown of each dollar of computer expenditures is

Hardware	35 cents
Staff	30 cents
Updating present system	15 cents
New applications	20 cents

The money spent on new applications of the computer system is the only amount subject to significant short-term management control. Yet the impact of computer applications on future benefits and costs is enormous.

Summary: Spend more money on new applications and development than the average firm does.

Pitfall 3: Letting Computer Salesmen and Data Processing Managers Make Major Decisions About the Computer

The natural inclination of computer salesmen and data processing managers is "to sell you a Cadillac when you need a motorcycle." They want you to have the biggest and the best; they do not think of how to improve managing.

Summary: Just as wars are too important to be left to generals, computer hardware decisions are too important to be left to specialists.

Pitfall 4: Installing an MIS Without an MS

It is absurd to process data and call it an MIS instead of first developing a management system (MS). The management system is the basis for managing with selected information.

Summary: Do not waste computer power.

Pitfall 5: Underestimating the Time and Expense of Developing a System

The inclination of hardware managers is to underestimate the time required for hardware installation and debugging. Training of personnel and the great length of time required to generate needed software are often overlooked or optimistically planned.

Summary: Plan carefully the *total* design, installation, training, and software preparation. Double your time estimate and you will probably come close to this new end date.

SUMMARY

In this chapter we have shown the close analogy between a manual process and the computerized process. This analogy explains the basic functions of the computer as (1) accepting input, (2) performing arithmetic, (3) storing data until they are needed, (4) controlling the sequence of its own operations, and (5) transmitting output.

The basic components of a computer system can also be matched with components of a manual system to show the similarity.

A wide variety of input and output devices exists for the central processing unit of the computer to make contact with the computer user. These devices are increasing steadily in type and sophistication. (We even have "intelligent terminals.")

Minicomputers are gaining in processing power and memory, challenging older giant computers or supporting the new ones. On the other hand, the transmission of data over long distances with ever-increasing efficiency makes possible the use of one central powerful computer.

Finally we have suggested several common and major pitfalls for management to avoid when hardware is being bought for an MIS.

QUESTIONS AND PROBLEMS

1. Explain in a sentence or two the following concepts related to the computer:
   a. Input
   b. Magnetic tape
   c. CPU
   d. Logic section
   e. Computer storage
   f. External storage
   g. Direct access
   h. Outputs
   i. System description
   j. Flow chart
   k. CRT display
   l. Data communications system
   m. Minicomputers

2. Three input alternatives for a computer system are _____, _____, and _____.

3. Match the following:

_____ a. System description

_____ b. Input document

_____ c. Output document

_____ d. File design

_____ e. Program flow chart

_____ f. Compiler

(1) Punched card carrying sales data

(2) Aggregations of records composed of fields

(3) High-level language translator

(4) Flow chart or narrative of information flow and operations

(5) Diagram of the logical steps for a program

4. In the IBM System/360 and 370, 1 *bit* is the storage of 0 or 1. One *byte* is 8 bits treated as a unit with a single address. One *word* is 4 bytes treated as a unit.
   a. How many bits in a word?
   b. A half-inch-wide magnetic tape storing 8 bits across its width is called an 8-track tape. If each *track* carries 1600 bits per inch (b.p.i.), how many bytes are carried in one inch of tape? (Usually there is an extra track for another purpose so that tapes are 9 tracks wide.)

5. List five pitfalls in acquiring computer hardware.

chapter six

Planning
for
MIS Development

CHAPTER 6   tells how to prepare a plan for the development of an
MIS.

When you have finished studying

PLANNING FOR MIS DEVELOPMENT

you should be able to

1. Explain the need for system planning instead of piecemeal design of MIS
2. Explain how the establishment of systems objectives improves MIS planning and design
3. Describe the characteristics of a "project"
4. Outline a typical project proposal for an MIS
5. Develop a simple plan for MIS development based on objectives, work breakdown structure, schedule, budget, and reporting format.

So far we have dealt with the basic ideas and philosophy of information systems and MISs. In the remaining chapters we shall set forth a procedure for the development of an MIS.

In this book we have divided the MIS development work into four phases:

OVERLAPPING
PHASES OF
MIS DESIGN

1. *Planning and programming*. This phase, covered in the previous chapter, is concerned with the planning, organizing, and control of effort devoted to MIS development.
2. *Gross design*. Sometimes referred to as feasibility study or conceptual design, gross design is the development of alternative MISs in preliminary form for evaluation and selection of the most promising. It is comparable to the rough sketches that engineers and architects make. Sufficient investigation is made to determine which designs are "feasible," that is, can be produced to operate (Chapter 7).
3. *Detailed design*. Once the critical decision—the selection of the gross design—has been made, the detailed design work is conducted to develop the operational and information systems in detail. The steps in this process are covered in Chapter 8.
4. *Implementation*. The output of design work is a set of specifications; implementation is the conversion of these specifications to a working system (Chapter 9).

As in all systems work, phases are overlapping or cyclical rather than simply separate steps. For example, we start with a total plan for the development in terms of the last three major phases. However, after we have come fairly well along on the detailed design we must revise and amplify on our plan for installing (implementing) the MIS. Further the gross design is not clearly separated from detailed design. It is possible to change some basic information flow patterns as the detailed design is carried out.

The approach to planning the development of an MIS given here must therefore be viewed as the first approximation. That is, replanning may be required if later significant changes in the development appear necessary.

THE NEED FOR SYSTEM PLANNING

PIECEMEAL
APPROACH OR
TOTAL SYSTEMS
PLAN?

Little more than lip service has been given to the idea of a total companywide MIS. Instead, we have seen the development of unrelated "islands of mechanization," quick payoff projects to automate payroll and clerical functions, or perhaps production of tons of computer data output distributed to managers without regard for needs.

This piecemeal approach to systems development has no unifying framework. It has several disadvantages. One of these stems from the unrelated nature of the subsystems developed. Frequently departments and divisions have developed individualistic systems without regard to the interface of such systems elsewhere in the organization. The result has been communication barriers between systems.

Failure To
Relate
Subsystems

A fairly common example of failure to relate subsystems is the way personnel information is structured. Several departments (sales, production, accounting, personnel) may maintain employee files that overlap with other similar files but do not provide for interface between them. In one instance, critical engineering and labor skills shortages developed in several geographically separated divisions of a multidivision company. But despite the fact that these skills were available elsewhere in the company, no identification could be made because of the lack of a common personnel-skills information system.

A second and serious disadvantage is the cost involved—cost in time, resources, and money. The longer a master plan is put off, the more costly will be the inevitable need to overhaul, unify, and standardize the approach to integrated systems design. Many companies have invested in the automation of clerical records and subsequently discovered that a complete overhaul of the system is necessary when it becomes integrated with a larger effort. A popular one-for-one conversion in the past has been the materials inventory *tab* system, which frequently requires complete rework when a production planning and control system is implemented.

Why Not Use the
Integrated
Approach to MIS
Design?

The following questions arise: First, why has the piecemeal approach been allowed to develop? And second, what should be done to improve the design situation so that an improved, integrated approach can be taken?

The answer to the first question is complex. The major reason probably is that managers have generally failed to realize in the early stages of systems development the scope of the computer and information systems, the investment it would represent, and the impact it would have on the operations of the business. Belatedly, many firms have realized the need for integration through the implementation of a master plan. Evidence seems to indicate that future systems development will be characterized by four improving trends:

FUTURE MIS
DEVELOPMENT

Emphasis on
Managerial
Functions of
Planning and
Control

1. A much greater share of systems effort will be devoted to the planning and control of operations rather than, as previously, to the clerical and routine paper work of finance and administration. Operations, marketing, product or process development, and personnel management are among the areas expected to have increasingly sophisticated applications.

More Investment
in MIS

2. An increasing percentage of expenditures for new plant and equipment will be spent on data processing equipment and activities. This trend reflects primarily the growing recognition on the part of management that information systems are a vital resource. Moreover, increasing expenditures will be made on managerial applications, the surface of which has barely been scratched.

3. An increasing fraction of computer and related expenditures will be devoted to design and *software* as opposed to mainframe and hardware. This changing "mix" of systems expenditures reflects the relatively unsophisticated state-of-the-art in systems design in most companies and the recognition that greater efforts under a master plan are needed.

Greater Tying
Together of
MIS Subsystems

4. The tendency toward the integration of subsystems will accelerate. Integration not only is economical but yields much more effective information for management planning, operating, and control. More and more companies realize this and are moving in that direction.

The answer to the second question, what should be done, lies clearly in the adoption of a master plan. Working according to a long-range blueprint is desirable. Indeed, the same reasons that can be advanced for business planning in general can apply to the argument for systems planning.

These four special reasons for systems planning are

REASONS FOR
PLANNING SYSTEMS
WORK

1. *To offset uncertainty.*
2. *To improve economy of operations.*
3. *To focus on objectives.*
4. *To provide a device for control of operations.*

Aside from the uncertainty of business operations and the resulting need for better forecasting information, the special need for a systems plan is evident because of advancing computer technology and its widespread effect on business operations. Both software (programming languages, systems design, etc.) and hardware (computers, related devices, data transmission equipment, etc.) have become so complex that the job of selection and utilization is much more difficult. As a result, the majority of organizations have fallen far short of their potential to use computers for processing the information necessary to manage the company effectively. A master plan may not remove the uncertainty, but it will almost surely place the firm in a better position to deal with the unknowns and to take advantage of developments as they occur.

Planning the overall approach to an integrated systems timetable is also *economical*. Design effort in most companies reflects the short-term approach of automating those clerical operations. These offer an immediate payoff in terms of reduction of paperwork and staff. Customer billing, payroll, accounts payable, and inventory records (not inventory control) are favorite targets for automation of clerical tasks. However, experience has shown that in the long run this approach is likely to be more costly than proceeding under a predetermined plan. Once one job or function has been automated, the need for the design and automation of contiguous functions frequently becomes obvious. Take, for example, the well-designed production planning system whose inputs come from a manual sales order and forecasting system and whose outputs are largely ignored by purchasing and personnel. It becomes obvious that money can be saved and performance improved by an effective linking together of these neighboring functions through a good plan for integrated systems design. However, if adjacent or interacting systems are not considered under a plan, costly rework will almost surely result.

Economies surrounding organizational changes, personnel considerations, and equipment purchase or rental may also be realized by working according to a predetermined grand scheme rather than permitting systems applications to "grow like Topsy."

A good plan for systems development also serves to *focus on company and systems objectives.* Conversely, firms without explicit organizational objectives and explicit plans for achieving them, that make expedient responses to environmental factors, are unlikely to have definite systems objectives and a plan for their attainment. We know that planning cannot proceed in any area of endeavor until adequate objectives have first been set. It follows that development of a master systems plan forces examination and definition of objectives.

The question arises, What are the objectives of an information system plan? Although we shall discuss this in detail later in this chapter, it is appropriate at this time to point out that if systems objectives are to be

A Good Plan
Brings Company
Objectives Into
Focus

supported, those in charge of systems development will have 'to ask the following questions: What will be the nature of the firm in the future, and what information will be needed to assist in the satisfaction of the needs arising from management of the company in the future changing environment? What will be our products . . . our customers . . . our competition . . . our distribution channels? What kind of sales forces will be needed . . . what facilities, etc.? Only after these questions are answered can the designer begin to determine the objectives of the systems plan and the specifics of information needs and sources.

Systems development, implementation, and operations are among the most difficult of activities within the company to control. The fourth major advantage of the development of systems effort under a predetermined plan is that the plan provides a means for subsequent *control.* Plans and objectives also provide the means for measuring progress of MIS development. If systems development activities and events are organized on a project basis with specific objectives (e.g., minimize cost of raw materials inventory) to be achieved within a certain time period and at a predetermined cost, then these goals can be used as yardsticks to measure subsequent accomplishments.

Yet despite the fact that the real reason for the development of management information systems is their use to improve the management of organizations, the planning and control of systems development efforts are frequently left to chance. Perhaps those responsible for this effort should take their own advice: "What you need is a system!"

OBJECTIVES OF MIS PLANNING

Planning involves the development and selection from among alternatives of the necessary course of action to achieve an objective. The objective is therefore the essential prerequisite to planning, and planning can be useful and commence only when objectives are properly selected. Therefore, systems planning cannot proceed according to a master plan or any other constructive scheme unless the objectives of the information systems plan are detailed and well understood.

START WITH
PLANNING
OBJECTIVES

We are referring not to specific *objectives* of subsystems but to overall *systems planning objectives*—in other words, to the characteristics of the information systems that should be developed for both the near-term and long-range effort. An excellent framework of objectives for the systems planning function has been developed by Blumenthal:

> The systems-planning function must therefore encompass the review of proposed systems in terms of planning criteria designed to minimize the number of systems, to broaden their scope, and to place them in the proper sequence for development. All these requirements can be expressed by the following list of systems-planning objectives:

1. To avoid overlapping development of major systems elements which are widely applicable across organizational lines, when there is no compelling technical or functional reason for difference.

2. To help ensure a uniform basis for determining sequence of development in terms of payoff potential, natural precedence, and probability of success.

3. To minimize the cost of integrating related systems with each other.

4. To reduce the total number of small, isolated systems to be developed, maintained, and operated.

5. To provide adaptability of systems to business change and growth without periodic major overhaul.

6. To provide a foundation for coordinated development of consistent, comprehensive, corporate-wide and interorganizational information systems.

7. To provide guidelines for and direction to continuing systems-development studies and projects.[1]

Balance MIS Benefits and Cost

Every company has limited resources to apply to its various activities. The amount of money spent on MIS development should be determined by (1) benefits obtained vs. costs and (2) benefits obtained vs. benefits obtained if the same money were spent instead on some other activity (such as advertising or research).

The benefits of any one or group of applications is not always self-evident. Many companies have tended to take the easy way out by automating the routine bookkeeping and clerical functions because these appear to be the "obvious" areas and because personnel replacement costs can be estimated. This approach is rarely the correct one, however. There are a few organizations (perhaps the Social Security Administration or Internal Revenue Service) whose clerical displacement savings outweigh the savings to be realized in the improvement of planning and control applications. Although the benefits in these managerial areas are intangible and difficult to measure, it is in these types of applications that system development effort has the most impact on costs and on company operations.

Orlicky identifies three areas that consistently yield the greatest benefits in industry:

1. Planning and control of finished goods in the distribution network.

[1] Sherman C. Blumenthal, *Management Information Systems: A Framework for Planning and Development*, Englewood Cliffs, N.J.: Prentice-Hall, Inc., 1969, p. 13.

2. Planning and control of the use of materials, machines, and labor in manufacturing operations.

3. Planning and control of the material procurement function.[2]

PROJECTS, PLANNING, AND MIS

MIS development is termed a *project* because it is a unique effort with a starting date and ending date. Generally, the flow of work in business is a continuous process except for major changes from time to time. Major changes usually result from major innovations (new ideas). The introduction of a new MIS is such an innovation.

A number of tasks related in a complex fashion to achieve a one-time objective, such as design of an MIS, is called a *project*. Projects differ from processes because they are discrete—they have a beginning and an end, as opposed to company functional operations such as marketing, manufacturing, or accounting. Projects are complex because they require a wide variety of skills. Moreover, they cut across traditional organizational lines and involve a substantial number of interrelated activities. And because each project is a one-time effort, unusual problems arise that call for nontraditional solutions. In addition, projects usually require the development of new techniques and advances in the state-of-the-art while the project is in progress.

Projects are carried out under the leadership of project managers. Because of the complexities and high costs of completing projects, these managers must provide coordination and leadership of an unusual order. Good functional managers may fail miserably as project managers. In particular, when a project manager operates from a staff position, as MIS project managers usually do, the difficulties are greatly compounded.

The basic foundations for successful project management are good planning and control systems within the project management cycle. This chapter focuses on the techniques for project management as related to the development, design, and implementation of MISs.

If MIS designers know how to design systems to assist management with planning and control, they should put this knowledge to work in conducting their own projects. Prior to the entire MIS design project or to any major step, the project manager should develop an overall plan, a detailed program for implementing the plan, and a method for controlling the progress, cost, and time variables of the project. The planning/controlling project cycle is indicated in Figure 6-1. This chapter covers the method and techniques of project management and how they are used for planning and programming MISs.

PROJECTS AND
PROJECT
MANAGEMENT

[2] Joseph Orlicky, *The Successful Computer System*, New York: McGraw-Hill Book Company, 1969, p. 96.

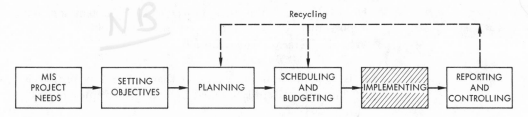

Figure 6-1 The planning-controlling cycle for project management.

NEEDS RESEARCH

START A PROJECT
BY LOOKING FOR
NEEDS TO BE
FULFILLED

The first stage in the MIS project management cycle is the search for MIS *needs*. If needs of managers are not identified, many thousands of dollars may be lost by developing systems that serve little purpose. Management then finds it necessary to return to the starting point again and again until needs are properly defined. The identification of needs, in terms of MISs, consists of

1. The search for planning and operating problems.
2. The search for areas of recurring difficult decisions or erroneous decisions.
3. The search for company opportunities that depend on expanded information systems.
4. Delineation of problems and opportunities (No. 3) so that priorities may be ranked.
5. Selection of projects whose payoff in terms of cost and limitations of resources is justified.

Let us amplify some of these concepts. Each company should have an MIS manager or a counterpart whose job is to search continuously for major company problems and opportunities. He must, of course, rely heavily on personal contacts with line managers and top managers as sources. His job is primarily that of gathering together problems, stimulating managers to think about opportunities, and generally getting managers to look beyond their daily jobs, both outside and inside the company. From problems and opportunities thus identified, MIS needs can be recognized in a general way. MIS projects may then be identified by summary descriptions and crude cost estimates, after which they must be evaluated with regard to three basic criteria:

1. How valuable is the solution to the problem or the opportunity (for expansion, market penetration, acquisition program, new production system, reorganization, etc.) to the company?

2. How valuable is the MIS project to the problem solution or the opportunity achievement? What is the net payoff?
3. What is the technology required?

It is evident from these criteria that before any project is undertaken it should be carefully assessed by asking such questions as

1. What are management's purposes? In what direction is it guiding the company in terms of products, services, market position, and return on investment? In other words, what is the corporate shape intended to be?
2. What possible MIS projects will aid management in planning, controlling, problem-solving, and decision-making? Is a "total system" feasible, or are the projects so large that only a few may be undertaken at a time?
3. Is the scope of each project defined? Unless descriptions of the project, its contribution, and its required utilization of resources are spelled out, the projects cannot be evaluated and ranked.
4. What are the major assumptions underlying each project? These assumptions relate to the environment, to management's needs, to available resources within the company, to desired goals of managers, and to time.
5. What are the short-term and long-term objectives of the MIS project? Too often MIS systems are proposed and designed to solve today's problems with no consideration for changes in organization, environment, and operations in the next five years.
6. What specific criteria should be used to evaluate and rank projects? The aggressive viewpoint of "What will the system do to advance the company in the long run?" should be used. Criteria are often based erroneously on cost and savings.
7. Is the project technically sound? That is, is it practical in terms of the state-of-the-art of management science, computer science, organizational behavior, and other relevant factors?
8. Are there deadlines or simply desired times for completion of the project?

The needs-research stage is sometimes called the preliminary analysis, or the preproposal stage.

SETTING PROJECT OBJECTIVES

As opposed to the definition of overall MIS planning objectives discussed earlier, in the planning-programming-control cycle objectives must be in more detailed form for each potential project. Needs research indicates the general nature and scope of MIS projects that are required, but once a project is selected, its purposes must be developed to fulfill the needs. An objective is an end result that is to be accomplished by the execution of the plan.

Objectives of information systems may vary widely in scope and direction. Objectives might be

1. Unify the financial and accounting system of a multidivision company or conglomerate.
2. Develop an environmental scanning system to keep corporate management alerted to new market opportunities and competitive strategic moves.
3. Develop a production and inventory control system that interfaces with the current purchasing and marketing information systems.
4. Develop an on-line information system for companywide materials and finished goods in terms of in-transport and warehouse location.
5. Develop an engineering management information system for control of technical work, costs, and schedules.
6. Develop an MIS for manpower inventory and long-range needs.
7. Update the current MIS for marketing to bring to bear new forecasting techniques and to adapt the system to the new computer being installed.
8. Revise the present financial reporting system to supply more decision-oriented information and to provide it on a weekly basis instead of a quarterly basis.

Besides such major objectives as suggested, each MIS project will have a number of supporting or secondary objectives. It is not enough, as in the first example, to simply specify unification of financial and accounting information. Objectives must be set regarding the nature of reports for each level of the organization, who gets what reports, and how frequently reports are to be issued. Secondary objectives might be enlarging and automating the data master file, relating sales information to production planning, or obtaining measurements of morale through classification of reasons for absenteeism and resignations. A complete list of objectives at the lowest level in the hierarchy of objectives is established subsequently during the planning of specific tasks. The topic of systems and project objectives will be expanded in Chapters 7 and 8.

PROJECT PROPOSAL

Two alternative sequences of action are possible for developing project proposals and obtaining management approval. As various projects are identified by needs and objectives, a preliminary definition of the scope of the project work, scheduling, costs, and benefits may be prepared as a *project proposal*. The projects are then evaluated by management and selections made on the basis of criteria discussed previously. Subsequent to this, detailed plans are prepared and reviewed once again by management.

In the second alternative, an MIS project is singled out. Then the complete and detailed planning, scheduling, and budgeting for the implementation is worked out. At this point a detailed project proposal is presented to management for acceptance or rejection. Because of the cost of preparing such proposals for all known projects, only those likely to be approved are developed in this much detail. Management thus does not have an opportunity to evaluate a broad range of proposals.

MAKE A FORMAL
PROPOSAL TO
MANAGEMENT

The format for the MIS project proposal consists of an introduction, a management summary, a system description, and an estimate of the cost and schedule. The detail given in each section depends on whether a brief proposal is prepared for a large number of projects (alternative 1) or whether a single project is selected on a judgmental informal basis and a proposal developed for management's approval (alternative 2). The nature of information contained in a proposal is outlined in Table 6-1.[3]

PLANNING TECHNIQUES

For very small projects, common-sense techniques for planning and documenting the plans for the MIS project are sufficient. We shall discuss here the more elaborate techniques for planning for larger projects. Most of these techniques and tools have been borrowed from engineering project-management theory and practice, where they originated.

The planning techniques rest on some fundamental management premises. The first is that all work can be planned and controlled. The second is that the greater the difficulty in planning the work, the greater the need for such planning. Techniques exist for a rational approach to planning the design and implementation of large systems. The third premise is that the assignment of project management to a project manager with wide responsibilities is an important factor in increasing the probability of success of a project. The project manager must control all funds required for the project. However, the project manager may direct the activities of a program without having direct-line command over all persons involved in the program. He achieves this by means of a clearly defined work breakdown structure for the project.

PLANNING
TECHNIQUES FOR
BETTER PLANS

3 See also David I. Cleland and William R. King, *Systems Analysis and Project Management*, New York: McGraw-Hill Book Company, 1968, Appendices; and W. Hartman, H. Mathes, and A. Proeme, *Management Information Systems Handbook*, New York: McGraw-Hill Book Company, 1968, Chap. 22.

Table 6-1 MIS project proposal outline.

---

1. Introduction
   a. A brief, clear statement of the problem or technical requirement.
   b. Purposes of the proposed MIS.
   c. Conservative estimate of the performance of the proposed system, its limitations, its life, and its cost.
   d. Premises and assumptions upon which the MIS is to be developed. These give organizational limitations; special requirements imposed by managers, vendors, or customers; environmental restrictions; or other ground rules.

2. What Is Offered
   a. Description of present method of operation and its weaknesses and problems.
   b. Information requirements, present and future. General description of proposed data base.
   c. Hardware, present and future, available within the company.
   d. Alternative aproaches to the information-decision-operational systems. A brief summary of each approach is given and the advantages and disadvantages of each are discussed to show why the proposed system is being offered.
   e. A somewhat more detailed description of the proposed MIS is given. The general plan of action, the budget estimate, and the schedule are provided.
   f. Management action required for adoption of the proposal and for planning and implementing the MIS are stated.

3. Method of Approach
   An outline of the plan of attack on the gross design, detailed design, and implementation. This demonstrates that the project manager has a practical approach for planning and executing the project.
   a. Method of data gathering and analysis.
   b. Personnel assignments.
   c. Programming techniques to be used for the project.
   d. Project reports and review. A description of the type and frequency of reports to keep management abreast of progress on the MIS project.

4. Conclusion
   This is not usually required. If an MIS project looks especially good from a highly technical viewpoint, the conclusion may summarize the strong points to give additional emphasis.

5. Appendices
   Organization charts, schedules, flow charts, quantitative analyses, and other detailed substantiating data of a technical or detailed nature that will aid management or technical staff personnel in evaluating the proposal.

Work Breakdown Structure

A fundamental concept in project management is the work breakdown structure, which starts with the total end result desired and terminates with the individual detailed tasks. The project breakdown structure is a natural *decomposition* of the project end result. It is created in a level-by-level breakdown from

1. System to subsystem.
2. Subsystem to task.
3. Task to subtask.
4. Subtask to work package.

The manner in which the project is broken down into tasks is illustrated in Table 6-2.

Table 6-2   Standard task list of the work breakdown structure for project control.

I.   Study Phase
    Task 1   Study organization goals and problems
      Subtask   1.1   Interview managers and study internal documents.
      Subtask   1.2   Survey operating problems.
      Subtask   1.3   Study informational problems.
    Task 2   Study company resources and opportunities.
      Subtask   2.1   Evaluate company resources.
      Subtask   2.2   Study needs of the market and environmental trends.
      Subtask   2.3   Evaluate competitive position.
    Task 3   Study computer capabilities—equipment and manpower skills.
    Task 4   Prepare proposal for MIS design study.

II.   Gross Design Phase
    Task 1   Identify required subsystems.
      Subtask   1.1   Study work flow and natural boundaries of skill groupings and information needs.
      Subtask   1.2   Develop alternative lists of subsystems.
      Subtask   1.3   Develop conceptual total system alternatives based on the lists of subsystems.
      Subtask   1.4   Develop scope of work to be undertaken based on need of the company and estimated resources to be allocated to the MIS.
      Subtask   1.5   Prepare a reference design showing key aspects of the system, organizational changes, and computer equipment and software required.

III. Detailed Design Phase
    Task 1   Disseminate to the organization the nature of the prospective project.
    Task 2   Identify dominant and principal trade-off criteria for the MIS.
    Task 3   Redefine the subsystems in greater detail.
      Subtask   3.1   Flow-chart the operating systems.
      Subtask   3.2   Interview managers and key operating personnel.
      Subtask   3.3   Flow-chart the information flows.
    Task 4   Determine the degree of automation possible for each activity or transaction.
    Task 5   Design the data base or master file.
      Subtask   5.1   Determine routine decisions and the nature of nonroutine decisions.
      Subtask   5.2   Determine internal and external data required.
      Subtask   5.3   Determine optimum data to be stored in terms of cost, time, cross-functional needs, and storage capacity.

Task 6   Model the system quantitatively.

Task 7   Develop computer support.
  Subtask   7.1   Develop computer hardware requirements.
  Subtask   7.2   Develop software requirements.

Task 8   Establish input and and output formats.
  Subtask   8.1   Develop input formats (design forms).
  Subtask   8.2   Develop output formats for decision makers.

Task 9   Test the system.
  Subtask   9.1   Test the system by using the model previously developed.
  Subtask   9.2   Test the system by simulation, using extreme value inputs.

Task 10   Propose the formal organization structure to operate the system.

Task 11   Document the detailed design.

IV. Implementation Phase

Task 1   Plan the implementation sequence.
  Subtask   1.1   Identify implementation tasks.
  Subtask   1.2   Establish interrelationships among tasks and subtasks.
  Subtask   1.3   Establish the performance/cost/time program.

Task 2   Organize for implementation.

Task 3   Develop procedures for the installation process.

Task 4   Train operating personnel.

Task 5   Obtain hardware.

Task 6   Develop the software.

Task 7   Obtain forms specified in detail design or develop forms as necessary.

Task 8   Obtain data and construct the master files.

Task 9   Test the system by parts.

Task 10   Test the complete system.

Task 11   Cut over to the new MIS.

Task 12   Debug the system.

Task 13   Document the operational MIS.

Task 14   Evaluate the system in operation.

The work breakdown structure, referred to as WBS, starts with a word description of the entire project and is then decomposed by word descriptions for each element of each subdivision. The organizational structure should have no influence on the development of the WBS. The primary question to be answered is, What is to be accomplished? Next, an acceptable way of classifying the work must be found. The classification should be such that natural systems and components are identified and milestone tasks for accomplishing their design are related. Neither gaps nor overlaps must be allowed, yet the structure should interlock all tasks and work packages.

The Work Package
Is a Unit of Work
Required to
Complete a
Specific Job
Within the
Responsibility of
a Lowest-Level
Organizational Unit

The smallest element in the WBS, usually appearing at the lowest level, is the work package, a paragraph description of the work that is to be done to achieve an intermediate goal. Requirements of time, resources, and cost are listed, including definite dates for starting and completing the work—a short duration compared to that of the total project. The breakdown of the project into work packages, each assigned to a single responsible manager, provides the means for control of the entire project. A typical list of items of information contained in a work package form is given in Table 6-3.

Sequence Planning

The relationships among tasks must be set forth by a chronological ordering, starting with the terminal task of the project and working backward. As each task is set down, it is necessary to determine what immediately preceding tasks must first be completed. When a network of events has been established, estimates of the time required to complete each event, based on the work package information, may be entered.

There are a number of time paths through a network that run from the starting event to the terminal event. The longest is called the *critical path*. On the basis of management decisions, resources may be added or redeployed to change the length of time of a current critical path to yield a new one, thus gaining time by a trade-off involving increased costs. The final network is sometimes called the *master project network plan*.

Master Program Schedule

The master program schedule (MPS) is a management document giving the *calendar dates* for milestones (major tasks and critical-path minor tasks), thus providing the control points for management review.

Table 6-3   Work package information checklist.

1. Project identification, title, and number
2. Title and number of work package
3. Responsible organization and manager
4. Interface events and dates
5. Start and end date for work package
6. Dollar and labor estimates, projections of dollars and labor on a weekly or monthly basis, and a schedule of actual application of resources maintained as current
7. Contract or funding source identification
8. Account charge number
9. Work order or shop order, to be opened when authorization is obtained to expend a specified amount of money under a particular account number

The MPS may be in the form of a Gantt chart for small MIS projects or in machine (computer) printout for large projects whose networks have been programmed for computer analysis and reporting. In the latter case, the MPS is derived from the network schedule by establishing a calendar date for the starting event.

While the above complex methods may be used to represent the MIS development plan, a simple plan may often be adequate. For example, a simple list of activities with completion dates is shown below to illustrate such a plan:

Activity	*Completion Date*
1. Establish MIS objectives	2/6/77
2. Prepare and submit project proposal	3/4/77
3. Conduct a detailed study of present MISs and information needs of managers	4/24/77
4. Develop the gross design	5/29/77
a. MIS gross flow chart	5/21/77
b. Centralized information needs	5/19/77
c. List of files needed	5/23/77
d. Extent of model bank needed, if any	5/29/77
e. Scope of computer hardware and software	5/29/77
5. Develop the detailed design	10/11/77
a. Detailed flow charts	8/7/77
b. Data base	8/10/77
c. Computer equipment and software	8/20/77
d. Procedures manual	9/5/77
6. Implement or install the new system	12/11/77
a. Complete training	12/5/77
b. Switch over to new MIS	12/11/77
c. Debug the MIS	12/18/77

Budgeting

The establishment of cost and resource targets for a planned series of periods in advance is project budgeting. Although cost constraints may be applied in a top-down fashion during planning, such constraints must be reconciled with a *bottom-up* approach through the work breakdown structure. Reconciliation is accomplished by either (1) allocating more funds or (2) narrowing and reducing the scope of the work and redefining the objectives of the project.

Budgets Tie Cost
and Performance
Together over
the Duration of
the Project

Cost and resource targets must be established for a work package by

1. Performing organization.
2. Funding organization.
3. Elements of cost: labor, materials, and facilities.

Only direct costs are included in the project budget, because they are the only costs over which the project manager has control.

Cushioning should not be added to the resource costs because meaningful measures of control depend on realistic goals. However, because experience has shown that project cost overruns are far more common than underruns, a contingency fund should be budgeted to cover unanticipated problems. The project manager's use of the contingency fund is also a measure of his performance.

REPORTING AND CONTROLLING

PROJECT PLANS
AND PROJECT
CONTROLS ARE
CLOSELY RELATED

Control of the project means control of performance/cost/time (P/C/T). These elements, P/C/T, must be reported in a way that ties them all together; otherwise the report is meaningless. Consider, for instance, a project in which performance and costs are on target. It is possible for such a project to be behind and in trouble from the time standpoint. On the other hand, a project may show an overrun of costs as of a particular date, yet if the work performance is ahead of schedule, this is good news instead of bad news.

Reporting Techniques

The reporting system for a project is its own MIS. Some methods of project reporting are

1. Integrated P/C/T charts as shown in Figure 6-2.
2. Financial schedules and variance reports.
3. Time-scaled network plans and computerized reports based on them.
4. Problem analysis and trend charts.
5. Progress reports.
6. Project control room and computerized graphic systems.[4]

Project Reporting
for Control Uses
Highly Developed
Techniques

7. Design-review meetings and reference designs. A common *reference design* must provide a formal description of system specifications and goals at any particular time. All designers work on the basis of assumptions about parts of the system other than theirs. If they are not

[4] See, for example, Irwin M. Miller, "Computer Graphics for Decision Making," *Harvard Business Review*, Nov.–Dec. 1969, pp. 121–132.

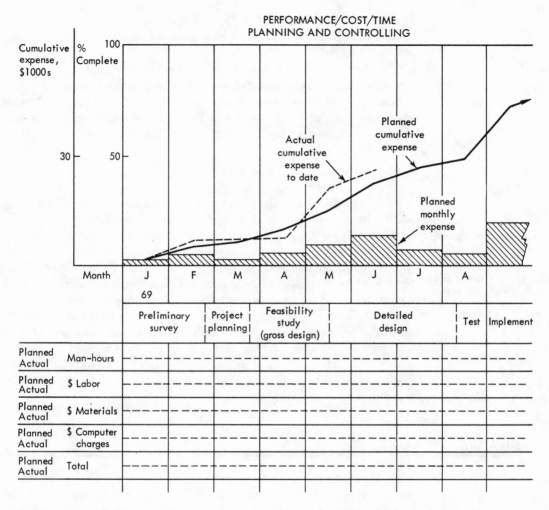

PERFORMANCE/COST/TIME
PLANNING AND CONTROLLING

Figure 6-2 Integrated P/C/T Chart.

working on the same assumptions, chaos results. The reference design may change with time, and the design review meeting of all key personnel is a good time to make formal changes.

Reporting Problems

Control is difficult if the only reports are written narratives requiring interpretation by management. At the other extreme, reams of computer data reports are equally poor. Managers prefer graphic displays, which reduce large amounts of complex information into easily understood pictorial form. Comparisons and trends of major variables are also effective in communicating. Graphic display must be designed to guard against too gross a level of reporting, however, or else growing problems may be obscured.

Other problems in reporting are the use of complex grammatical structure; high "fog index" of writing; excessive and unexplained abbreviations, codes, and symbols; and too much technical jargon.[5] Projects may fail if the project manager and his technical specialists do not make clear to management what is happening and how the money is being spent.

Control Through "Completed Action"

Every Manager Up the Project Line Is Accountable for Performance of Work Assigned to Him

A manager in a chain of command cannot divest himself of accountability for a task that is delegated to him. Responsibility for a work package may be delegated to the lowest level in the organizational hierarchy, but each manager up the line is evaluated on the basis of completed action on the work package. The worker who has responsibility for a work package should be supplied with adequate reports of P/C/T. As variances are reported to the responsible performer, the burden is on him to take corrective action. His ultimate responsibility is "completed action," the presentation of a completed job to his manager. Only in emergencies and cases of wide variances from planned action should the managers at various levels in the organization step in to reclaim delegated responsibility. The control in a well-run project is essentially self-control, based on a good reporting system.

SUMMARY

The design and implementation of an MIS cannot be carried out on an unplanned trial-and-error basis. The complex assemblage of tasks involved and the cost of the design and implementation are such as to constitute a major project. Project management is conducted with special management techniques of its own, techniques related to establishment of project needs and objectives and to planning, scheduling, budgeting, reporting, and controlling.

The outstanding characteristics of these techniques are the breakdown structure, the network approach to defining task relationships, and the integration of performance/cost/time for planning and control. The detailed techniques for implementing these major-project management techniques have provided powerful aids to management. We have summarized the project planning and control cycle in Figure 6-3.

[5] Robert Gunning, *The Technique of Clear Writing*, New York: McGraw-Hill Book Company, 1952. Fog index = 0.4 (average number of words per sentence) + 0.4 (average number of three-syllable words excluding capitalized words and words made up of easy words). Use several samples of about 100 consecutive words.

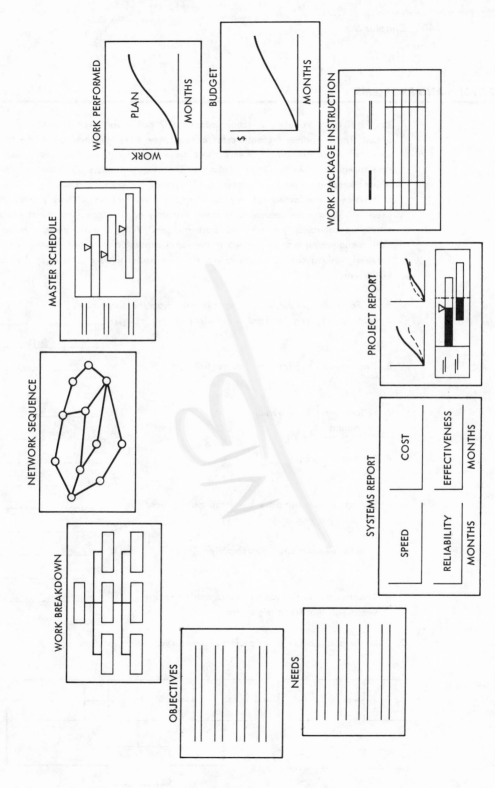

Figure 6-3 Project planning and control cycle.

QUESTIONS AND PROBLEMS

1. The P. P. Trang variety store chain opened 602 new stores over a recent ten-year period. The executives responsible for opening new stores did not consult the firm's own real estate division and hence chose many poor locations. They also failed to consult with the merchandising executives. The store managers operated the stores without keeping inventory, cost, and profit records for each department. The Trang EDP systems were located at corporate headquarters and served only headquarter executives. Corporate accounting concentrated only on total company results without setting up control systems for each store and each type of department in a store. Cash management was not related to the rapid expansion in number of stores or to required working capital. Financial reports were issued three months after the close of the operating period.

    For each item below, give two examples from the above case:

    a. Evidence of need for total corporate planning   (1) _____

       (2) _____

    b. Evidence of need for corporate control   (1) _____

       (2) _____

    c. Failure to relate subsystems in company operations   (1) _____

       (2) _____

    d. Piecemeal actions   (1) _____

       (2) _____

    e. Key information not available to top management for planning and control   (1) _____

       (2) _____

    f. Possible objectives for the company   (1) _____

       (2) _____

    g. Uncertainties in the economic and marketing environments that Trang might face   (1) _____

       (2) _____

2. Label the blocks below in the project planning cycle:

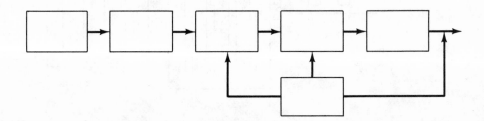

3. Match the following columns by placing the correct number before each letter:

_____ (a) Need for systems planning

_____ (b) Reasons for planning

_____ (c) How establishing systems objectives improves planning

_____ (d) Maximizing benefits/costs of the MIS

_____ (e) Project

_____ (f) Needs research

_____ (g) Project proposal

(1) Application of an MIS to managerial planning and control

(2) To offset uncertainty, improve efficiency, focus on objectives, and provide a basis for control

(3) A unique work program with definite starting and completion dates

(4) Reduces overlapping, sets priorities, and provides a basis for control

(5) Description of a potential MIS project for the purpose of obtaining management approval

4. Consider the following activities and dates:

	Start	Finish
(1) Establish MIS objectives	1/4/76	2/6/76
(2) Conduct a preliminary study of present operations and MIS	1/10/76	4/24/76
(3) Prepare a flow chart for the gross design of the MIS	4/25/76	5/21/76
(4) Prepare a list of files needed	5/15/76	5/23/76
(5) Develop the detailed design of management information and sources	5/21/76	8/26/76
(6) Develop the data base and subsidiary file specifications	5/21/76	8/2/76
(7) Develop software programs	5/27/76	8/20/76
(8) Develop specifications of hardware and software	6/15/76	8/20/76
(9) Prepare complete detailed design specifications	8/15/76	9/30/76

a. Prepare a Gantt chart plan.

b. For the corresponding network showing completion of activities, show the times for each activity (arrow) and find the critical (longest) time path.

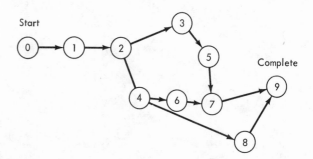

MIS Design: Developing the Gross Design

CHAPTER 7 tells how to create the concept or gross design of the MIS.

When you have finished studying

MIS DESIGN: DEVELOPING THE GROSS DESIGN

you will be able to

1. Describe a set of objectives for an MIS
2. Identify typical MIS constraints
3. Develop approximate information needs
4. Determine current management information sources in a company
5. Develop simple management and operating information system flow charts
6. Describe typical formats for MIS inputs and outputs
7. Identify some important considerations for selection of MIS hardware
8. Describe, in general, the documentation of the gross design.

If you were planning to build your "ideal home," you would probably first look at layouts of many homes. Then you would take your
sketch pad and block out the arrangement of rooms you have decided
upon. This is a rough or "gross" design of your home.

Much more work would need to be done to *detail* the house. Dimensions of rooms would have to be set. Some reshaping of the rooms may
be required. Then, all the hundreds of construction details would need
to be worked out to produce a final "system." This is the *detailed* design.

The gross design of an MIS has the same purpose as the rough
sketches that you would draw for your home. It establishes the basic
parts and their relationships within the system. In this chapter we shall
give a procedure for developing the gross design. Since developing a
gross design is a highly creative process and the results are very complex,
we can really only present some guidelines.

STUDY THE COMPANY AND DEFINE ITS PROBLEMS

**WHAT IS THE
TRUE DIRECTION
OF THE FIRM?**

To start developing a gross design for the MIS, we should first agree
upon the description of our business firm. This is not so easy as it may
seem at first glance. Executives often do not communicate with each
other about basic objectives and the direction of their company. Identification of major problems and a priority for solving them are often lack-
ing. As a result, executives are working in conflicting or nonintegrated
directions.

**What Are Current
and Long-Range
Problems?**

Current problems are not the only concern. MIS design should be
related to long-range planning for the company. Long-range plans are
dependent on MIS capabilities, and, at the same time, MIS design concepts must be based on the future reference business. A reference business description is the blueprint for the company at some particular time.

144

For MIS gross design, we must look at alternative potential reference businesses for the firm *one year, three years,* and *five years* hence.

Without giving a complete directory of every item in a long-range plan, we have listed below a few of the key items for management to consider in the development of MIS design concepts:

Sales in units and dollars
Products, sales by product, share of the market
Number of customers and location
Plants—location and size
Warehouses—location and size
Number of employees
Key executives—identification of each
Number of middle executives
Number of vendors and locations
Working capital and cash inventory
Identity of competitors and share of the market of each
Computer capabilities and locations
Communications network within the company
Environmental factors, such as general business conditions, political/legal factors, and social factors

Management must take the first step in MIS development by thus clarifying the business itself. This description of objectives, role, and problems, once understood and agreed upon by management, is sometimes called the *reference business.* It must be referred to by all concerned with MIS development time and again to make sure the MIS will serve the business. Figure 7-1 summarizes the idea of the reference business.

Management Must Clarify the Business for Everyone

SET OBJECTIVES FOR THE MIS

It would be nice to set the objective of the MIS as supplying each manager with all the information he needs when he needs it. This is not very practical, however. First, the information may not be available within the company. Second, the cost of preparing the information or of supplying it promptly and frequently may be too great. Third, the cost of obtaining information from outside the company may be far too high. For example, test-marketing a product or conducting a probability sample survey to obtain market information may cost hundreds of thousands of dollars in some cases.

THE OBJECTIVES OF MIS MUST BE DIRECTED TOWARD INCREASING THE MANAGERS' EFFECTIVENESS

The manager must define system objectives in terms of increasing his effectiveness in achieving company objectives. This takes into account

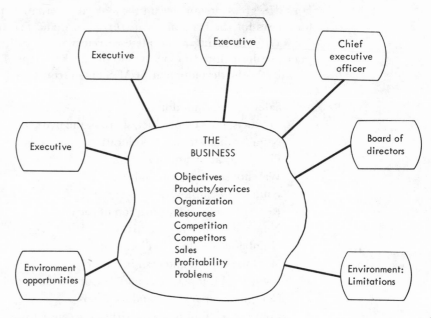

Figure 7-1   Developing the reference business.

both benefits and costs of the MIS. While an MIS may increase efficiency by automation of clerical work, the real value of the system is the degree to which it increases *management effectiveness*. We introduced the idea of project objectives in Chapter 6 and shall now explain them further.

Managerial effectiveness may be increased by (1) early warning signals from the MIS, (2) decision-assisting information, (3) programmed decision making, and, last and least, (4) automation of routine clerical activities. Thus objectives for the MIS are usually established in these four areas. An example of each is shown in Table 7-1. Each objective is based, of course, on some objective of the company.

Despite its difficulty, being specific is necessary. System objectives must ultimately be stated in terms of the objectives of the department, group, function, or manager to be served or in terms of the functions the information system is to perform. In other words, system objectives should be expressed in terms of what managers will be able to do after their information requirements have been met. Such expression may use descriptive statements, flow charts, or any other means that will convey to management the objectives. If possible, the objectives should be stated in quantitative rather than qualitative terms so that alternative system designs as well as system performance can be measured for effectiveness. That is, a statement of objectives should include exactly what it is that the system is supposed to accomplish and the means by which it will subsequently be evaluated. Table 7-2 shows an example of such a statement.

Managers Are More Effective if They Have Advance Warning of Trouble

. . . if They Have Information That Will Help Make Better Decisions

. . . if as Many Decisions Are Programmed as Possible

. . . if Clerical Activities Are Automated to Reduce Time Required for Supervision

Table 7-1 Examples of MIS objectives.

Type	MIS Objective	Related Company Objective
1. Early warning signals	(a) Prevent a long-term gap between average plant capacity and demand for the firm's product	Minimize production costs with expansion of plant capacity
	(b) Prevent surprises due to technological breakthroughs affecting the firm's products	Avoid crash development programs or loss of market share
	(c) Maintain awareness of top-management succession problems	Plan for orderly change of top managers over the next 10 years
2. Decision-assisting information	(a) Supply financial trends and ratios to management	Make good cash and capital investment decisions
	(b) Provide a model and computer hardware and software that will answer managers "What if . . . ?" questions on profits for combinations of products	Achieve a profitable product mix within company constraints
3. Programmed decision making	(a) Assignment of orders to machines and scheduling of orders	Lower production costs
	(b) Allocating advertising expenditures among selected magazines	Provide economical and broad support for salesmen
4. Automation of routine clerical operations	(a) Automation of payroll computations	Timely and accurate pay of employees at minimum cost
	(b) Automation of inventory status and reports	Up-to-date accurate records of inventory to serve customers without delays

This table contains a statement of objectives for the material control system of one of the nation's major electrical manufacturers. Notice how specific objectives are defined.

Listed in Table 7-3 are an additional group of functional subsystems and a hypothetical statement of objectives for each. *These examples will be used for illustration throughout the remainder of this chapter.*

Table 7-2 Objectives of material control system: major electrical manufacturer.

Subsystem	Objective
Routings	Capture routing information and time values that can be used by manufacturing for cost of completed work, labor status by contract, effect of changes by rerouting, etc.
Status	Establish a system that can be used by manufacturing to determine work load in the shop, effect of accepting additional work, overload in various cost centers, status of self-manufactured work in process, etc.
Tools	Capture all tool information that can be used by manufacturing to determine tool status *prior* to release of work to shop, and maintain a tool inventory by contract for auditing purposes both by the company and the government on government contracts.
Cost control	Establish an overall system that can be used by manufacturing to very quickly determine labor costs, material costs, tool costs, overruns, etc., by contract.
Scheduling	Determine effect of engineering changes, lack of material, tool shortages, etc.
Make or buy	Make decisions on those items to subcontract, based on cost, load, schedule, etc.
Request for proposal information	Establish a system that can be used by manufacturing to produce immediately the necessary information needed for customer requests and requests for proposals.
Elapsed time	Analyze, improve, and prepare an orderly procedure that can be used by manufacturing to report elapsed time, if required by contractual obligation.

WHAT WILL THE MIS DO?

In summary, the first steps in systems design attempt to answer the following questions: Why is it needed? What is the purpose of the system? What is it expected to do? Who are the users, and what are their objectives? These questions relate to the *what* of systems design, and the remainder of the steps relate to *how* it is to be achieved.

Finally, the establishment of MIS objectives cannot be divorced from a consideration of organizational objectives, near term and long range. Over the near term, system objectives can usually be framed in terms of management planning and control and decision making: lowering costs, strengthening operating controls, improving data flow, and meeting customer and external requirements. These short-range system objectives must, however, take into account the environment in which a business will be operating five to ten years hence. *Today's* system design must take *tomorrow's* environment into account.

Table 7-3

Subsystem	Objective
Inventory	Optimize inventory costs through the design of decision rules containing optimum reorder points, safety stock levels, and reorder quantities, each capable of continuous and automatic reassessment.
Accounts payable	Pay 100% of invoices before due date.
Purchasing	Provide performance information on buyer's price negotiations with suppliers in order that purchase variance can be controlled within set limits.
Production control	Identify cost and quantity variances within one day in order to institute closer control over these variables.
Project control	Identify performance against plan so that events, costs, and specifications of the project can be met.

IDENTIFY SYSTEM CONSTRAINTS

CONSTRAINTS ARE
LIMITATIONS ON
THE MIS

Constraints are simply limitations of the MIS or requirements of the MIS imposed by either management or other groups. Constraints are usually classified, however, as internal or external. See Figure 7-2.

Internal Constraints

If *top-management support* is not obtained for the systems concept and for the notion that computer-based information systems are vital for management planning and control, the type of design effort discussed in these chapters cannot be implemented. A good environment for information systems must be set, and one essential ingredient is the approval and support of top management. This constraint definitely influences the kind of system the manager-user may design.

Some
Constraints
Are Set by
the Company

Organizational and policy considerations frequently set limits on objectives and modify an intended approach to design of a system. The structure of the organization and the managers occupying various positions influence information flow and use of system outputs. In a decentralized multiplant organization with a wide product line, the design of common systems in cost accounting or production control is obviously less acceptable than in a more centralized organization with fewer products. An additional organizational difficulty is related to the turnover of managers. More than one head of computer operations has stated that his major difficulty is the abandonment or redesign of systems due to the turnover among manager-users. Also, company policies frequently define or limit the approach to systems design. Among these policies are those

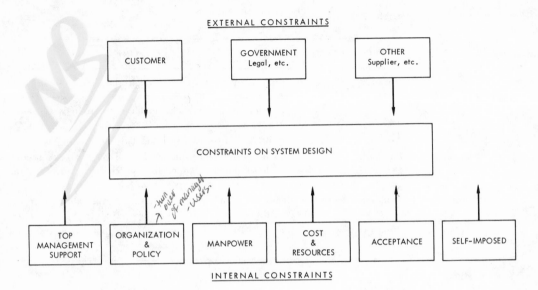

Figure 7-2 Constraints on MIS design.

concerned with product and service, research and development, production, marketing, finance, and personnel. For example, a "promote from within" personnel policy would have an impact on the type of systems design to build a skills inventory. Other important considerations in design are those concerning audits.

Manpower needs and personnel availability are a major limiting factor in both the design and utilization of information systems. Computer and systems skills are among the most critical in the nation; rare indeed is the manager who admits to having sufficient personnel to design, implement, and operate the systems he desires. Additional considerations concern the nature of the work force and the skill mix of users. Elaborate and sophisticated systems are of little value if they cannot be put to use.

Perhaps the most significant constraint of all is the one concerning *people.* "People problems" is probably the factor most often mentioned where failure to achieve expected results is concerned. Here we have the difficulties associated with the natural human reaction to change, the antagonism, and the lack of interest and support frequently met in systems design and operation. Automation, computer systems, and systems design often call for the realignment of people and facilities, organizational changes, and individual job changes. Therefore, these reactions are to be expected and should be anticipated in designing systems to achieve the objective.

Cost is a major *resource* limitation. The cost to achieve the objective should be compared with the benefits to be derived. You do not want to spend $20,000 to save $10,000. Although a cost-benefit analysis is frequently difficult, some approach to priority setting must be undertaken. Considerations similar to those surrounding cost apply also to the use of other resources. *Computer capacity* and other facilities relating to operation of data processing systems should be utilized in an optimum way.

Self-imposed restrictions are those placed on the design by the manager or the designer. In designing the system to achieve the objective, he may have to scale down several requirements in order to make the system fit with other outputs, equipment, or constraints. Usually, he will also restrict the amount of time and effort devoted to investigation. For example, he may want to design a pilot or test system around one product, one plant, or one portion of an operation before making it generally applicable elsewhere. Functional requirements also define constraints placed on the system by its users. The data requirements, the data volumes, and the rate of processing are constraints imposed by the immediate users. More remote users impose constraints by the need to integrate with related systems.

External Constraints

Many Constraints Are Set by Outsiders Such As the Customers, the Government, Unions, and Suppliers

Foremost among the considerations surrounding the external environment are those concerning the *customer*. Order entry, billing, and other systems that interface with systems of the customer must be designed with his needs in mind. If certain outputs from the system are not acceptable to the customer, a definite limitation must be faced up to. He may require that bills be submitted in a form that provides input to his system of accounts payable. For example, standard progress reporting and billing procedures are among the requirements imposed for processing data under many military procurement programs.

A variety of additional external constraints should be considered in addition to the customer. The *government* (federal, state, local) imposes certain restrictions on the processing data. Among these are the need to maintain the security of certain classes of information (e.g., personnel) in order to comply with law and regulation in the conduct of business (e.g., taxes, reporting) and to meet certain procedures regarding record keeping and reporting to stockholders (e.g., outside audit). *Unions* can and do affect the operation of systems involving members in matters such as compensation, grievances, and working conditions. *Suppliers* are also an important group to be considered when designing information systems because these systems frequently interface with that group.

In summary, it is important to recognize the constraints that have an impact on systems design. Having recognized them and made appropriate allowance in the design function, the manager will then be in a position to complete the remaining steps toward the design of an operating system that will achieve the objective he has previously determined.

The nature of constraints is illustrated here by stating a hypothetical constraint for each of our selected functional subsystems:

Subsystem	*Statement of Constraint*
Inventory	Regardless of reorder points and reorder quantities, the supplier will not accept orders for less than carload lots for raw materials 7 and 12.
Accounts payable	The individual who prepares the check for payment of invoices must not be the same individual who approves payment.
Purchasing	It is not necessary to negotiate purchases in amounts under $500.
Production control	System output for shop control will be identified by department only and not by the individual worker or foreman.
Project control	We are required to report weekly to the U.S. Department of Defense any slippages in time or cost exceeding 10% of any event in the project control critical path.

DETERMINE INFORMATION NEEDS

A clear statement of information needs is fundamental and necessary to good systems design. Too many companies spend lavish sums on hardware and software to perpetuate existing systems or build sophisticated data banks without first determining the real information needs of management: information that can increase the perception of managers in critical areas such as problems, alternatives, opportunities, and plans.

INFORMATION
NEEDS MUST
BE DESCRIBED

Unless managers can provide the specifications for what they want out of an information system, the design effort will produce less than optimum results. If, on the other hand, the manager-user can define his objectives and spell out the items of information that are needed to reach the objective, he is then at least halfway home in systems design. Failure to be specific on these two steps probably accounts for the downfall of more design efforts than any other factor. If systems design begins without such clear-cut statements by the manager, the systems analyst or technician will provide *his* objectives and *his* information needs.

Yet it is not easy for a manager to spell out the specific information requirements of his job, and therein lies a basic frustration in the improvement of systems. In an attempt to get a clear statement of information needs, the analyst frequently meets with an interviewing situation somewhat like this typical exchange:

It Is Difficult
for a Manager to
Describe His
Information
Needs

ANALYST

Could you tell me what the objectives of this cost accounting system are, as you see them?

FINANCIAL MANAGER

Sure . . . to get the reports out faster . . . to do something about keeping the costs in line . . . to keep management informed. . . .

ANALYST

Yes, I understand . . . let me put it another way. What are your responsibilities as you see them?

FINANCIAL MANAGER

Whatta you mean? I'm in charge of the treasury department.

ANALYST

Yes, I know, but we need to get a better statement of your department's objectives, how the cost accounting system can further these objectives, and what information is needed to do this.

FINANCIAL MANAGER

Well, we need the information we've been getting, but we need it faster and with a lot more accurate input from those fellows in operations.

Three Ways to Help Managers Define Their Information Needs

This hypothetical conversation reflects the difficulty of getting managers to be specific about information needs. One approach, sometimes used by consultants, is to get top management to require in writing from subordinate managers a statement containing (1) a list of four or five major responsibilities for which the manager believes himself to be accountable and (2) the four or five specific items of information that are required to carry out the responsibilities. These requirements could be framed in terms of duties performed or decisions made; the idea is to get the managers to think of information needs. If this can be done, the information systems is well on the way to being designed.

Another approach is avoidance of the direct question, What information do you need? Instead, the designer requests that the user describe what occurs in the decision-making process; then the designer concerns himself with the identification of the questions that are to be resolved in the activity for which the system is being designed. This approach is also a good one for the manager-user, because he is intimately familiar with his operation and presumably with the difficult decision operations in it.

One way of determining what managers do *not* need in the way of information is to cease issuing selected periodic reports or reduce their circulation list. If a manager really uses a report, he will complain, and his name may be restored to the circulation list.

A manager needs information for a variety of reasons concerned with the management process. The type of need that he will have at various times and for various purposes depends largely on two factors that we shall examine briefly: the personal managerial attributes of the individual manager, and the organizational environment in which decisions are made.

PERSONAL ATTRIBUTES

Knowledge of information systems. If the manager is aware of what computer-based systems can do, his information requests will probably be more sophisticated and more specific. His knowledge of capabilities and costs places him in a much better position to aid in the design of a good system.

Managerial style. A manager's technical background, his leadership style, and his decision-making ability all affect the kind and amount of information he requires. Some prefer a great amount of detail; others like to decide with a minimum of detail and prefer personal consultation with subordinates.

Manager's perception of information needs. "You tell me what I need to know" and "Get me all the facts" represent two opposite perceptions of information needs. This dichotomy is due partly to the fact that many managers are ignorant of what information they need. Another dimension of the problem is the widely differing views of managers regarding their obligation to disseminate information to subordinates and to groups outside the firm. The manager who cannot or will not delegate authority is likely to keep information closely held.

In Table 7-4, we have shown a format for collecting and listing basic information needs of managers as the managers perceive them.

Table 7-4 Information needs of several managers in a manufacturing company at the gross design level.

Manager	Function or Objectives	Principal Information Needs
President	Short- and long-run profitability, expansion, stability of earnings	Summary reports: 1. Financial 2. Sales 3. Marketing 4. Public relations 5. Consumer division 6. Industrial division 7. International operations 8. Engineering/research 9. Forecasts of the future Exception reports: Major problems affecting company operations and deviations from plans, competitive actions posing a threat, government activities of major significance

Manager	Function or Objectives	Principal Information Needs
Vice president and treasurer	Direct all financial matters for the company and is responsible for all financial reports, budgets, and their analysis	Revenue and costs Cash flow Tax liabilities Gross insurance budgets Capital structure factors such as bond rates, cost of floating new equity, and trends in financial markets
Senior VP, marketing and sales	Directs all marketing functions and public relations	Summarized sales forecast Summarized market research reports on 1. Attitudes and buying habits of customers 2. Analysis of past marketing strategies 3. Competitors and their products Exception reports on sales significantly above or below plans, by product, region, or sales group
Manager, national sales training	Conducts training seminars in the field to strengthen the sales force and its supervision	Number and location of new sales and new salesmen Areas of weakness in sales improvement Training needs
Traffic manager	Directs traffic activities for incoming and outgoing materials	Location of warehouses Location of supplies Train, truck, water, and air rates Differences in quality of service provided by various carriers
Data processing manager	Responsible for the equipment and staffing of the data processing center; provides data processing service to all managers, particularly, the financial, MIS, marketing, and engineering organizations	Forecasts of services required from each organization New equipment coming on the market Forecasts of growth of services required Format of reports and media of reports desired by users Data base specifications Sources of input data

To help the managers focus on their needs, rather than on information actually received, they were first asked to give the basic objectives of their positions.

ORGANIZATIONAL ENVIRONMENT

Nature of the company. Problems in communication and in controlling operations seem to be a function of the company's size and the complexity of its organization. The larger, more complex firms require more formal information systems, and the information needs of these systems become more critical to operations.

The Nature of the
Company Affects
the Manager's
Information Needs

Level of management. We outlined in Chapter 2 the three levels of management (i.e., strategic planning, management control, operational control) and the varying needs for information at each. Each level needs different types of information, generally in different form. Top levels need the one-time report, the summary, and the single inquiry. The management control level needs the exception report, the summary, and a variety of regular reports for periodic evaluation. The operational control level requires the formal report with fixed procedures, the day-to-day report of transactions, in order to maintain operational control of actions as they occur. Managers at *all* levels have changing information needs, depending on the nature and importance of the particular decision

Structure of the organization. The more highly structured the organization, the easier it is to determine the information needs. Where authority and responsibility are clearly spelled out, relationships understood, and decision-making areas defined, the information needs of managers can be determined more easily.

Returning to our illustrative subsystems, some information needs at the operating subsystem level of management might be stated:

Subsystem	*Information Needs*
Inventory	Daily report on items that have fallen below minimum inventory level, in order that expediting action can be taken.
Accounts payable	Incoming invoices coded according to "days to due date," because invoices should be paid no sooner than 2 days prior to due date in order to conserve cash.
Purchasing	The performance of each individual buyer, indicated by comparing actual purchases with hypothetical purchases at base or standard prices.
Production control	Exception report to identify by shop order and lot number the variances in cost and quantity that are over or under by 5%.
Project control	Weekly report on progress against plan for the events in critical path. Also need to know where float exists in other events so that resources may be shifted.

DETERMINE INFORMATION SOURCES

Once we have identified managers and their principal or "gross" information needs, the next design step is to determine the source of this information. Managers may receive information from

1. External sources such as customers, vendors, other businessmen, business publications, newspapers, and government and industry documents.
2. Other managers or other organizations within the company such as data processing.
3. Their subordinates.
4. Files of data.

Such information must be generated according to managers' needs. This means that operating systems must produce, from transactions, this needed information. Operating systems and hence organizational units must be modified or designed anew to serve the information needs of managers.

OPERATING SYSTEMS MUST BE DESIGNED TO YIELD INFORMATION THAT MANAGERS NEED

Let us illustrate with a simple example. A company has a system for aiding management to make capital budgeting decisions. The system gathers recommendations from marketing, production, engineering, and corporate management. These recommendations are tabulated and ranked by a committee. A total capital budget constraint is then imposed by top management, and a final selection of investments is made. At one of these annual reviews, a conversation starts:

ENGINEERING MANAGER
Our unit manufacturing costs seem to be creeping up. Why do we have so many rejects?

PRODUCTION MANAGER
Our equipment is aging, Jim. You know I've tried to get some new numerical controlled modern lathes and drill presses in the budget for the last five years.

MARKETING MANAGER
That's true, Bill, but when is a machine old or obsolete? And what is the average age of each class of machines that you have?

PRODUCTION MANAGER
I don't know. We'd have to research that, Sam.

This shows that the capital resource subsystem was not designed to produce information that managers need. In fact, if the records on the purchase date of the equipment were not kept for a period of 10 to 15 years, it might be very difficult to determine the average age of classes of equipment. The subsystem needs to be redesigned to furnish such information at capital budgeting time.

How To Locate Sources of Information That Managers Need

During this step in systems design, the determination of information sources, the form of the new system begins to take shape. We must not only uncover information sources for the particular subsystem under consideration but also take into account how they fit into the overall integrative sources of information and techniques of analysis.

Information Sources Must Be Matched to Needs

Sources of information may be categorized:

1. *Internal and external records.* Internal records most often take the form of written materials and could include examples of inputs or outputs, file records, memoranda and letters, reports containing information about the existing system, and documentation of existing or planned systems. External data may come from a variety of sources such as trade publications, government statistics, and the like.

2. *Interviewing* managers and operating personnel is a valuable method of identifying possible sources of information and of analyzing the existing system. This form of data gathering can be the most fruitful method of securing information, provided it is conducted properly. Unlike the reading of written records, the gathering of facts from an interview involves human communication problems; these can be largely overcome by proper planning and by gaining the confidence of persons interviewed.

3. *Sampling and estimating* methods may become necessary when the accumulation of data is so large that only a portion of it can be examined. The major advantages of sampling techniques lie in the savings of time and cost, particularly on nonrecurring events where data are not available. One frequently used form of sampling is *work sampling*, which can be used to analyze the actions of people, machines, or events in terms of time. Estimating is an acceptable method of analysis and is a time-saver; however, estimates should be checked to control totals or be verified by interview where possible.

4. *Input/output analysis* is demonstrated in Figure 7-3 with the input/output chart, a visual portrayal of information inputs to a system and the information output that results. With a listing of inputs along the left side and outputs across the top, the relationship can be established by the dot at the point of intersection. For example, to produce an output of invoices, the information designated by the dots for company order number, tax data, net price, and shipping papers is required as input.

Figure 7-3 also demonstrates how data can be reduced and subsystems integrated through proper design. The top half, or "before analysis" portion, reveals that several items of output appear also

OUTPUT DATA

Input/output chart — BEFORE ANALYSIS

INPUT & SUPPORTING DATA	Invoices	Shipping papers	Shipping labels	Quantity shipped	Back orders	Replenishment orders	Net price	Shipping terms	Shipping register	Stock ledgers	Stock bulletin	Stock report	Billing & cost dist.	Price realization	Tax reports	Royalty reports	Face sheets	Unfilled orders	Orders entered ($)	Statistical analysis
Customer orders																				
Order number		•	•				•													
Quantity ordered				•	•					•							•	•	•	
Item ident.		•			•					•							•	•	•	
List price							•										•	•	•	
Company ord. no.	•	•	•			•			•	•										
Customer reg. record																				
Pricing policy (Dis.)	•						•	•									•	•	•	
Traffic routing		•						•												
Tax data	•																			
Quantity shipped		•																		•
Net price	•																			•
Invent. cost at stand.												•	•	•						•
Stock replen. proc.				•	•					•										•
Receipts				•	•					•										•
Invoices													•	•	•	•	•		•	•
Shipping papers	•		•					•	•											
Stock ledgers				•	•					•	•	•								•
Price & cost refer.													•	•						
Peg board forms													•	•		•	•			
Royalty ident. codes																•				

OUTPUT DATA

Input/output chart — AFTER ANALYSIS

INPUT & SUPPORTING DATA	Invoices	Shipping papers	Shipping labels	Quantity shipped	Back orders	Replenishment orders	Net price	Shipping terms	Shipping register	Stock ledgers	Stock bulletin	Stock report	Billing & cost dist.	Price realization	Tax reports	Royalty reports	Face sheets	Unfilled orders	Orders entered ($)	Statistical analysis
Customer order no.	•	•	•						•											
Cust. ident. no.	•	•	•		•		•	•	•						•			•	•	•
Item ident. no.	•	•		•	•	•	•	•		•	•	•	•	•	•	•	•	•	•	•
Quantity ordered	•	•		•	•	•		•	•	•	•	•	•	•	•	•	•	•	•	•
Receipts	•	•		•	•	•		•	•	•	•	•	•	•	•	•	•	•	•	•

Source: Paul R. Saunders in Victor Lazzaro, ed., *Systems and Procedures*, 2nd ed. Englewood Cliffs, N.J.: Prentice-Hall, Inc., 1968.

Figure 7-3 Input/output chart (customer order processing).

as input, indicating rehandling and reprocessing of the same information to produce an output. The bottom half of the figure illustrates how consolidation and integration can reduce the number of information sources (i.e., input items). Figure 7-4 demonstrates the multiple uses of information sources and how information requirements may be identified and combined in a systems design that can serve more than one user. Files of input can be utilized by various organizational elements and various information subsystems.

5. *Multidimensional flow* is an additional technique of organizing information sources or depicting the existing design of a subsystem. A flow chart can be constructed to trace the routing or flow of information from origin to destination and to arrange this flow in a chronological sequence that shows the progression of information through the organization. Although they are not specifically required for identification of information sources, the factors of frequency, volume, time, cost, and physical distance can also be shown on such a chart.

Information Sources—Summary

Now that information sources have been identified with information needs, the next design step is to prepare a list that matches needs and sources. Such a list is evaluated and reevaluated until a final valid list of information sources is generated to match against previously determined information needs. This matching can take the form of a matrix diagram, a valuable device for the integration of subsystems as well as for use in the remainder of the systems design process. Figure 7-5 illustrates how such a matching process might be useful for the economic order quantity subsystem of the inventory management system.

Information sources can be further illustrated by giving examples of our selected subsystems:

Subsystem		*Information Sources*
Inventory	NEED	Items falling below minimum inventory level
	SOURCE	Stock-level determination subsystem compares current balance against minimum inventory level
Accounts payable	NEED	Code invoices "days to due date"
	SOURCE	Coded upon entry into accounts payable subsystem
Purchasing	NEED	Performance of individual buyers
	SOURCE	Purchasing system compares outgoing purchase prices against predetermined standards
Production control	NEED	Cost variances over or under 5%
	SOURCE	Integration of costing with manufacturing applications: shop control, stores requisitioning, labor distribution, etc.
Project control	NEED	Progress against plan for events in critical path
	SOURCE	Project control subsystem

Figure 7-4 Multiple uses of information.

Courtesy of Motorola, Inc.

	ORGANIZATION COMPONENT							MASTER FILES																		
	Sales	Production	Quality control	Engineering	Material control	Accounting	Personnel	Customer file	Vendor file	Open order file	Open purchase order file	Sales data file	Product file	Plant master schedule	Master parts list	Supply file	Operations file	Design file	Inventory and price file	Raw materials file	Accounts receivable / Credit and collections	Accounts payable	Employee master file	Payroll file	Labor planning file	Ledger balance file
Order processing	◁			◁	◁	◁		◁		◁			◁	◁					◁	◁	◁					
Product design and documentation		◁		◁					◁	◁			◁		◁			◁		◁						
Customer product modifications	◁	◁		◁									◁													
Contracting	◁			◁		◁		◁	◁	◁	◁		◁	◁	◁				◁			◁			◁	◁
Selling	◁					◁		◁				◁	◁													
Promotion	◁							◁				◁	◁													
Pricing policies	◁			◁	◁	◁				◁		◁	◁		◁		◁		◁	◁						
Product scheduling	◁	◁			◁			◁		◁		◁	◁		◁											
Production and inventory	◁	◁	◁	◁	◁	◁			◁	◁	◁	◁	◁	◁	◁				◁							◁
Plant capacity	◁	◁	◁	◁						◁		◁		◁												
Product quality and control			◁	◁									◁				◁	◁								
Personnel accounting						◁	◁									◁							◁	◁	◁	◁
Receiving function			◁						◁		◁															
Purchasing					◁	◁			◁		◁				◁					◁		◁				
Finance	◁				◁	◁		◁		◁		◁	◁		◁			◁	◁		◁	◁			◁	◁
Shipping	◁	◁	◁			◁		◁		◁	◁	◁	◁	◁	◁							◁				◁
Management	◁	◁	◁	◁	◁	◁	◁	◁	◁	◁	◁	◁	◁	◁	◁	◁	◁	◁	◁	◁	◁	◁	◁	◁	◁	◁

Figure 7-5 Data worksheet.

	Strategic planning center	Operations manager	Personnel manager	Production planning mgr.	Customer service	Engineering manager	Marketing manager	Data processing manager	Assembly manager	Inventory control	Manufacturing manager	Purchasing manager
Personnel statistics	X	X	X	X	X	X	X	X		X	X	X
Bill of materials				X		X						
Parts list				X		X						
Proposed time and cost schedule		X		X		X	X		X		X	
Contract verification		X						X				
Contract rejection		X						X				
Time schedule		X		X		X	X			X		
Cost schedule		X		X		X	X					
Design specifications	X					X	X					
Time and cost progress reports		X		X		X	X		X		X	
Inventory reports		X		X								X
Sales forecast (manual)	X											
Shipping invoice		X			X							
Assembly schedule									X			
Performance summary report	X	X		X			X					X
Project order		X				X	X					
Fabrication order											X	
Work order		X		X								
Contract	X											
Time cards												
Master change order		X		X	X							
Repair order	X											
Customer complaints	X											
Purchase order												X
Vendor invoice												X
Computerized sales forecast	X	X		X				X				
Purchasing report	X	X		X								X

DEVELOP ALTERNATIVE GROSS DESIGNS

WHAT ARE POSSIBLE
PATTERNS OF
INFORMATION
FLOW, FILE SYSTEMS,
AND DATA
PROCESSING?

The development of a *concept* of a system is a creative process that involves synthesizing knowledge into some particular pattern. In our case, the concept of an MIS would consist of the major decision points, patterns of information flow, channels of information, and roles of managers and competitors. The concept must also include the relationship of the MIS to all functional operating systems, both existing and planned. The concept is a sketch of the structure or skeleton of the MIS, guiding and restricting the form of the detailed design. If gross design is the skeleton, then detailed design is the flesh.

Let us present two very simplified examples of alternative gross designs. For the first example, consider a company that wishes to introduce a new compact car. Two teams of engineers are put to work to conceive a design. One concept produced is a sketch showing a three-wheeled vehicle of a specified maximum length, weight, and horsepower, with the engine in the rear. The other team produces a sketch and description of a four-wheeled vehicle with front-engine drive and a specified minimum length, maximum weight, and horsepower limits.

In the second example, a company has 20 warehouses scattered about the United States to provide rapid shipment to customers. Headquarters and production facilities are at a single location. An MIS is needed to regulate production and inventories because of constant crises that have arisen with respect to deliveries. Two teams are asked to develop an MIS. The first team proposes that all orders from customers be sent directly to marketing at company headquarters. Marketing management will then provide demand forecasts to the factory and shipping instructions to the warehouses. A computer at company headquarters will maintain a perpetual inventory of all products in all warehouses. The second team proposes an MIS whereby orders are transmitted by the customers directly to the nearest warehouse. Each warehouse maintains its own inventory records; each forecasts its demand for the month ahead and transmits it to the factory.

Alternative Flow Charts

Now let's take a small case example of alternative gross designs of an inventory and accounts receivable system. In Figure 7-6, the inventory status is stored on punched cards in a master file. New orders and the master file must be read into the computer for calculation of new inventory and billing. The outputs are inventory report, invoices, and a new master file.

In Figure 7-7, a central data base accessed directly by the computer contains all current files. When new orders are read into the computer, the reports are issued and the files are automatically updated.

General System Flow

The system flow chart is a common method of indicating the general structure of a computer-based information system. Shown in such a chart is the description of the information flow in general terms. The system flow also reflects the design efforts that have gone on before this step: setting objectives, establishing constraints, and determining information needs and sources.

The system flow, as illustrated by a flow chart, is quite general in nature and indicates only the main components of the system. At this stage in the design, the chart does not indicate what processing occurs at particular steps in the flow or what specific data, equipment, or people are involved. However, the chart is extremely important because it pro-

Figure 7-6   Inventory and accounts receivable—punched card or tape.

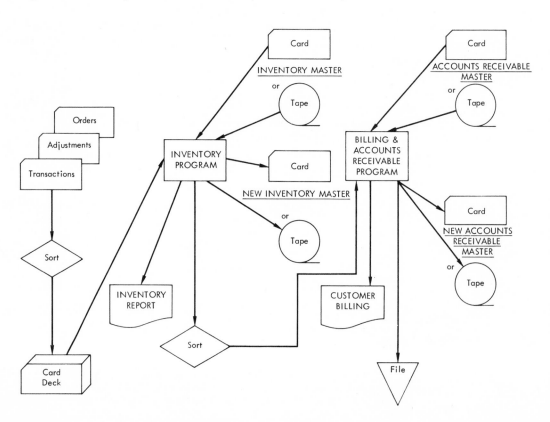

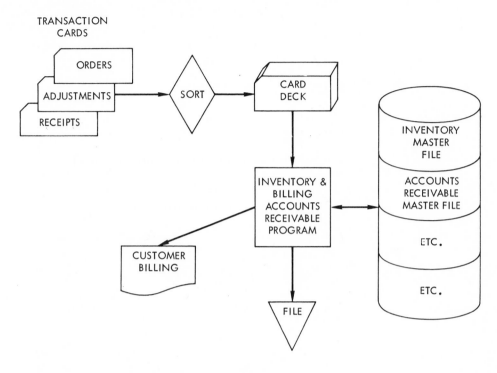

Figure 7-7   Inventory and accounts receivable—direct access.

vides the foundation upon which a great many detailed specifications will follow. All managers should appear on the gross design flow chart to show information they must receive.

In Figure 7-8 we have sketched a rough or gross design flow chart. Different degrees of detail may appear in such a chart. Remember that its main purpose is to show the arrangement of managed subsystems and principal information flows to managers. Notice some important characteristics of the gross design flow chart:

Systems Flow Chart Shows Managers, Information Inputs to Managers, and Information Sources

1. System *objectives* are achieved and reflected in the flow diagram.
2. Information needs and information sources are designed into the system.
3. Decision rules and decision points are shown.
4. Inputs and outputs are designated.
5. Most important—*subsystems are integrated.*

In the gross design stage, clarity of presentation is more important than using a wide variety of standardized flow-chart symbols. Figure 7-9 shows the standard flow-chart symbols as they appear on plastic templates.

Figure 7-8 Information flow chart.

Courtesy of STP Corporation.

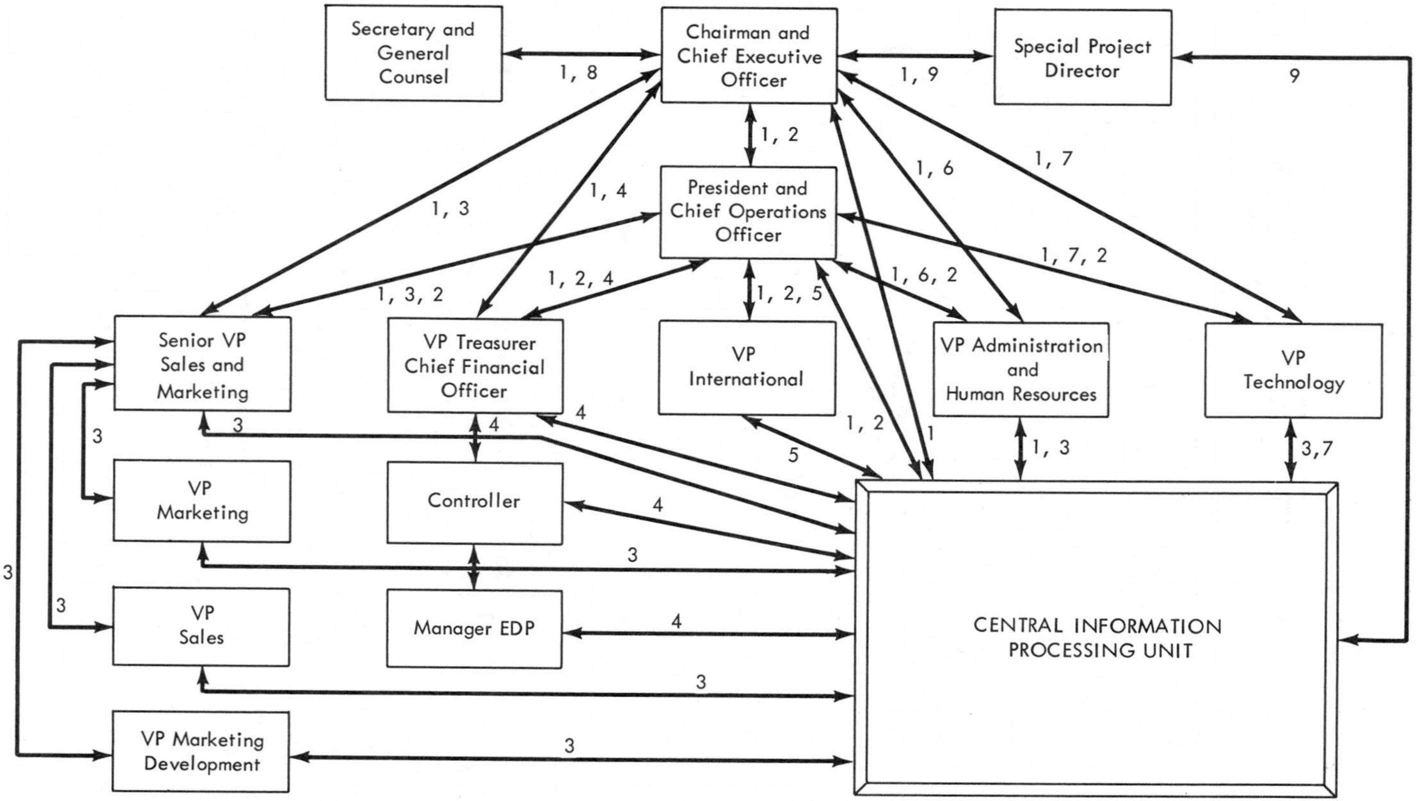

Figure 7-8 (continued) Code for information flow chart.

1. *General Operational Information and Reports*
   Profit center performance reports
   Variance analysis
   Profitability by product life
   Long-range & annual profit plans
   Overhead budget reports
   Financial position
   Market & economic trends
   Advertising & advertising quality
   Sales & sales promotion
   Long-term supplies agreements
   Personnel requirements
   Relevant issues
   General aspects of business
2. *Specific Operational Reports and Information*
   Inventory status
   Work-in-process backlog summary
   Cash position
   Orders awaiting shipment
   Pricing information
   Sales data
   Warehouse stock
3. *Marketing and Sales Information and Reports*
   Daily summary of selling (broken down by product and task)
   Budget performance forecast
   General administration information
   Sales & marketing status reports
   Sales trend analysis
   Share of market report
   Results of special promotions
   Reports on capital projects
   Revised forecast & variations
   Outstanding purchase commitments
   Marketing personnel analysis
   Advertising strategy & expenditure reports
   Marketing cost & deviation reports
   Life cycle analysis
   Promotional allowances
   Customer lists & new accounts
   Sales recapitulation report
   Buyer price analysis report
   Sales audit reports
4. *Financial Information and Reports*
   Budget & periodic reports on performance against budget
   Accounting control

Payroll by hourly & salaried groups
Payroll distribution reports
Inventories of products
Aged trial balance
Customer credit information
Accounting reports
Order & customer profile reports
Unfilled & back order information
Sales reports
Warehouse shipments information
Anticipated stockouts
Work-in-process backlog summary
Expediting information
Purchase orders & receiving data
Open purchase order status
Vendor delivery performance reports

5. *International Information and Reports*
Share of market report
Sales trend analysis
Revised forecast & variations
Overhead budget reports
Financial position
Profitability by product line
Item performance
Profit center performance reports
Variance analysis
Market & economic trends
Shipment reports

6. *Administration and Human Resources Information and Reports*
Personnel management reports
Manpower requirement reports
Personnel performance reports
Salary information
Labor distribution
Personnel requirement forecasts
Operating plans
Personnel training data
Personnel history

7. *Technology Information and Reports*
New product status reports
Schedules
Equipment inventories
Cost information
Research & development information
Item performance reports
Quality control reports
Market & economic trends
End-product requirements

8. *Legal Counsel Information and Reports*
   Legal documents
   Contracts
   Patent rights information
   Pension plans
   Government control information

9. *Special Product Director Information and Reports*
   Item performance
   Raw materials forecasts
   Overhead budget reports
   Financial position
   Variance analysis
   Profitability by product line reports

Data Bank

Data Banks Store
Data; Model Banks
Store Models

The nature of the data and model banks and of their relationships to the MIS subsystems helps to determine the gross design. Most companies have data stored in file cabinets and desks scattered throughout offices and plant locations. The development of the electronic computer and on-line storage have made possible the centralized storage of most company data. For example, the IBM 3850 Mass Storage System can expand a user's on-line data storage capacity to as much as 472 billion characters of information.

Centralized Data
Storage Is the
Data Base

As part of the gross design, the general nature of the data bank (or data base) should be described. This may be done by listing the files to be included in the data base. A file is simply a set of related records. In the detailed design, more specific information on each file must be developed, including the structure of records.

Figure 7-9   Program and system flow-chart symbols.

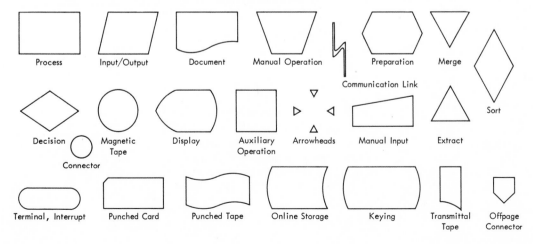

Process	Input/Output	Document	Manual Operation	Preparation	Merge

Communication Link

Decision	Magnetic Tape	Display	Auxiliary Operation	Arrowheads	Manual Input	Extract

Connector

Sort

Terminal, Interrupt	Punched Card	Punched Tape	Online Storage	Keying	Transmittal Tape	Offpage Connector

A list of files for a southeastern Florida bank is shown in Figure 7-10(a). The operational portion of this data base is expanded into subfiles as shown in Figure 7-10(b). The data base for a manufacturing company, a bank, or a public agency will vary greatly. The data base must therefore be designed to fit the particular organization. By eliminating duplicate files and providing prompt access to data, the data base is an important consideration in the gross design.

The Data Base Is Subdivided into Files

System Inputs

From the user's point of view, the inputs were structured when information sources were determined. However, there remains the task of design of input format. Because inputs frequently have to be accepted in the form in which they are received from outside the firm (e.g., sales orders, shipping documents, receiving papers, personnel information, etc.), input design becomes a matter of converting these to machine-usable form. Where inputs are from other subsystems within the firm,

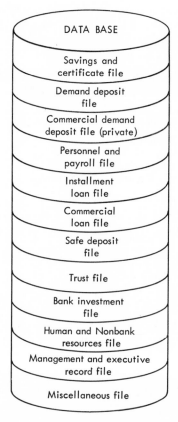

DATA BASE

Savings and certificate file

Demand deposit file

Commercial demand deposit file (private)

Personnel and payroll file

Installment loan file

Commercial loan file

Safe deposit file

Trust file

Bank investment file

Human and Nonbank resources file

Management and executive record file

Miscellaneous file

Figure 7-10(a) Florida bank.

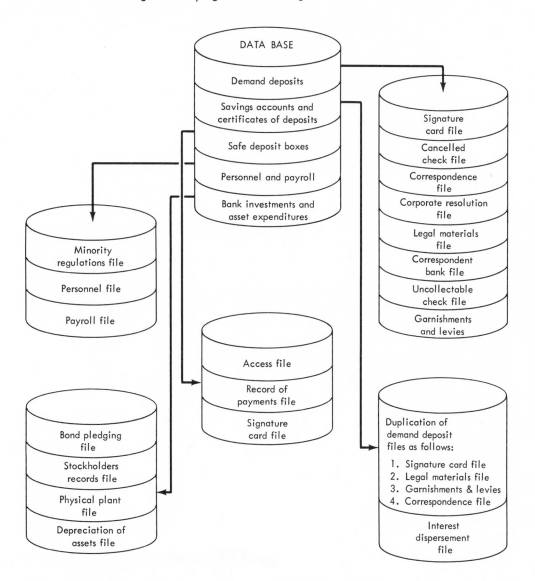

Figure 7-10(b) Operational area data base.

the problem becomes one of integrating these systems through common data elements and other means.

System Input Format More detailed input-data specification includes the sources of data —i.e., where they come from, what form they are in, and who is responsible for their production. Some inputs may be machine-readable and some may have to be converted. Because *forms* are so often used in collecting inputs and for other aids in operating a system, they are indispensable in modern business, and forms design is a primary concern of the systems designer.

Although the manager is not concerned in detail with these input specifications, he should be aware that the designer must specify the source of each input, its frequency, volume, and timing, plus its disposition after processing is completed. Because input must be checked for validity and volume, the editing procedures for accomplishing this are also required. Another important consideration is the specification of how inputs are to be converted into machine-readable form. These and other details of input design are usually contained on forms designed for that purpose.

System Outputs

System Output Format

From the technical standpoint, output-data definition includes the specification of destination—i.e., where they go, what form they take, and who is responsible for receiving them. Included in the specifications are the distribution of output (who gets what, how many copies, and by what means), the frequency with which output will be called for and its timing, and the form the output will take (tape, hard copy, data terminal, etc.). Questions that the designer will ask in the process of developing output specifications include

1. What form are the output reports to take? Can it be off-line?
2. Should the information be detailed or summarized?
3. What can I do with the output data that will be reused?
4. What kind of output form will be required? How many copies?
5. Are reports generated on demand? By exception? On schedule?

Despite the need to answer these details of output specification, the manager is concerned primarily with getting his information needs as previously determined in some type of output format. In other words, the consideration is how to *present the information to the eye or the ear of the manager,* and the answer lies in the content and form design of the output document. The form design is a direct function of information needs and should be constructed to fill those needs in a timely fashion. Care should be taken not to ask for *too much* information *too frequently.* "Management by exception" and "information by summary" should be the guiding principles.

Three illustrative subsystems that we have been using for design in this chapter are inventory management, production control, and purchasing. Figure 7-11 shows examples of outputs that might be designed to provide managerial information needs determined earlier in the design process for these subsystems.

Figure 7-11 Selected outputs for three subsystems: inventory management, production control, purchasing.

DAILY RAW MATERIALS EXPEDITE REPORT

Item Number	Description	Unit	EOQ	ROP	Bal	On Order	Del.	Received	Action
zz	Gasket Material	yd	900	400	327	900	6/6		Expedite with vendor
f73	Spring	doz	60	10	12	60	7/3	42	Check receipt

SHOP VARIANCE REPORT

No.	Lot	Description	Unit	Run	Start	Due Compl.	Shop		Variance ± 5%
3B2	R44	Alum. Tube	each	2	6/13	6/19	Weld		Cost variance + 7.2%
zzx4	R44	Alum. Tube	each	3	6/13	6/26	Bend		Time over 7 days

BUYER NEGOTIATIONS VARIANCE REPORT

Material	Unit	Part No.	Vendor	Standard Cost	Actual Cost	Variance	
Steel Pl.	Lb.	274345X	Bay Metals	.32	.35	.03	9.4% +
Dr. Shaft	ea.	B33–165	Zimmer	9.55	8.72	.83	8.7% **

Hardware and Software Considerations

In the gross design stage, consideration should be given to the type of computer, forms of file storage, forms of input to the computer, and forms of access to the computer. The last is becoming very important today as CRT displays become more common.

Outline the Hardware and Software Requirements Taking Costs into Account

The time and cost of preparing software (computer programs) must also be given consideration early in the design phase. While "What if . . . . ?" inquiries to computerized models are impressive, the cost of development may also be impressive.

Document the Gross Design

The alternative gross designs should be documented so that management may compare them and select one.

The documentation should consist of the following main ideas:

1. Background of the problem or need for the proposed MIS.
2. A list of managers, their objectives, and information needs.
3. Constraints on the design of the MIS.
4. Desired objectives of the MIS.
5. Alternative gross designs:

Prepare a Written Description of Possible Gross Design

   a. Information flow charts.
   b. Data base (lists of files).
   c. Information subsystems, their inputs and outputs.
   d. Rough descriptions of hardware and software requirements and related organization and facilities.
   e. A system narrative to integrate all elements of each gross design.

SELECT THE GROSS DESIGN

Different arrangements of information flow and operations as well as different file structures are developed as we have indicated. The next step is to select the "best" concept. Sometimes, one design will dominate all others, and the choice is easy. More often, a brief appraisal will indicate that some gross designs are not feasible or not very good. When there are two or three apparently good designs, the final choice may be made by

EVALUATE ALTERNATIVES FOR THE GROSS DESIGN AND SELECT ONE

1. Comparing the expected performance of each design with the objectives of the system as previously developed.
2. Preparing a rough cost/effectiveness analysis of each design. This forces some quantified comparisons among systems.

3. Examining flow charts and identifying the strong and weak points of each gross design. Examine the quality of the data banks and availability of data.

4. Expanding the gross designs in more detail if none of the above leads to preferred design.

The selection of the gross design is a managerial decision.

SUMMARY

The gross design represents the conceptual structure of the MIS. It specifies the performance requirements for those who will develop the detailed design. Because it sets the broad outlines of the MIS, the managers who will make use of the MIS must have a large role in the development and evaluation of alternative concepts.

Management must identify basic business problems and objectives of the MIS. System constraints may be of an environmental, basic business, or technical nature. Management is responsible primarily for specifying the first two. The needs of management for information are a function of the problems to be solved and of individual managerial style. Thus, only the managers can factor these into the gross design. Sources of information, on the other hand, are often best determined by the technical specialists.

The gross design is ultimately described by formal documents such as flow charts, input/output matrices, data bank requirements, hardware and software requirements, organizational changes, and time and cost refinements of the project program proposed.

QUESTIONS AND PROBLEMS

1. Relate the *planning and decision making* to the appropriate *manager* by placing a check mark in the correct boxes below:

Planning and Strategic Decision Area \ Manager Responsible	Marketing	New product planning	Promotion	Engineering	Manufacturing	Production planning	Human resources	Finance/accounting
Marketing								
Price								
Promotion								
Distribution								
Manpower								
Product								
Modification								
Quality								
Eliminate								
Add new								
Process/equipment								
Capacity								
Process								
Equipment								
Manpower								
Overhead								
Allocation								

2. Relate *information requirements* to *planning and decision making* by checking the correct boxes in the table below:

Planning and Strategic Decision Area \ Information Requirements	Market potential	Sales potential	Sales and price history	Market share	Distribution costs	Sales expense	Promotion costs	Product properties	Competitive edge	Technical development costs	Manufacturing capacity	Manufacturing costs	Break-even sales	Capital budgets	Cash flow plans	Indirect costs	Profitability by product	"Losing" businesses
Marketing																		
Price																		
Promotion																		
Distribution																		
Manpower																		
Product																		
Modification																		
Quality																		
Eliminate																		
Add new																		
Process/equipment																		
Capacity																		
Process																		
Equipment																		
Manpower																		
Overhead																		
Allocation																		

3. In the portion of the gross design of an MIS shown below, match the numbers with information items listed below:

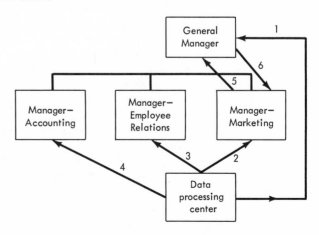

_____ a. Turnover, number of employees, salary statistics

_____ b. Summary financial statements

_____ c. Labor and material costs for all departments

_____ d. Analysis of sales by product, salesman, area, projection of trends

_____ e. Product policies, market share objectives.

_____ f. Sales forecast

4. **Case Study: The Artcraft Company**

The Artcraft Company was formed in 1924 to service sign painters with supplies required by their trade. The company began simply as a jobber; sales were made through a simple 24-page catalog directed to sign painters and to stores dealing in such supplies.

In 1928, Mr. E. C. Parsons, Artcraft's owner, developed a lettering device suitable for use by draftsmen, advertising art studios, sign painters, and others. At first, Artcraft had the parts made on the outside and then assembled and packaged the item. Subsequently, they undertook manufacture of a number of the component parts.

The lettering device filled a particular market need; it was successful on its own and also was responsible for attracting business to the company's general line of supplies. Although the general economy deteriorated following 1928, Artcraft's sales went from $750,000 to $1.8 million by 1935.

Following World War II, popular interest in painting escalated, and Artcraft's sales increased greatly, particularly with art supply stores. By 1960, their sales were nearly $10 million, of which $6 million was in items they manufactured—paints, brushes, palettes, and related items. The balance was imported or purchased domestically and packaged under Artcraft's name.

In 1962, E. C. Parsons II entered the business after his graduation from business school. From the outset it was clear that he was both alert and aggressive. He concluded rather quickly that the company had been the fortunate victim of circumstances, that it had been carried along by the tides of a generally improved economy and the growing popularity of art as a hobby. In line with his belief that the company was far from having reached its potential, he proposed that the product line be increased, by amplifying the art supplies offerings and by extension into engineering and drafting supplies, and that a sales force be added to reinforce the catalog.

In 1964, the elder Parsons died. Young Parsons took over and immediately set the wheels in motion to move the company onto higher ground. He decided it would be too much of a financial strain on the company to both increase manufacturing activity and develop a sales force, and so it was decided to increase the line by jobbing rather than manufacturing additional items and to concentrate on sales force development.

By 1969, company sales had reached $18 million. Company strategy had taken hold. There were now 300 employees, handling 100,000 orders annually from distributors, art supply and drafting supply stores, hardware and paint stores, college book stores, advertising agencies' art departments, and industrial and research firms. In all, Artcraft had 18,000 customers, of whom 500 had annual purchases of $15,000 or more, and a line of nearly 12,000 items. Further increases in the range of 10% per year were expected.

Artcraft's accounting and information systems, which relied on manual and mechanical methods, were under the direction of Ed Simpson, who had been with the company for 20 years. Recently a number of problems had arisen. Although none were of a critical nature, in the aggregate they suggested that with further growth, present methods were likely to prove inadequate. The situation was reflected in comments by various company executives and workers:

George Saunders, sales vice president: "Our catalog is vital, both for mail orders and to support our salesmen. Considering the thousands of items we carry, a salesman could not function without it. Our problem here is our inability to get a catalog out on time even once a year. Even then it is filled with items that should have been dropped, and new items are often omitted. Under pressure of getting it out, we do not change prices to reflect cost changes. Actually, we should produce two catalogs a year, with supplements quarterly."

Al Beven, production vice president: "I'm spending too much time putting out fires. Most of our production problems are a matter of deciding between Urgent, Very Urgent and Extra Very Urgent. This business was built on service to the customer. We still think this is the most important thing. Consequently, we make one short run after another just to have something in stock. The high cost of short runs takes a back seat to customer service.

Joe Dean, purchasing agent: "We now have many low-value, low-volume items on which we can't afford to keep unit inventory records. The warehouse is supposed to notify us when items reach reorder quantities. They don't; they either forget or don't care. You know, there is a lot of turnover in help there. In any event, most of my buyers spend half their day on the phone expediting shipment. They should be shopping for prices and new items and helping me with the catalog."

Al Parker, credit manager: "We have a lot of small accounts that I believe should be written off if they do not pay after a couple of reminders. Understand, I'm not sure our collection costs exceed our collections for small accounts, but it is my educated guess they do. Actually, just going through customer-account ledger cards to flag delinquent accounts costs us a fortune. On top of this, half the reminders that go out should never have been sent; during busy seasons it takes three days or more between receiving a collection and getting it onto the customer's records."

Mitch Webber, warehouse supervisor: "We keep feeding the order-editing department lists of items going out of stock and to be taken off back order status. It doesn't seem to make any difference. Practically every order we get lists out-of-stock items, and this means retyping and refiguring these invoices. Even worse, they are backordering items we have presently in stock. By the time they release the back orders, the items will be out again."

Artcraft's sales are firm; they are making money. In fact, they are having the best year in their history by a considerable margin.

Notes in the file of Al Beven, Production VP of Artcraft:

No. of Units in a Production Run	No. of Runs
1–99	13,510
100–500	18,050
600–900	3,100
1000 and over	220

Major Product Line*	Units of Sales/Product Line	Sales in Dollars
A	220,000	$ 3,000,000
B	191,000	5,200,000
C	165,000	2,900,000
D	160,000	1,981,000
E	98,000	3,800,000
F	40,000	520,000
G	25,000	310,000
H	4,000	30,000
I	4,000	19,000
J	1,000	400,000
		$18,160,000

*A product line may have between 1 and 180 items in the line to yield the 12,000 items Artcraft produces.

Notes in the file of George Saunders, Sales VP:

Year	Artcraft Sales (millions)	U.S. Disposable Personal Income (billions)
1935	1.81	58.5
1940	2.10	75.7
1945	2.90	150
1950	4.83	—
1955	6.95	—
1965	13.9	469
1970	20.4	—

Notes in the file of Al Parker, Credit Manager (Industry Data):

Bad-Debt Accounts	Approximate Debt/Equity	Years Business Has Been in Existence
12	0.85	1.5–2.0
25	0.75	1.0–2.0
30	0.75	0.5–1.0
10	0.50	0.5–1.0
3	0.85	3.0–5.0

a. List the management problems.

b. List management's information needs.

c. Draw a gross design flow chart showing flow of information to managers.

chapter eight

MIS Design: Detailed System Design

CHAPTER 8   explains how to develop your gross MIS design into more detailed form and how to document (describe) the design.

When you have finished studying

MIS DESIGN: DETAILED SYSTEM DESIGN

you will be able to

1. List steps to be taken to develop the design of an MIS so that it will be acceptable to the organization
2. Explain the meaning of dominant and trade-off criteria that limit the final design
3. Identify and describe briefly the subsystems of a business for which managers need information to plan and control
4. Explain how to obtain information to carry out the design work
5. Explain how to develop and describe the data base
6. Develop detailed operating subsystems and their information flows
7. Describe typical information output formats from the MIS going to managers
8. Identify hardware and software considerations
9. Organize the report describing the detailed design.

DETAILED DESIGN
OF AN MIS IS A
COMPLEX PROCESS;
DESCRIBING IT IS
LIKE DESCRIBING
WHAT HAPPENS
WHEN A CUSTARD
PIE HITS A FAN

Once the scope and general pattern of the MIS have been expressed as the gross design, the detailed design work may be started. A step-by-step explanation of how to develop the detailed design is not possible for the following reasons:

1. There is no clear separation between the end of gross design work and start of detailed design work. The gross design is considered done whenever enough detail is developed in the flow chart, data base, and data processing systems to select a feasible and rewarding design.

2. A designer may base his procedures on present technology (in managerial decision making and computer hardware) or on future technology that he anticipates will be available when the design is completed.

3. Designing a system requires many interrelated activities all going on concurrently. Our textbook description of a procedure can follow only one sequence of steps at a time.

4. It is not possible to anticipate and describe the organizational reactions that occur and require modification of design in an actual situation. Therefore, we find our procedures limited to the "rational" aspects of design modified only by general organizational behavior theory.

5. If we try to present all the details of the procedure for design and of an actual system, the general approach to design would be lost among thousands of details. On the other hand, if we present generalizations, the reader gains no idea of the many specific items making up the design.

6. An explanation of a detailed system design procedure must be interrupted frequently by descriptive essays on some aspect with which the designer deals.

The Nature of
Systems Design
with Selected
Samples of the
Work Will Be
Given

Within the limitations of clarity and objectives imposed by these considerations, we shall attempt to present the nature of systems design at the "edge of the art." The edge of the art is broad, with part in the present and part in the near future. A general approach will provide the framework, but frequent resort to detailed procedures and descriptions will bring substance to the framework.

INFORM THE ORGANIZATION OF THE PURPOSE AND NATURE OF THE SYSTEMS DESIGN EFFORT

IF PEOPLE KNOW
WHAT IS GOING
ON, THEY WILL
PARTICIPATE; KEEP
THE ORGANIZATION
INFORMED ABOUT
MIS PLANS

The first step in systems design is not a technical one. It is concerned with gaining support for the work that follows. Systems designers must have the support of most members of the organization in order to obtain information for the design of the system and to obtain acceptance of the final system. At a minimum, members of the organization should be informed of the objectives and nature of the study. It is preferable, if possible, to draw many members into the study, at least in some small way. Furthermore, it is desirable to reassure the employees, if possible, that changes will benefit them or that they will not suffer financially from the implementation of the system. Even so, the natural human resistance to change requires that sufficient information on general progress be disseminated to gradually accustom the employees to their future roles.

The contrary approach, that employees should not be disturbed during the system design, can be quite hazardous. When people are not informed, they seize upon bits of information, construct concepts that may be completely erroneous, and in consequence often take up detrimental activities. The final system, when announced, may be met with shock, resentment, and both open and secret resistance.

AIM OF DETAILED DESIGN

The detailed design of an MIS is closely related to the design of operating systems. Sometimes, it is true, the operating system must be accepted without change and a new MIS appended to it. However, it is preferable to design both systems together, and as we discuss the detailed design of the MIS, this parallel effort will be apparent, even though our principal focus is on the MIS.

By drawing upon the analogy of engineering design, we can clarify the meaning of detailed design. The direct goal of engineering design is to furnish a description of a tested and producible product. Engineering design consists of specifications in the form of drawings and specification reports for systems as a whole and for all components in the system.

Further, justification documents in the form of reports of mathematical analysis and test results are part of the detailed design. Enough detail must be given so that engineering design documents and manufacturing drawings are sufficient for the shop to construct the product. The production of operating and maintenance instructions is also considered part of the design output.

The analogy of detailed design of MIS readily follows. The aim of the detailed design is to furnish a description of a system that achieves the goals of the gross system design requirements. This description consists of drawings, flow charts, equipment and personnel specifications, procedures, support tasks, specification of information files, and organization and operating manuals required to run the system. Also part of the design is the documentation of analysis and testing, which justifies the design. The design must be sufficiently detailed that operating management and personnel may implement the system. Whereas gross design gives the overall general specifications for the MIS, the detailed design yields the *construction* and *operating* specifications.

DETAILED DESIGN GOES FROM THE GROSS CONCEPT TO THE "NITTY-GRITTY" DETAILS

PROJECT MANAGEMENT OF MIS DETAILED DESIGN

Any effort that qualifies as a system design has the dimensions of a project. The first step in the detailed design is therefore a planning and organizing step. For small projects, all phases may be planned for, as described in Chapter 6, *before t*he gross design is undertaken. Often, in larger projects, not enough is known about the prospective system in advance of the gross design to plan for the detailed design project. Further, if the gross design indicates that a new system design is not appropriate at this time, any project planning for the detailed design in advance would be wasted.

To Build a System Start with a Plan

Once the project manager and key project personnel have been designated, the steps in project management fall into two classes: *planning* and *control*. The amount of effort expended in each step is obviously a function of the size of the MIS project and the cost of developing the detailed design of the project. The key steps in planning and control of detailed design, based on Chapter 6, are recapitulated here.

Project Planning

1. Establish the project objectives. This involves a review, subdivision, and refinement of the performance objectives established by the gross design.
2. Define the project tasks. This identifies a hierarchical structure of tasks to be performed in the design of the MIS and may be documented by work package instructions for large projects.

3. Plan the logical development of sequential and concurrent tasks and task activities. This usually requires a network diagram of events and activities.
4. Schedule the work as required by management—established end date and activity-network constraints. Essentially, the work and schedule are tied together by completion of the PERT (Program Evaluation and Review Technique) diagram.
5. Estimate labor, equipment, and other costs for the project.
6. Establish a budget for the project by allocating funds to each task and expenditures month by month over the life of the project.
7. Plan the staffing of the project organization over its life.

Project Planning Leads to Control of Performance, Time, and Cost

Project Control

1. Determine whether project objectives are being met as the project progresses.
2. Maintain control over the schedule by changing work loads and emphasis as required by delays in critical activities.
3. Evaluate expenditure of funds in terms of both work accomplished and time. Revise the budget as required to reflect changes in work definition.
4. Evaluate manpower utilization and individual work progress, and make adjustments as required.
5. Evaluate time, cost, and work performance in terms of schedules, budgets, and technical plans to identify interaction problems.

IDENTIFY DOMINANT AND PRINCIPAL TRADE-OFF PERFORMANCE CRITERIA FOR THE SYSTEM

Dominant criteria for a system are those that make an activity so important that it overrides all other activities. For example, a dominant criterion might be that the system operate so that there is never a stockout. This overrides the criterion of minimizing inventory cost. Such a criterion might hold for a company selling human blood, life-preserving drugs, or electric power. It might even hold for a company selling a consumer product where loss of a customer is permanent and all competitors have a no-stockout policy.

WHAT LIMITS THE MIS EFFORT?

Examples of other dominant criteria might be one-day customer service, zero-defect product, specified price range for products, maintenance of multiple sources of supply for all materials and components purchased, or conformity of all research and engineering to long-range corporate plans. It is obvious that identification of the dominant criteria is necessary before subsequent design steps can proceed.

Trade-off criteria are those in which the criterion for performance of an activity may be reduced to increase performance of another activity. For example, the criterion of low manufacturing costs might be balanced against that of long-range public image of the firm achieved by reduction in environmental pollution. Again, the criterion of producing styles or models for many segments of the market might be balanced against that of maintaining low manufacturing and service costs.

The reason for identifying dominant and trade-off criteria is that as the detailed design is developed, decision centers (managers or computers) must be identified to achieve such criteria or to permit trade-offs.

DEFINE THE MANAGED SUBSYSTEMS

DEFINE THE
SUBSYSTEMS
CAREFULLY SO THAT
MANAGERIAL
RESPONSIBILITY
CAN BE DEFINED
We start the process of defining the subsystems with two principal blocks of information: (1) the gross design concept and (2) the dominant and trade-off performance criteria. Although the gross design requires some assumptions concerning the subsystems, it is necessary now to review these subsystems and to redefine them if it seems appropriate. Based on the gross design, investigation of the detailed activities of each management decision subsystem and operating subsystem must be made.

Levels of Management Subsystems

Top management, middle management, and first-line management each have different perspectives and objectives. In Chapter 2, we noted the general strategic view of top management. Middle management is concerned with intermediate-range planning and control. First-line managers and supervisors focus on people doing technical or functional work.

The difference among these levels is related to the "time span of discretion." That is, managers at each level make decisions and use discretion. At the top level, if a top manager makes a mistake, it may take as long as five to ten years before it becomes apparent. At the lowest level of management, an error in judgment will probably be evident within a few months at the most.

It therefore appears that activities of the company may be divided into subsystems based on level of management. Information must be supplied to managers at each level to permit decision making appropriate to this level. (See Table 8-1 and Figure 8-1.)

Functional or Project Subsystems

If management is to manage the business, it must have information to manage each functional area (engineering, marketing, operations, etc.). In other words, just as we split the business into subsystems by levels of

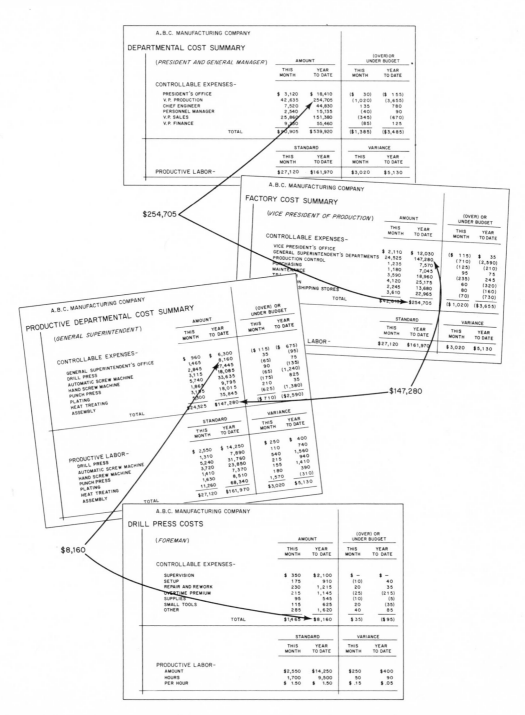

Source: John A. Higgins, "Responsibility Accounting," *Arthur Andersen Chronicle*, April 1952, p. 151.

Figure 8-1

management, we must also split the business into functional subsystems. These subsystems must be managed properly. To do so, we must focus on the planning, organizing, and controlling of each of these subsystems.

It is not enough to focus on management-level subsystems alone. We must be certain that our MIS provides information to manage the functional subsystems. When companies are organized by product or project, then product or project MISs must assist managers. (See Table 8-1 and Figure 8-2)

Figure 8-2   Engineering functional subsystem.

Source: E. Ralph Sims, Jr., "Automating Administrative and Engineering Activities," *Automation*, June 1968, p. 94. Reproduced with permission of The Penton Publishing Co., Cleveland, Ohio.

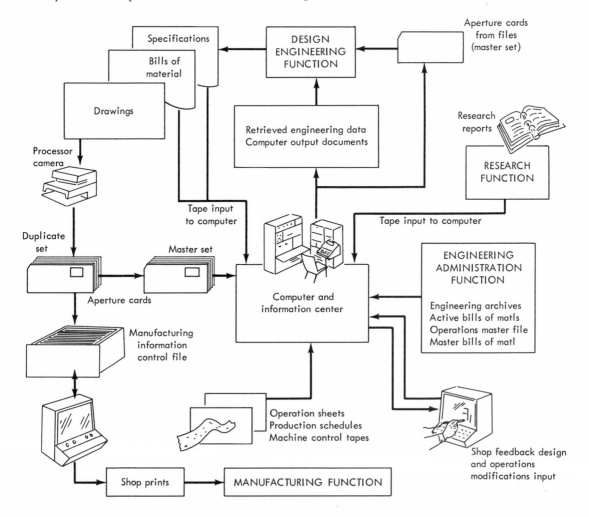

Resource Subsystems

Who Is
Responsible for
Each Resource
Subsystem?
Looking at the company as divided into levels of managing or divided into functional activities still may not provide integration of other subsystem activities. There are major resource subsystems that managers in most companies consider:

Human resources
Capital resources

Courtesy of Xerox Corporation.

Figure 8-3   Capital resource subsystem. Management of capital expenditures at Xerox Corporation.

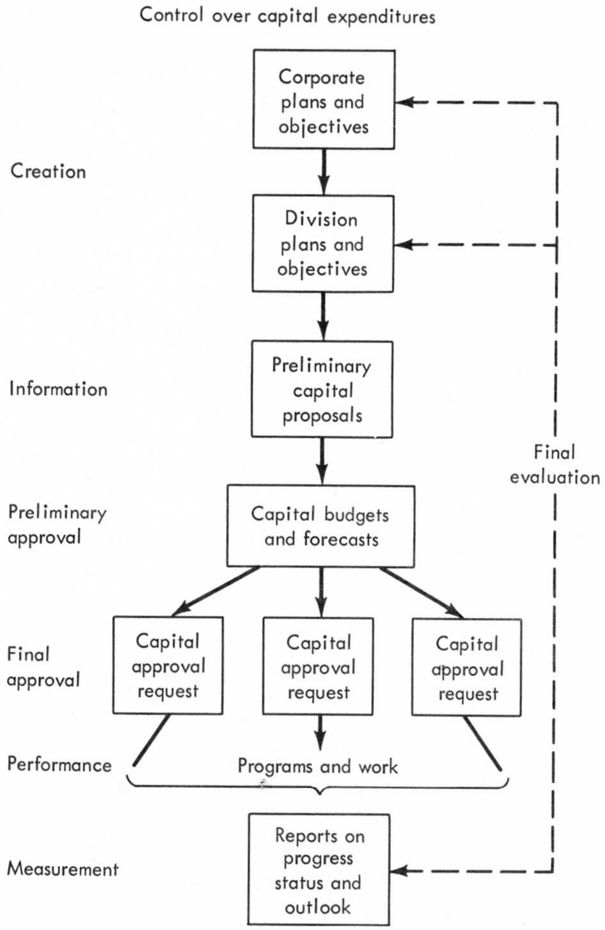

Control over capital expenditures

Materials
Liquid assets
Intangible resources

Information must be supplied to management by the MIS to permit proper management of these subsystems. (See Table 8-1 and Figure 8-3.)

Phase Subsystems

If we consider the business as a processor (a system), it acts on inputs in a series of steps to yield outputs. These steps represent, roughly, phases of the business. Each phase may be considered a subsystem to be managed. In a manufacturing firm they are

Who Is Responsible for Each Phase Subsystem?

Forecasting
Financing
Material handling and processing
Distribution

(See Table 8-1 and Figure 8-4.)

Figure 8-4   Phase subsystems.

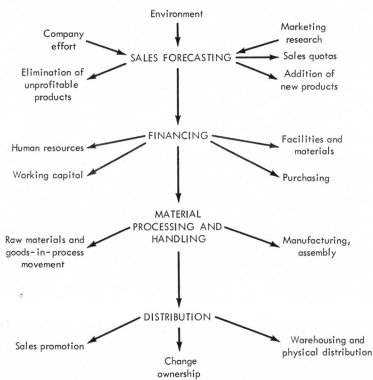

Degree of Detail in the Detailed Design

The degree of detail developed at the detailed design stage depends on the complexity of the company and information needed to select a good design. In small simple companies, relatively little detail will be required to "block out" the nature of the MIS.

If we consider the activities of a company subdivided as below, we would develop the detailed MIS down to the operation element level.

System
    Subsystem
        Functional (specialized) activity
            Task
                Subtask
                    Operation element

SUMMARY

Managing just one set of the business subsystems does not guaranty that the other subsystems will be properly managed. In the detailed design, responsibility for each subsystem must be identified. The person responsible for each subsystem must then obtain the information required to manage it. Most companies manage these subsystems on a hodgepodge basis. For example, companies frequently have a capital budgeting activity but fail to maintain equipment records or develop long-range equipment plans.

Table 8-1 indicates the nature of activities for the various subsystems so that detailed information needs may be determined.

OBTAINING INFORMATION

The designer utilizes four principal sources for the development of the MIS:

1. Task force meetings.
2. Personal interviews.
3. Internal and external source documents.
4. Personal observation of operations and communications, when feasible.

TASK FORCE MEETINGS

For the design of large systems, the use of task forces for the development of information and ideas is usually advantageous. The task force

Table 8-1 The controlling subsystems of a business.

Subsystems	Examples of Activities Within the Subsystem
A. Levels of management subsystems	
Top management (management or enterprise systems)	Strategic planning, company policy setting
Middle management (operating or functional subsystems)	Short-range planning and control, functional and product tactics
First-line management (transaction subsystems)	Control of daily operations and transactions, supervision of individual operators, supervision of utilization of machines and materials
B. Functional or project subsystems	
Marketing engineering	Promotion, research, forecasting, project management, product development, product safety, and reliability
Operations	Production planning and control, production, allocating men and machines to meet priority of customers' orders and total demand
Finance/accounting	Fund raising, debt control, cash flow, planning, budgets, financial records, and reports
Human resources	Staffing planning, maintaining inventory skills systems, wage and salary administration, developing companywide personnel policies
Project or product	New product development and launching, managing competing brands within the company
C. Resource subsystems	
Human	Organization planning and staffing, appraising and regarding people, motivating, training
Capital	Capital budgeting; equipment replacement, planning; maintaining equipment records; maintaining land inventory records; acquisition and disposition of capital assets
Materials	Purchasing, inventory planning and control, materials forecasting, movement and storage of materials
Liquid assets	Cash investment, cash inventory
D. Phase subsystems	
Forecasting	Environment, economic, political, technology, opportunity, resource, and sales forecasting
Processing of inputs	Planning of plant capacity, level of operations, operations, warehousing, inventory, logistics
Financing	Maintaining adequate cash reserves, maintaining lines of credit
Costing	Relating costs to labor, materials, leases, subcontracts, and time; costing of products and operations
Human resource	Setting objectives and monitoring performance, organizing and staffing

for a single subsystem should consist of both managers and key specialists. The designer should chair the task force meetings. His function is to draw out ideas and information, synthesize ideas, including his own, and present in diagrams and documents the synthesis for evaluation and modification. The task force meetings serve to bring out information gaps, operating needs, and controversial points. In repeated meetings, the design of a subsystem is hammered out.

A Task Force
Brings Key
People
Together To
Answer Key
Questions

INTERVIEWS

Instead of, or in addition to, task force meetings, the designer may conduct interviews with key managers at top and intermediate levels, with key specialists, and with a sampling of operating employees. Although it appears obvious, it cannot be emphasized enough that the designer *must use tact in interviews*. Whether he is interviewing the top manager or the lowest-level employee, his role is that of *a searcher* for knowledge, *not a lecturer* on systems.

In interviews with managers, the designer should seek information on

1. Objectives of the firm or organizational component.
2. Major policies in force or needed to accomplish these objectives.
3. The categories of information the managers desire.
4. Speed of access to the various categories of information desired by managers.
5. Intervals of time desired between receipt of various types of information.
6. Format desired for information presented.
7. Style of decision making of the managers.
8. Resources that will be committed for the implementation and operation of the system.
9. Degree of manager involvement in classes of decisions: individual decision making, participative decision making, or partially routine (programmed) decision making.
10. Organizational relationships that would facilitate system operation and management decision making.

Interviewing Permits
Probing for
Answers

Systems designers should not expect too much from managers in the way of defining information needs. Rather, they should work with managers to identify objectives and develop plans. The identification of necessary information will follow from this.

INTERNAL AND EXTERNAL SOURCE DOCUMENTS

The use of internal source documents primarily provides the systems designer with a point of departure. From a practical viewpoint, it is likely that many traditional operations and reports must be retained simply to provide some continuity of operations; and this is appropriate, because the current methods are usually the result of continued minor improvements. Modification or regrouping of activities or data batches is still feasible for the systems designer, however. The number of internal source documents may be great, depending on the company, so that no complete listing is given here. Organization and policy guides, procedures manuals, master budgets and account structure, and the many functional reports of engineering, manufacturing, marketing, purchasing, and employee and public relations should be examined according to their relevancy to the system being designed. Sometimes, reports such as records of customers' complaints or of service calls may provide the key to system design needs.

Documents May Uncover Leads to Decision Processes

External source documents provide economic, marketing, industry, and financial information related to the firm that may be of assistance. A review of the company by a securities analyst in a financial journal may provide very valuable insights.

DIRECT OBSERVATION

The designer should not isolate himself in his office to sketch out designs; he should make on-the-spot surveys of operations in action. It would be foolish, for example, to develop a systems design in which foremen in the factory provide hourly personal reports to a planning/control center if the factory were a half-mile in length or if the planning/control group were in a building some distance away. Similar absurd situations could be conjectured for sales reports or physical distribution reports. On-site inspection will reveal the physical and environmental restraints that may have to be accepted in a new system. Conversely, however, such inspection may also lead to a major revision of the physical facilities to suit the system design.

Direct Observation Shows Decision Making in Action

The designer should record, as he goes along, the relevant (and probably much irrelevant) data he is gathering. In the case of large documents, he would, of course, merely make notes of points vital to his investigation. At the end of certain phases, he should try to organize the data so that future information may be related to that already gathered. Finally, at some point, he sketches alternative designs for the operating subsystems.

DETAIL THE INFORMATION NEEDS OF MANAGERS

The basis for developing information needs of managers is shown in Figure 8-5. The objective of the MIS is to get to the manager, on a timely basis, information he needs that is most important. The cost of

Thomas R. Wilcox became CEO [Chief Executive Officer] of Crocker National Corp. in 1974. Crocker is the twelfth largest banking system in the United States. Warren R. Marcus, bank analyst, said, "Recognizing what is wrong is half the battle. The previous management didn't even know their problems."

Wilcox's first challenge at Crocker was merely finding out what was going on. The bank's management information system was so primitive that he could not even get answers to basic questions on costs, profitability, and management responsibilities. "I don't think those who designed the information system," says Wilcox wryly, "anticipated the requirement that management intercept the information flow." The first key outsider that Wilcox brought in was Arthur B. Hall, a specialist in management information systems at Touche Ross & Co.

Business Week, Aug. 11, 1975, p. 41.

information provides one of the limits to making the upper right square in Figure 8-5 as large as possible. The amount of information that a manager can absorb within a given time period provides another limit.

IS THERE AN INFORMATION-NEED PROFILE FOR EACH MANAGER?

The upper left square in Figure 8-5 should be as small as possible. *Managers should not receive reports and data unless they have a need for them at some particular time.* They may always obtain available data upon their own requests if they need it.

Procedure for Developing Information Needs

The procedure for developing the information needs of a manager is shown in Figure 8-6. Developing such needs is a difficult and frustrating task. Generally, the manager cannot at first identify the range of his information needs. The systems designer must explore tactfully the objectives of the manager's position, his relationships with other company activities, and the kinds of problems and decisions he himself is actually involved with. What reports does the manager receive that he rarely or never reads?

The next step is to develop a detailed description of each item of information the manager needs. This involves specifying

Get Details of Information Needs of Each Manager

Level of detail or aggregation

Frequency of the report

Media (written, oral, display device, etc.)

Format (organization of the report)

Time (monthly reports could, for example, be issued on the first of the month or the fifteenth of the month)

Acceptable levels of reliability and precision

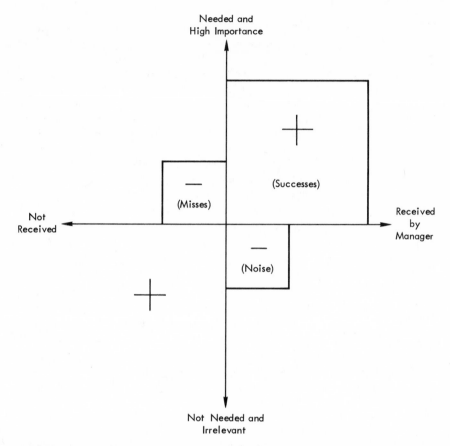

Figure 8-5 Measure of the information storage and retrieval system.

Information Sources

As Thomas R. Wilcox noted at Crocker, managers must be able to tap into the data system of a company to get their information. After the information needs have been specified, the sources of the information must be determined (Figure 8-6). The manager obtains his information from

Given a Need, What Is the Likely Source?

1. External sources.
2. Superiors and subordinates.
3. Reports issued from other organizations in the company.
4. Files (data base).

External sources may be casual conversations, publications, customers and vendors, and meetings. The MIS can only attempt to formalize such flows. For example, specific publications could be sent to the manager or information request forms could be developed to seek information from outsiders.

Communications between the manager and his superior and subordinates may be specified, as, for example, weekly staff meetings. At the same time, the manager must ensure that operations that are his responsibility lead to reports that he can use for planning and controlling.

The MIS designer should work with managers to make sure that interorganizational information is transmitted according to needs.

Finally, the systems designer and management must make sure that a good system of company files is established. Centralized files, the data base, are the source of both formal routine reports and answers to inquiries placed by managers.

DEVELOP THE DATA BASE

The data base is the data that must be obtained (sometimes called "captured") and usually stored for later retrieval for managerial decision

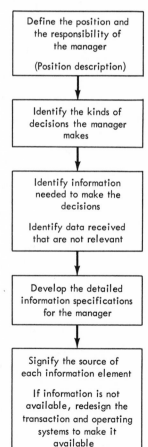

Figure 8-6 Developing information needs for a manager.

making. It also consists of data that will be utilized in programmed decision making and real-time control. The data base is derived from the needs of management for information to guide the total business system. We shall start with the study of management's problems and information needs and then detail the data requirements of the systems.

How Do You
Develop a
Companywide
Data Base?

A systematic approach to the development of the data base is as follows:

1. Identify all individuals and activities that require data inputs. These consist of managers, operating personnel, automated transactions, as well as decision tables or modeling operations.
2. Prepare a data or file work sheet for each data element, giving
   a. Source of data.
   b. Length and form.
   c. Current and potential frequency of updating.
   d. Retention schedule for the data.
   e. End use of the data.
3. Group all data work sheets by system and check for omissions.
4. Group all data work sheets by activity and by organizational component and note duplications. A matrix approach to this analysis along the general lines indicated by Figure 8-7 is very helpful.
5. Eliminate duplicated data requirements to develop an integrated data base for which cross-functional use of the master file is employed. See Figure 8-7.
6. Evaluate the items in the master file for frequency of need and value of the data to the system versus cost of obtaining the data. Judgment must now be used to prune the file for possible revision of the system design if the cost of file construction and file maintenance exceeds the estimated value of the system or the available resources.

In Figure 8-8 we have shown how files may be listed in preparing the centralized data base.

DEVELOP DETAILED OPERATING SUBSYSTEMS
AND THEIR INFORMATION FLOWS

The description of an operating system is essentially a description of what is done and what order it is done in. In addition, some system descriptions are charted to show who does it.

IDENTIFY THE
OPERATING
SUBSYSTEMS

The information system description shows the information flow that is necessary to relate one operation or transaction to the following one.

Both of these descriptions may be shown on the same chart, if desirable. Further, the level of detail shown on either chart may vary significantly. To further confuse matters, charts drawn for explanation

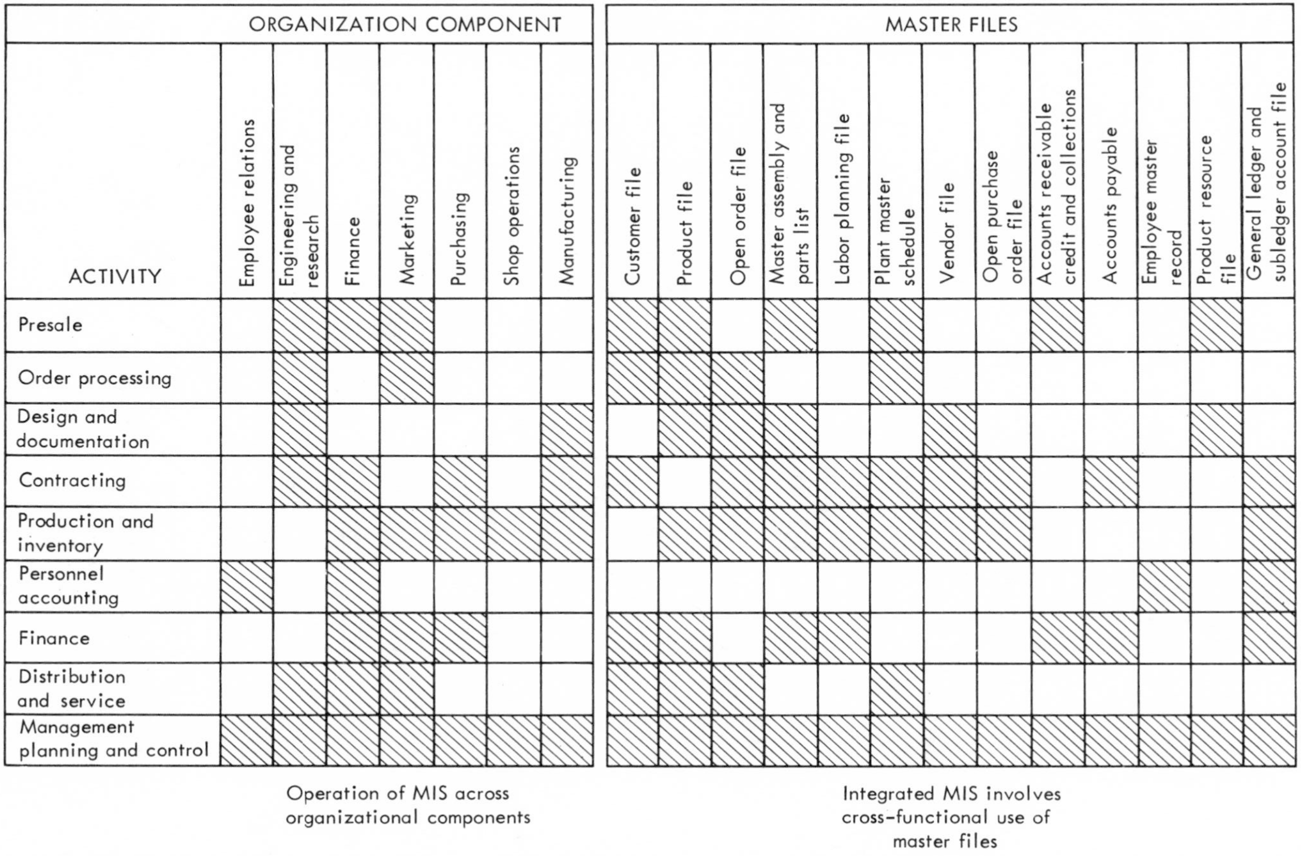

MASTER FILES

Integrated MIS involves cross-functional use of master files

Operation of MIS across organizational components

ORGANIZATION COMPONENT

ACTIVITY	Employee relations	Engineering and research	Finance	Marketing	Purchasing	Shop operations	Manufacturing	Customer file	Product file	Open order file	Master assembly and parts list	Labor planning file	Plant master schedule	Vendor file	Open purchase order file	Accounts receivable credit and collections	Accounts payable	Employee master record	Product resource file	General ledger and subledger account file
Presale		▨	▨	▨				▨	▨		▨		▨			▨			▨	
Order processing				▨				▨		▨			▨							
Design and documentation		▨	▨		▨	▨	▨	▨	▨		▨			▨	▨				▨	▨
Contracting									▨											▨
Production and inventory					▨	▨	▨		▨	▨	▨				▨					▨
Personnel accounting																				
Finance			▨									▨				▨	▨			▨
Distribution and service	▨			▨																
Management planning and control	▨	▨	▨	▨	▨	▨	▨	▨	▨	▨	▨	▨						▨		▨

Source: Based on a figure by John Ryan, Manager of Internal Automotive, General Electric Co., in *Automation*, May 1964. Reproduced with permission of The Penton Publishing Co., Cleveland, Ohio.

Figure 8-7 Development of the master file.

Figure 8-8   List of files and contents for a municipal police organization.

I. Chief
   A. City manager
      1. City manager
      2. City commission
      3. Civil service board
      4. City planning board
   B. Appreciation letters
   C. Cadet training procedures
   D. Pension fund records
   E. Procedure orders
   F. Information on school guards and safety patrols

II. Inspector
   A. Current laws
   B. Disciplinary action
   C. Citizens complaints
   D. School incidents

III. Major
   A. Records of resistance of arrest
   B. Bars that become nuisances
   C. Memos to divisions
   D. Auctions
   E. List of bondsmen
   F. Civil defense and disaster procedures

IV. Administrative division
   A. Building maintenance
   B. Equipment status
   C. Accounts (for control only)
   D. Division personnel data

V. Training division
   A. All training procedures
   B. Target practice records
   C. Division personnel data

VI. Detective division
   A. Photographs of known offenders
   B. Modus operandi files
   C. Organized crime associations
   D. List of pawn shop transactions
   E. List of unions
   F. Nickname file
   G. Division personnel data

VII. Traffic division
   A. Accident and fatality reports
   B. Radar enforcement data
   C. Special services (auditorium and football game patrol)

    D. School patrol
    E. Jitney and traffic cab licenses
    F. Division personnel data

VIII. Patrol Division
    A. Shift assignments
    B. Crowd control procedures
    C. Evidence collection procedures
    D. Arrest Procedures
    E. Division personnel data

IX. Central file
    A. Investigative file
      1. Criminal
      2. Noncriminal
    B. Identification file
      1. Traffic accident reports
      2. Misdemeanors
      3. Fingerprints
        a. Criminals
        b. Civilians

of management systems and MIS look quite different from charts drawn by computer programmers, and yet they are given the same name.

The MIS designer is concerned most with management flow charts. The manager of electronic data processing utilizes computer flow charting to implement the requirements of the MIS designer. (See the Appendix.)

In most practical situations, the MIS designer accepts the operating systems as developed or modified by the managers. He then prepares detailed information flow charts and tables that represent the information inputs to each manager, its source, and its flow or method of transmittal. In essence, the diagrams come from breaking up the gross design of the MIS into subsystems and providing considerably more detail.

Although because of space limitations we cannot show all the detail desired, we have shown in Figure 8-9 a management or *operating system* flow chart. In Figure 8-10, we show an *information* flow chart. Finally, in Figure 8-11, we show part of a detailed *management information* flow chart. As an MIS designer, you should be more interested in clarity of presentation than following some rigid rules in representing your MIS. These examples of flow charts are only shown to stimulate your thinking rather than to serve as models.

What Are Three Kinds of Flow Charts?

ESTABLISH THE INFORMATION OUTPUT FORMATS FOR MANAGEMENT

Too little attention is paid to the format and timing of information communicated to managers to assist their decision making. Too often

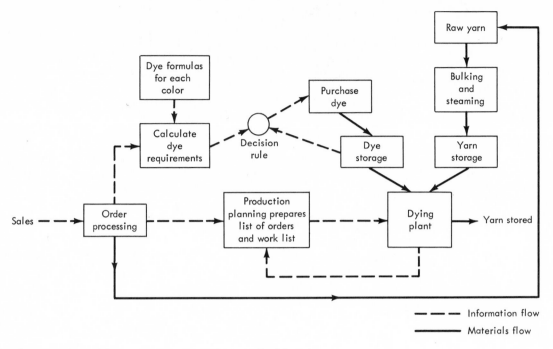

Figure 8-9 Production operations system for a textile dying plant.

Figure 8-10

Source: *Forms for the 9 Key Operations of Business*, Moore Business Forms, Inc.

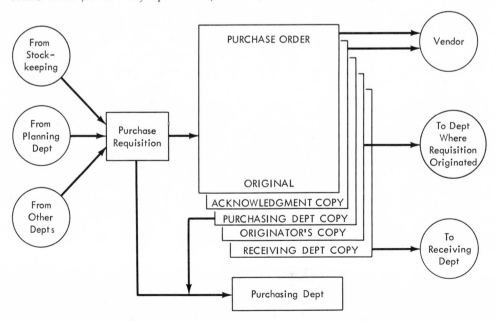

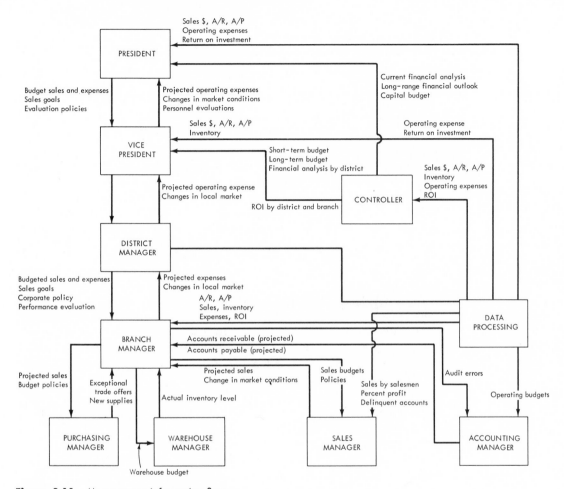

Figure 8-11 Management information flow.

managers are swamped with raw computer printouts, neatly bound to impress them. They are routinely fed reports that occupy their time in the search for problems when operations are progressing smoothly. Finally, when a crisis does occur, a day or more is required to collect the relevant information.

Management reports should be of two kinds: brief summaries of the total system for which the manager is responsible and relevant information on specific problems he has selected to work on. Problems may be brought to his attention in three principal ways. His superiors may detect a future or current problem arising from factors other than his own system. The manager himself may identify problems from summary reports or needs of the future. Subordinates may bring problems to him as part of their functioning in his system.

A system of reports should be established, not to isolate the manager from routine detail but to provide him with increasing detail at each level of operation as he needs it to solve problems and make decisions. Managers may receive

1. Routine reports such as monthly earnings statements, sales of individual products, cash flow, and available plant capacity. The purpose is to permit managers to monitor operations and trends.
2. Special reports of problems or out-of-control situations.
3. General management summaries of the state of the total business system for strategic and tactical planning purposes.

Most reports are still typed, printed, or computer-produced. A system of reports showing the shift in detail and emphasis of reports for a finance company is outlined in Figure 8-12. Another example, that for a materials producing company, is shown in Figure 8-13.

A CENTRAL
INFORMATION AND
DECISION ROOM

The written report is, however, rapidly being replaced with terminal devices, particularly visual display devices.[1] At its ultimate, large electronic display devices on the walls of the business "war room" enable top management to review information and call for information easily visible to the group. This is particularly effective for dealing with major problems and company strategy. (See Figure 8-14.)

The growing computer sophistication of today's managers is increasing the use of time-sharing terminals as a means of getting information to managers. High-level managers of a number of companies now have these terminals in their offices at work, at home, or at both. They are able to utilize models to ask the "What if I do this . . . ?" type of question and receive the information within seconds or minutes.

In general, the format should be established to *save the manager's time.* A wide variety of new communications and display equipment is being developed, and the systems designer should remain abreast of these developments.

SPECIFY THE EDP HARDWARE AND FACILITIES

RED WARNING!
TOP MANAGEMENT
MUST MAKE
HARDWARE
DECISIONS AND
NOT LEAVE THEM
TO TECHNICIANS

Management must make the decision as to the hardware and also as to whether it should be purchased or leased. It is a big mistake for top management to throw up its hands in ignorance and abdicate these decisions to the EDP manager and his technicians. The EDP manager should prepare alternative proposals, and top management should demand answers to questions such as

[1] See, for example, "The Terminal Takeover," *Infosystems*, May 1975, pp. 38–40.

Baffled by Snow Job

I've seen the ablest and toughest of executives insist on increased productivity by a plant manager, lean on accounting for improved performance, and lay it on purchasing in no uncertain terms to cut its staff. But when these same executives turn to EDP they stumble to an uncertain halt, baffled by the snow job and the blizzard of computer jargon. They accept the presumed sophistication and differences that are said to make EDP activities somehow immune from normal management demands. They are stopped by all this nonsense, uncertain about what's reasonable to expect, what they can insist upon. They become confused and then retreat, muttering about how to get a handle on this blasted situation.

Harry T. Larson, "EDP, a 20-Year Ripoff," *Infosystems*, Nov. 1974, p. 27.

Here Are Some Tough Questions Management Should Ask. What Are Some Others?

1. What is the total cost of purchase vs. lease over a ten-year period?
2. Why can't we use a smaller and cheaper computer? Name the next smaller one and its price, and give the disadvantages of selecting it.
3. What are the annual operating costs of the proposed hardware system vs. those of an alternative smaller system?
4. Can we start with a very small system and expand as usage develops? Why not use only minicomputers?
5. For several alternatives, what are the reliability, availability, throughput/dollar, compatibility of components, ease of upgrade, modularity, and expected maintenance costs?
6. For several alternatives, what are the software characteristics such as user's library, time for preparation of our applications, and ease of translation to other program languages?
7. What support do the vendors provide in terms of education, consulting, promptness in maintenance, and technical manuals for operations?

While there is no necessity for management to become expert in the technical characteristics of computers and peripherals, management should familiarize itself with criteria and processes for selection.[2]

Next, management should ask pointed questions about the size and quality of the organization that are proposed for the computer center. The same is true for the floor space, facilities, and location of the computer center.

---

[2] There are a number of easy-to-read short books for the nontechnical manager who must participate in computer acquisitions. See, for example, the excellent book by Jerome Kantor, *Management Guide to Computer Selection and Use,* Englewood Cliffs, N.J.: Prentice-Hall, Inc., 1970.

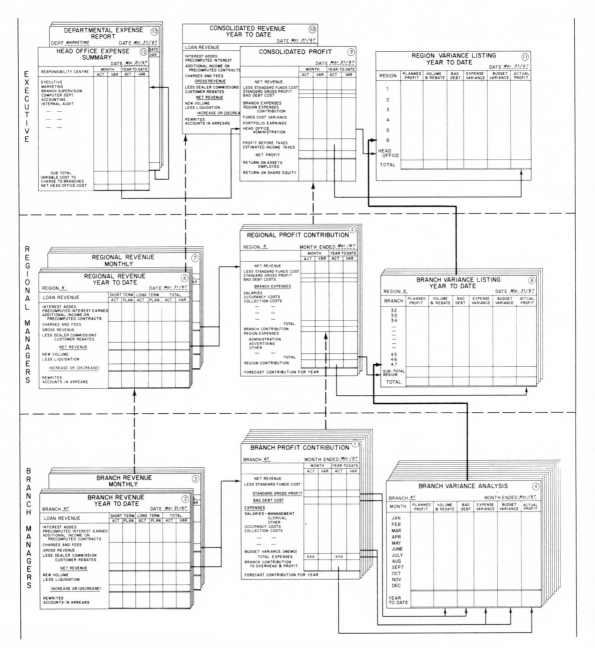

Source: R. Wolfman, "Management Information for Financial Institutions—Opportunities for Improvement," *Canadian Charted Accountant*, July 1968, p. 23.

Figure 8-12 System of reports for a finance company.

CAPITOL AGGREGATES CORPORATE OPERATING SUMMARY

	Period 1	Period 2	Period 3	Period 4	Period 5
OPERATING INCOME:					
...AREA .01 ...	418036				
...AREA .02 ...	1947960				
...AREA .03 ...	97451				
TOTAL	2463447				
GEN+ADMN	238989				
EXPLORATION	14207				
OTHR INC+EXP	(37015)				
PRFT SHRING	264334				
TOT ADMN EXP	480515				
OPER INC	1982932				
INTEREST	485042				
INC BEF FIT	1497890				
FED INC TAX	718987				
INVEST CRT	(331722)				
NET INC	1110625				
PERCENTAGES:					
NT INC/SALES	11				
PERC R O A I	17				
NET INC/EQTY	18				
EQTY/T ASSET	47				
AVG ASSETS	12013204				

CAPITOL AGGREGATES CORPORATE CASH FLOW SUMMARY

	Period 1	Period 2	Period 3	Period 4	Period 5
NET INCOME	1110625				
DEPRECIATION	948047				
SHT TRM DEBT	0				
DEPLETION	6080				
NEW L T DEBT	3354000				
TOTAL AVLBLE	5418752				
ASSET REPLMT	448890				
PRPSED ASSET	4290000				
SHT DEBT RTR	300000				
SCH DEBT RTR	1087846				
REC REQRMNTS	477280				
INV REQRMNTS	(97734)				
LAND INVESTM	0				
OTHER ASSETS	0				
ACCTS PAYBLE	335271				
TAX LIABLTS	0				
TOTAL RQRMNT	6841553				
NET CASH FLW	(1422801)				
DEBT/ASSETS	.53				
TOTAL DEBT	6960254				
POLICY DEBT	6717607				
AVAILABLE	(242647)				

CAPITOL AGGREGATES CORPORATE BALANCE SHEET

	Period 1	Period 2	Period 3	Period 4	Period 5
CASH	(1122801)				
RECEIVABLES	1566772				
INVENTORIES	420477				
CURR ASSETS	864448				
PLT+EQUP	13637602				
ACUM DPRCTN	3941461				
NET PLT+EQUP	9696141				
LAND	2016370				
OTHER ASSETS	593920				
TOTAL ASSETS	13170879				
SHT TERM DEBT	0				
CRR PORT LTD	1168440				
ACCTS PAYBLE	664729				
FIT PAYBLE	0				
CURR LIABLTS	1833169				
LNG TRM DEBT	5127085				
TOTL LIABLTS	6960254				
OWNERS EQTY	6210625				
LIABLTS+EQTY	13170879				
CURRENT RATIO	.5				
	.47				

CAPITOL AGGREGATES CORPORATE OVERVIEW REPORT

	Period 1	Period 2	Period 3	Period 4	Period 5
CURRENT RATIO	.5	.9	1.5	1.9	2.4
EQTY/ASSETS	.47	.30	.35	.38	.45
TOTAL ASSETS	13170879	25191364	25247775	28770269	28953701
NT CASH FLOW	(1422801)	819801	476423	1129449	1329290
AREA 01 P/L	418036	349993	427268	498695	556177
PERC R O A I	17	10	13	15	17
AREA 02 P/L	1947960	1550535	3495365	3978810	4356416
PERC R O A I	25	11	17	19	20
AREA 03 P/L	97451	106518	112772	116939	116016
PERC R O A I	242	148	190	219	227
NET INCOME BEF INT+TAXS	1982932	1664312	3438134	3904374	4262708
R O A I BEF INT+TAXS	17	9	14	14	15
NET INCOME	1110625	1205395	1114257	1603144	1552675

Figure 8-13

Figure 8-13

Area Level Summary Report

OPERATING SUMMARY, AREA 01 AUSTIN

	Period 1	Period 2	Period 3	Period 4	Period 5
PLANT 01	280211	251442	266468	280805	294453
PLANT 03	30657	32730	35611	41317	43245
PLANT 04	201112	0	0	0	0
PLANT 06	117611	134145	149651	162477	171631
PLANT 10	16606	17144	19173	22299	22793
PLANT 12	0	0	0	0	0
PLANT 14	0	148187	196800	242445	285649
TOT OPR INC	646197	583648	667703	749343	817771
AR SPRT COST					
ADMIN+SALES	228161	233655	240433	250649	261595
TOT AD+SL EX	228161	233655	240433	250649	261595
TOT AR INC	418036	349993	427270	498694	556176
OPR RATIOS					
INC/SALES	17	14	16	17	17
PLANT ASSETS	3569915	3419370	3297306	3220333	3174439
OVHD ASSETS	62471	62934	66620	70265	73164
TOT ASSETS	3632386	3482304	3363926	3290598	3247603
AVG ASSETS	2533934	3557345	3423115	3327262	3269101
PERCH R O A	16.5	9.8	12.5	15.0	17.0

> Perfect computer environments, like perfect computers, don't exist. However, within the narrow parameters of equipment requirements, human engineering, and corporate budgets, careful planning is the key to reliability and capacity for growth.
>
> "The Computer Environment: No Room for Error," *Infosystems*, Aug. 1974, p. 24.

DEVELOP THE SOFTWARE

We are concerned in this book primarily with the managerial and decision-making aspects of MISs. Although software programming development in the technical sense is not a primary concern of management, management does have the responsibility of ensuring that the software is an economical and effective part of the MIS. Software development, particularly good programming, is an expensive activity that cannot be slighted.

Don't Ignore Software Decisions; The Results Can Be Disastrous

Generally it is not advisable to prepare computer programs until management has approved the detailed design and directs implementation of the MIS. This means that programming is carried out in the implementation stage.

A catalog of descriptions of proposed programs should be prepared. This forces an evaluation of time and cost of software in the implementation stage. An example of program description is shown in Figure 8-15.

Figure 8-13

Plant Level Reports

COST DETAIL, PLANT NO. 14 NEW AUSTIN GRAVEL PLANT

	Period 1	Period 2	Period 3	Period 4	Period 5
FIXED COSTS:					
DIRECT LABOR	0	137280			
DEPRECIATION	0	221286			
TOT FXD COST	0	358566			
VAR COSTS:					
OPER SUPPLIES	0	1847			
KILN BRICK	0	9233			
ELEC POWER	0	23294			
REPAIRS	0	33237			
ROYALTY	0	51702			
SHOP CHARGES	0	7386			
GRAVEL PURCH	0	80876			
MISC EXP	0	7386			
TOT VAR COST	0	214961			
TOTAL COST	0	573527			

PLANT INCOME, PLANT NO. 14 NEW AUSTIN GRAVEL PLANT

	Period 1	Period 2	Period 3	Period 4	Period 5
SALES:					
SAND	0	167918	176415	185341	194720
GRAVEL	0	204422	214767	225633	237049
FILL MATRL	0	58559	61522	64635	67906
TYPE I SACK	0	91260	95878	100729	105826
I C GRAVEL	0	199555	209653	220261	231406
TOTAL SALES	0	721714	758235	796599	836907
DEDUCTIONS	0	0	0	0	0
NET SALES	0	721714	758235	796599	836907
FIXED COSTS	0	358566	334573	314700	298487
VRBLE COSTS	0	214961	226862	239454	252771
TOTAL COST	0	573527	561435	554154	551258
OPRTG INCM	0	148187	196800	242445	285649

Source: Eileen Mackenzie, "An Operations Room for Fast Decisions," reprinted by special permission from the January 1972 issue of *International Management.* Copyright © McGraw-Hill International Publications Company Limited. All rights reserved.

Figure 8-14   An operations room for fast decisions.

PROPOSE AN ORGANIZATION TO OPERATE THE SYSTEM

The development of a new organization structure when the company executives and organization are in place is fraught with practical obstacles. Managers would consider it an imposition if the MIS group were to suggest regroupings, particularly if an individual manager's position may be abolished. The MIS group should work with incumbent and top managers to *suggest* organizational changes that will correspond to requirements of the new system. The group should not attempt to press or sell a reorganization. Major changes in organization are the prerogatives of top management.

SOMEBODY HAS TO
MIND THE STORE—
GET ORGANIZED

Organization for systems management requires an outlook different from that of organization for functional component management. Subsystem managers should recognize that their main objective is that the subsystem should function in a way that is best for the whole system. Subsystem management requires a knowledge of the dynamics of systems and of the need for trade-offs to optimize system performance. The manager must be able to interface his subsystem operations effectively with coupled subsystems.

The hierarchy of management should follow the hierarchy of systems and subsystems, rather than of technical disciplines. Assignment to

---

Date: March 20, 1977

Identification:	**BEG**
Full Name	Branch expense generator
Status:	Proposal
Language:	**COBOL**
Computer:	IBM 360/40
Run time:	16–22 minutes
Runs per year:	12

Description: BEG produces expense detail reports at the branch level. It utilizes sales and lease data, population statistics, and manpower factors. It provides expenses by product line for up to a 24-month period.

The program will produce hard copy and also a tape for linkage with other programs.

Figure 8-15   A program proposal for a single model.

activities by technical discipline should be primarily at the lower level, except for some overlay service systems such as financial planning and control.

DOCUMENT THE DETAILED DESIGN

The end product of the detailed design project is production of the documents that specify the system, its operation, and its design justification. Documentation consists of

THE DESIGN IS NOT COMPLETE UNTIL IT IS DESCRIBED IN A WRITTEN REPORT TO MANAGEMENT

1. A summary flow chart.
2. Detailed flow charts.
3. Operations activity sheets showing inputs, outputs, and transfer functions.
4. Specification of the data base or master file.
5. Computer hardware requirements.
6. Software (programs).
7. Personnel requirements by type of skill or discipline.
8. Final (updated) performance specifications.
9. Cost of installation and implementation of the system.
10. Cost of operating the system per unit of time.
11. Program for modification or termination of the system.
12. An executive digest of the MIS design. This is a report that top management can read rapidly in order to get the essence of the sys-

tem, its potential for the company, its cost, and its general configuration. We point out that a high-level MIS official at General Electric remarked, "If the MIS can be justified on the basis of cost savings, it isn't an MIS." The executive digest should be directed toward showing how the system will aid managers' decision making by gains in information or in time.

Some documentation should be on standardized forms. Input/output/activity diagrams or listings are an example. Obviously, standard symbols should be established for flow charts, and guidelines should be established for flow-chart format. Some documentation is unique to a project, such as the data base, and the format and classification of items should be determined by the needs of the particular user. Other documentation should simply follow good reporting style.

For further details of typical forms which may be developed to document the design, refer to the Appendix. Also in the Appendix is a comprehensive list of items to be documented and the likely format.

In Figure 8-16, we have shown a table of contents for an actual MIS design project. (Implementation was not included in this report but rather was in a separate report.)

Figure 8-16 PTS Corporation, Table of Contents.

PTS Corporate Background
Recent developments in company background
Organizational chart
Conceptual Design
List of objectives by major subsystems
    Marketing subsystem
    Accounting and finance subsystem
    Distribution and warehousing subsystem
    Inventory control subsystem
    Illustration of internal and external constraints of system
List of Managers and their information needs/sources
Conceptual design flow charts
    Operational information flow
    Strategic information flow
    MIS flow chart
Identification of major files
Detailed Design
Detailed outline of data base
    Inventory file
    Accounts payable file
    Master customer and accounts receivable file
    General ledger file

Marketing research and sales file
Distribution and warehousing file
Technology research results file
Vendor file
Legal records file
Personnel file

File and manager-user matrix

Chart of accounts

Detailed flowchart of information flows

Key to detailed flowchart

Contents description and format of reports received by each manager

EDP function
Organization and personnel
Hardware
Software requirements

Procedures manual, general contents

SUMMARY

Detailed design of the MIS system commences after the conceptual framework of the gross design has been formulated. Detailed design begins with the performance specifications given by the gross design and ends with a set of specifications for the construction of the MIS. Unless the operating system is to remain unchanged, the design of the MIS must be developed in conjunction with the design of the operating system.

A unique recipe for detailed design cannot be given, because design work is a creative, problem-solving activity. Blind alleys, iterative cycling processes, and new techniques are developed during the design process itself. We have tried here to describe major phases and activities of the design process. The prospective MIS professional must develop in-depth skill in the problem-solving, decision-making, and management science areas by further study. He must develop his skill in systems design through actual experience. A textbook can only point the direction.

QUESTIONS AND PROBLEMS

1. Many managerial reports are required for the planning and control of each subsystem in a business. Examples of reports are given in the right-hand column below. Match each report with the system it belongs with.

Company Subsystems	Report

Organizational-level subsystems

_____ (1) Top management	a. Program status
_____ (2) Middle management	b. Work list
_____ (3) First-line supervision	c. Capital budget

Functional subsystems

_____ (4) Engineering	a. Inventory of raw materials
_____ (5) Marketing	b. Evaluation of profitability of a new plant
_____ (6) Manufacturing	c. Laboratory projects
_____ (7) Financial	d. Labor market status
_____ (8) Personnel	e. New-accounts summary

Resource subsystems

_____ (9) Human resources	a. Daily investment position
_____ (10) Capital assets	b. Distribution of inventories
_____ (11) Materials	c. Average age of equipment
_____ (12) Liquid assets	d. Organizational development plan
_____ (13) Intangible resources	e. Manpower planning

Product subsystems

_____ (14) Large appliances	a. Personal disposable income
_____ (15) Small appliances	b. Forecast of home construction
_____ (16) Recreational products	c. Consumer preference study of toasters
_____ (17) Office equipment	d. Trend of sales of filing cabinets

Phase subsystems

_____ (18) Forecasting	a. Correlation of personal selling and advertising with sales volume
_____ (19) Financing	b. Average time from receipt of raw material to shipment of finished goods
_____ (20) Material handling/ processing	c. Anticipated sales by product and customer for next year
_____ (21) Distribution	d. Debt/equity ratio

2. List principal sources for obtaining information in developing an MIS.

3. Rate the following characteristics of data bases as favorable (F) or unfavorable (U):

_____ a. Same data appear in the central file, the departmental file, and the financial file.

_____ b. Many forms are provided for control of data entry.

_____ c. A file system is integrated for all uses.

_____ d. Data are accessible by people outside the company.

_____ e. People would pay to see what is in my central files.

_____ f. The data base is patterned after organizational structure rather than business subsystems.

_____ g. The data base planning is centralized.

_____ h. The data base is largely independent of user program changes.

4. Below are lists of activities, inputs to subsystems, and outputs to subsystems. Place an (X) in the column that will relate activity, input, and output to the appropriate subsystem.

	Order Processing	Warehousing	Purchasing
Activities			
Correct inventory record balance	( )	( )	( )
Order delivered by salesman	( )	( )	( )
Prepare sales order form	( )	( )	( )
Stamp receipt time	( )	( )	( )
Pick item & deliver to shipping	( )	( )	( )
Mark "BO" (back order)	( )	( )	( )
Edit for customer account number	( )	( )	( )
Stamp shipping copy	( )	( )	( )
Edit requisition	( )	( )	( )
File requisition in open-order file	( )	( )	( )
Arrange requisition by buyer specialization	( )	( )	( )
Credit check	( )	( )	( )
Compare against company catalog	( )	( )	( )
File in sales order file	( )	( )	( )
Compare to vendor historical file	( )	( )	( )
Inputs			
Customer list	( )	( )	( )
Receiving report	( )	( )	( )
Sales order log	( )	( )	( )
Inventory records	( )	( )	( )
Requisition	( )	( )	( )
Master customer file	( )	( )	( )
Customer's invoice (copies 3, 4, 5)	( )	( )	( )
Warehouse sales order file	( )	( )	( )
Customer order	( )	( )	( )
Vendor historical file	( )	( )	( )
Catalog	( )	( )	( )
Customer credit file	( )	( )	( )
Price list	( )	( )	( )
Sales order	( )	( )	( )
Purchase order	( )	( )	( )
Back order production request for items to be manufactured (copy)	( )	( )	( )
Back order purchase request for items to be purchased (original)	( )	( )	( )

Outputs

Requisition for stock items	( )	( )	( )
Purchase order	( )	( )	( )
Bill of lading	( )	( )	( )
Sales order	( )	( )	( )
Customer's invoice (with items)	( )	( )	( )
Updated vendor performance history file	( )	( )	( )
Manual sales order marked with inventory check (to data processing)	( )	( )	( )
Updated customer credit file	( )	( )	( )
Updated master customer file	( )	( )	( )
Shipping order	( )	( )	( )

5. Refer to the Artcraft Case in Chapter 7. Develop the detailed design to the extent that you can based on the case material and your knowledge of business.

chapter nine

Implementation and Evaluation of the New MIS

CHAPTER 9 explains how to put the MIS into operation and evaluate it.

when you have finished studying

IMPLEMENTATION AND EVALUATION OF THE NEW MIS

you should be able to

1. List and describe four methods for putting a new MIS into effect in an organization
2. List and describe briefly the tasks required to implement the MIS design
3. Prepare a plan for implementation of the MIS
4. Describe the general nature of testing the new MIS
5. Describe briefly several approaches to evaluating the new MIS in operation.

Designing an MIS is a big project. Converting from the design description into a working system may be an even bigger project. This conversion is usually called *implementation* of the design.

The implementation phase is a period of constructing the arrangements of facilities, people, and equipment. It involves changing work habits of many managers and operating personnel. Since it is a period filled with many technical, financial, and human problems, careful planning will yield many rewards. In fact, we would state that careful planning is a necessity to prevent chaos.

Although the design of a management information system may seem to management to be an expensive project, the cost of getting the MIS on line satisfactorily may often exceed that of its design. The cumulative expenditures for the design and installation of an MIS follow the pattern sketched in Figure 9-1. The implementation has been accomplished when the outputs of the MIS are continuously utilized by decision makers.

There are four basic methods for implementing the MIS once work has been completed:

1. Cut off the old system and install the new. This produces a time gap during which no system is in operation. It is practical only for small companies or small systems where installation requires one or two days. An exception to this would be the installation of a larger system during a plant's vacation shutdown or some other period of inactivity.

2. Cut over by segments. This method is also referred to as "phasing in" the new system. Small parts or subsystems are substituted for the old. If this method is possible, some careful questions should be asked about the design of the new system. Is it really just an auto-

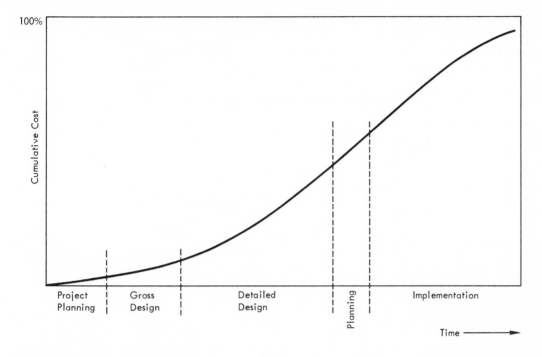

Figure 9-1 Growth of MIS project costs.

Putting in a
New System Is a
Complex, Messy
Affair; Select
One of Four Ways
that Fits the
Situation Best

mation of isolated groups of clerical activities? Generally, new *systems* are not substitutable piece by piece for previous *nonsystems*. However, in the case of upgrading old systems, this may be a very desirable method.

3. Operate in parallel and cut over. The new system is installed and operated in parallel with the current system until it has been checked out; then the current system is cut out. This method is expensive because of the manpower and related costs. However, it is required in certain essential systems, such as payroll or customer billing. Its big advantage is that the system is fairly well debugged when it becomes the essential information system of the company.

4. Implement the system as the design effort progresses. This is a piecemeal approach, but it has the advantages of involving users in a sort of implementation/test/redesign process. Such a process provides operational testing of the design on a continuous basis, but it limits consideration of major design alternatives. It is a trial-and-error process. Completion of conceptual and analytical design in advance of equipment installation offers many advantages besides cost.

Except for the timing and for obvious variations, the implementation steps for all four methods may be covered together. We now proceed to give step-by-step procedures for implementation, support, test, and control of the specified MIS. We assume that the specification provides the system description both in general and in detail, procedures for operation, forms and data base required, the new organization structure including position descriptions, and facilities and equipment required. The step-by-step procedures are given for major phases of the implementation that are usually conducted in a parallel or network time format.

PLAN THE IMPLEMENTATION

The three main phases in implementation take place in series; these are the initial installation, the test of the system as a whole, and the evaluation, maintenance, and control of the system. On the other hand, many implementation activities should be undertaken in parallel in order to reduce implementation time. For example, acquisition of data for the data base and forms design for collection and dissemination of information may be carried out in parallel. Training of personnel and preparation of software may be in parallel with each other and with other implementation activtities.

To Prevent Chaos During Implementation, Plan Thoroughly for the Changeover

It is apparent, then, that the first step in the implementation procedure is to *plan the implementation*. Although some analysts include the planning of the implementation with the design of the system, we believe it is operationally significant to include it in the implementation stage, for several reasons. First, the planning and the action to implement the plan should be bound closely together. Planning is the first step of management, not the last. Further, the MIS design and the urgent need for the system at the time the design is completed will weigh heavily on the plan for implementation. And finally, the planning process is a function of line management, at least as far as key decisions or alternative plans are concerned. The systems analyst may prepare plans to assist managers, but *managers must have the last say*. At the same time, managers require the services of the systems analyst to detail plans. The managers prefer to make decisions based on the most recent information: the MIS specifications, the proposed plans of the systems analyst, and the current operating situation.

The planning for the project of implementation should follow the procedures for project programming described in Chapter 7. Once the conversion method has been described, the specific steps are as we shall delineate here.

Identify the Implementation Tasks

The major implementation tasks, or milestones, usually consist of

1. Organizing the personnel for implementation.
2. Acquiring and laying out facilities and offices.

3. Developing procedures for installation and testing.
4. Developing the training program for operating personnel.
5. Completing the system's software.
6. Acquiring required hardware.
7. Designing forms.
8. Generating files.
9. Completing cutover to a new system.
10. Obtaining acceptance.
11. Testing of the entire system.
12. Providing system maintenance (debugging and improving).

Identify the Major Implementation Tasks for Your Company

The plans should list all subtasks for each of these major tasks so that individuals in the organization may be assigned specific responsibilities.

Establish Relationships Among Tasks

Which Tasks Must Immediately Precede Each Task?

For small projects, the order of performance may simply be described in text form. However, even in small projects, a Gantt chart or network diagram makes visualization of the plan and schedule much clearer. In large projects, many concurrent and sequential activities are interrelated, so that a network diagram must be employed in any good plan. Figure 9-2 shows a Gantt chart, and Figure 9-3 shows a network diagram (condensed) for illustrating task relationships.

Establish a Schedule

How Long Will It Take To Do Each Task? What Are the Start and End Dates for Each Task?

A first estimate of the schedule is prepared by having the system designers estimate the times between the events in the program network. The critical path (longest time through the network) can then be calculated. The end date is thus established once the starting date is specified. Figures 9-2 and 9-3 indicate how times are shown for the implementation activities.

The actual desired end date is then usually specified by management on the basis of this information. Obviously, management may apply pressure or provide additional manpower to shorten the network times.

Negotiating Realistic Target Dates with Management

In a somewhat simplified representation (although possibly true to life), the decision scenario might run like this:

[The top manager involved and the managers who report to him, the MIS design manager and an analyst, and the computer center manager and a programmer attend a conference.]

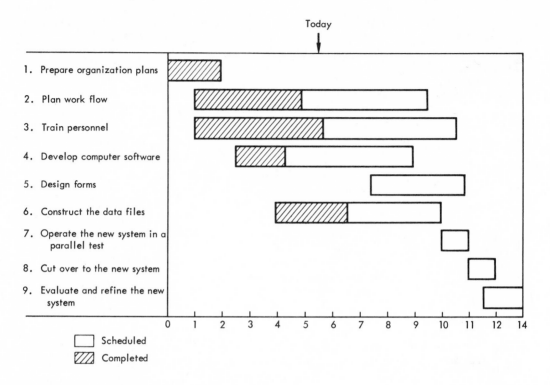

Figure 9-2 Gantt chart for MIS implementation.

TOP MANAGER (to
his managers):

> Well, you fellows have worked on this MIS to get rid of the prob-
> lems of lack of information and obsolete methods. Now's the time
> to see what you have really got. Bill [MIS design manager] has
> given us his plan for getting this MIS into action. I see from his
> plan that this will take seven months. That's a pretty long time.
> It seems to me that about three months of good, concentrated effort
> should swing it.
>
> [Bill has already estimated that it could be done in three months
> if nothing at all went wrong. His previous consultations with the
> computer center manager, Ken, have led to his present estimate.
> They have learned from past experience that the safe course is to
> double the estimated time required. They have also agreed pri-
> vately to add on another month for the purpose of the meeting.]

BILL:

> Ken and I have gone over this very carefully, and we think that
> the very best time we could make with full pressure applied by
> your managers would be six months.
>
> [The top manager plays this game every day and interprets this

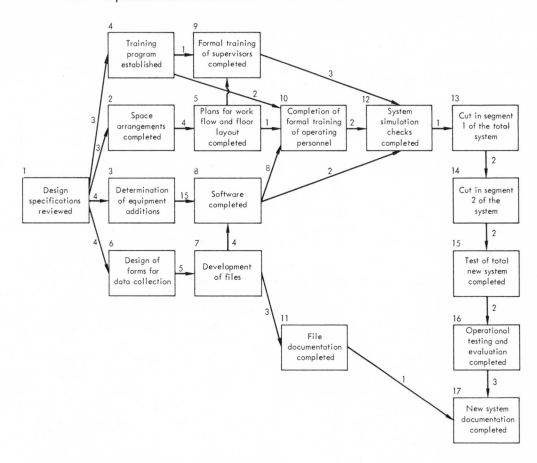

Figure 9-3 Network diagram for MIS implementation.

correctly as double the ideal time, but recognizes it as a schedule that could be met in practical circumstances. He also knows that most schedules tend to slip, so he continues.]

TOP MANAGER (to
his managers):

You guys are the ones that are going to have to live with this and spend time working on it. How about it, should this be cut back?

ONE OF THE
MANAGERS:

If we cut some corners and shoot for completing the data base at a later time, I think we could make it in four months.

TOP MANAGER:

Let's do it this way so that Bill has no complaints. We'll schedule complete installation in five months and really bear down. We *need* this system. If we get a little behind in our work over this period, we can more than make it up as soon as the system's in—OK? Let's start in immediately along the lines of Bill's plan. Bill, you revise the details of the schedule as you think necessary and get new copies of the plan out tomorrow. If there are no objections, that's all, then.

[Heads nod in agreement and murmurs are heard that "this is a great system but we're really going to have to sweat to get it in." The meeting ends.]

Do Not Be Optimistic; Prepare Realistic Cost Estimates by Detailing All Costs and Anticipating a Number of Problems

Prepare a Cost Schedule Tied to Tasks and Time

The cost for completing each milestone, and possibly each task required to complete a milestone, should be established as part of the plan; then the rate of expenditures should be budgeted. The techniques for this phase of planning were covered in Chapter 6.

Establish a Reporting and Control System

Establish a Formal Reporting and Control Process To Keep Implementation Tightly on Schedule

Reporting and control of the work in progress may be obtained by weekly meetings of the key people involved or by brief written progress reports. The financial personnel must make certain that report formats allow them to show cost and technical progress relationships as well as cost and time relationships. When large numbers of people are both conducting regular operations and introducing new equipment, arrangements, and operations, some confusion is inevitable. The object of the control system is to minimize this confusion and the associated delays and costs.

ACQUIRE FLOOR SPACE AND PLAN SPACE LAYOUTS

The installation of a new system to replace a current one may require a major revision of facilities as well as a completely new office, computer room, and production layouts. The MIS project manager must prepare rough layouts and estimates of particular floor areas he feels will be needed. He should then prepare cost estimates and submit a proposal for management's approval.

START TO IMPLEMENT BY OBTAINING THE FLOOR SPACE REQUIRED

Facilities and space planning should begin as soon as approval of gross space allocations has been obtained. The urgency for such planning is twofold. First, there may be a long lead time if new partitions, electrical work, air conditioning, or even new buildings are required. Second, the detailed work flow depends on the physical arrangements of the buildings. The training of operations personnel will be more successful if it is based on exact physical relationships among the people and the equipment.

Space planning must take into account the space occupied by people, the space occupied by equipment, and the movement of people and equipment in the work process. Related to these are the number and kinds of exits; storage areas; location of utilities, outlets, and controls; environmental requirements for the equipment; safety factors; and working conditions for the personnel. A large investment in good working conditions will repay its cost many times. It is a shortsighted and costly policy to scrimp on facilities and human environment when a major renovation is required to install a new system.

ORGANIZE FOR IMPLEMENTATION

Once the implementation tasks have been defined in the planning phase, management usually assigns a project manager to guide the implementation. A manager of management information systems may assume this responsibility by virtue of his permanent assignment. In smaller companies, someone from the finance/accounting department, or even the computer center manager, may be placed in charge. A project manager, who is responsible for the entire MIS development and implementation, as described in Chapter 6, usually works best.

The role of line managers must be made clear. Because the purpose of the MIS is to increase the amount and quality of their contributions, the system is really *their* system. Top management must take explicit steps to make the middle managers aware of this and of the necessity for their involvement in implementation. Essentially, the system specialists are there to *assist* management with the implementation; they are assigned to the project as needed for this purpose.

ASSIGN RESPONSIBILITIES FOR THE IMPLEMENTATION TASKS

Besides assigning responsibilities to line managers, systems specialists, and computer programmers, top management should make sure that line functional personnel have active parts in the implementation. These are the people who will operate the system, and they also must feel that it is *their* system.

Proper organization by assignment of specific leadership and task responsibility diffused widely throughout the whole organization can prevent the moans and wails so often heard after a new MIS is installed and fails. Mature people respond to work assignments that call forth their full talents. They resist the control that is implied when they are simply handed a system installed by specialists and told exactly how to operate it. But when they have a hand in shaping and constructing the system they must operate, employees react favorably. Without such acceptance, management finds that new systems fail because of inertia, apathy, resistance to change, and employee feelings of insecurity.

DEVELOP PROCEDURES FOR IMPLEMENTATION

The project leader has available the network plan for proceeding with the implementation. He must now call upon key people in the project to prepare more detailed procedures for system installation. For example, suppose the detailed design specification calls for the manufacturing manager to receive a report on raw materials stored on the factory floor at the end of each day. The source of data is the foreman, who will fill out forms and send them to a production planner for compilation. The systems analyst must develop the procedure for delivering instructions and forms to foremen, for coordinating and integrating this very small portion of the MIS with other parts of the manufacturing system, and for working out problems with the people involved.

As another example, suppose some files must be converted from filing cabinets to magnetic tape or to some kind of random-access storage. The systems analyst must develop the procedures for making this conversion without upsetting current use of the files.

Procedures for evaluating and selecting hardware must be spelled out. Procedures for buying or constructing software should be established. Procedures for phasing in parts of the MIS or for operating the MIS in parallel must be developed. Obviously there are *many* procedures that must be delineated in advance if the entire implementation is to be saved from chaos.

A major part of implementing the MIS is the testing of each segment of the total system as it is installed. So far, the only testing that has been done is a simulation of the system during the detailed design stage. The testing of segments of the MIS during installation requires application of line personnel to actual files, software, and hardware for either current operations or specially designed test problems. This is equivalent to the physical laboratory testing of parts of an engineered product after the theoretical evaluation (testing) and before construction of the parts.

It is necessary to develop the testing procedures on the basis of the design and test specifications. The procedures should prescribe

1. Which segments of the system will be tested.
2. When such tests are to be performed.
3. Test problems to be run.
4. Who will perform the tests.
5. How the tests will be run.
6. Who will evaluate test results and approve the system segment or recommend modification.

We might review at this time the sequence of test development and conduct up to the point before system acceptance. The steps are listed under the appropriate steps of system development.

1. *Detailed design stage:* Prepare a test description for each test. The test description is a concise statement of the ultimate objective of the test and the systems, components, and facilities involved in its accomplishment.
2. *Detailed design stage or implementation stage:* Prepare a test specification for each test. The test specification is derived from the test description. It is a completely detailed statement giving information on conditions under which the test is to be run, duration of the test, method and procedure to be followed, data to be taken and frequency, and analysis to be performed on the data.
3. *Implementation stage:* Prepare a test operating procedure for each test. A completely detailed procedure for the accomplishment of the test specification includes organization of personnel for conduct of the test; provision of necessary test forms and data sheets; statement of conditions to exist at the start of the test; a list of all equipment, software, and file data required for the test; and a step-by-step procedure for all the people participating in the test.
4. *Implementation stage:* Prepare an acceptance test program. This requires a test description, test specification, and test operating procedure for the entire MIS, to check out the system before it is accepted by operating personnel for sole continuous use.

TRAIN THE OPERATING PERSONNEL

A program should be developed to impress upon management and support personnel the nature and goals of the MIS and to train operating personnel in their new duties. In the case of management, many of whom participate in the development of the system, two short seminars are usually adequate. If the first meeting is held at a time when the detailed design is well along, some valuable proposals may be offered that can then be incorporated in the design. Another meeting near the end of the implementation stage may review the benefits of the system and the roles of the executives.

IF TRAINING HAS NOT STARTED BEFORE, IT SHOULD BE DONE BEFORE THE ACTUAL CHANGEOVER

Particular attention should be paid to the training of first-line supervisors. They must have a thorough understanding of what the new MIS is like and what it is supposed to do. Because, in essence, they oversee the operation of the system, they must learn how it will operate. They are faced with many changes in their work, and they must obtain acceptance of changes by their subordinates. Supervisors will therefore have an intense interest in the answers to the following questions:

1. What new skills must we and our people learn?
2. How many people do we gain or lose?
3. What changes in procedures do we make?
4. What are the new forms? Are there more or fewer?
5. What jobs will be upgraded or downgraded?
6. How will our performance be measured?

Certain professional support personnel—such as computer center personnel, marketing researchers, production planners, and accounting personnel who provide input to the MIS or are concerned with processing data and information—should also attend one or several orientation meetings. Because these people will be working with only a small part of the MIS, the seminars should be designed to provide them with an understanding of the complete system. This will furnish direction for their own jobs and give them a perspective that may reduce the likelihood of blunders.

Finally, longer and more formal training programs should be established for people who perform the daily operational tasks of the MIS. These are the clerks, the computer operators, the input and output machine operators, file maintenance personnel, and possibly printing production and graphic arts personnel.

In most medium and large companies, a training specialist arranges such programs. He schedules classes, arranges for facilities, and assists the technical people (in this case, the systems analysts) in developing course content and notes for distribution. In small companies, the MIS manager will probably have to develop the training program himself.

DEVELOP THE SOFTWARE; ACQUIRE THE HARDWARE

SOFTWARE SHOULD BE PREPARED—AND TESTED IF POSSIBLE; HARDWARE MUST BE BROUGHT ON THE SITE AND INSTALLED

A comprehensive discussion of the preparation of computer programs and the evaluation and acquisition of computer and peripheral equipment does not fall within the objective of this text. We are concerned rather with identifying the managerial considerations of MIS design. The *management* of automation of logic, communication, and display is important as a *basis for systems design* and as a *factor in systems implementation*. To a great extent the detailed design of the MIS has provided some criteria for the hardware and software, if it has not in fact specified it. One complicating factor in systems installation is that a new computer is often required along with the new MIS.

Systems designers and programmers provide the flow diagrams and the block diagrams during the detailed design stage. Some modification may be required, however, as the implementation stage progresses. In the implementation stage, coders convert block diagrams into sequences of statements or instructions for the processing (computer) equipment. The development of software consists of the following steps:

1. Develop standards and procedures for programming. Standardized charting symbols, techniques, and records should be maintained.
2. Study the gross system specifications and work with the system designers in the development of the detailed design. The computer programmers should be a part of the design team by contributing their expertise as needed.

3. Develop the data processing logic and prepare the programming flow charts. When the programming charts are completed, they should be reviewed by the systems design group.

4. Code the instructions given by the flow charts. This is the writing of detailed instructions to the computer. Good coding should balance gains from economical use of machine storage capacity with possible speed of machine operation. Another important goal for the coding process is to build error control into the machine instructions.

5. Test the program. The aim is to find, diagnose, and correct errors by running sample problems and checkout programs on the computer. Actually, this "debugging" often continues into the implementation phase, where it is a much more expensive process.

6. Document the programming, coding, and testing. This is an extremely important step. Too often rough sketches, preliminary programs and codes, and test results are not updated to the "final" or most recent status. Not only should documentation be maintained completely up to date, but the contents should be easily interpreted by anyone skilled in the field. It is management's responsibility to ensure that this proper documentation takes place.

The development of software and the acquisition of new equipment are usually the limiting items in getting an MIS implemented. When possible, these tasks should be started during the design state. There is, of course, some risk of loss in starting early, but it must be balanced against the considerable delay involved in the sequential approach to design and implementation of the MIS.

DEVELOP FORMS FOR DATA COLLECTION
AND INFORMATION DISSEMINATION

DESIGN FORMS FOR
THE COLLECTION OF
DATA TO GO INTO
THE FILES AND
COMPUTER DATA
BASE

A vast amount of detailed data, both external and internal to the company, must be collected for input to the MIS. If control over marketing is to be exercised or sales forecasting is carried out, then somewhere, every day, a salesman must sit in a room and fill out a form summarizing the day's activities. Obviously, the form ensures that the right information is supplied in a manner that simplifies processing for computer storage. We might ask, What about a truly modern firm in which the salesman may plug in his time-sharing terminal and transmit his information directly to a computer thousands of miles away? Even in this case, the salesman must have a form (or format) for his guidance.

Forms are required not just for input and output but also for transmitting data at intermediate stages. In a personnel system, input to the computer may consist of all known applicants for all known jobs within a company. The computer may provide sorted output to match jobs and applicants. The personnel recruiting specialist may then have to add a statement of his activities—*on a form*, which is attached to the computer output. The entire package is then forwarded to the manager of personnel.

Output forms of the MIS must be prepared at the implementation stage, when they can be both designed and tested. Further, the problems of printing and inventory size and location must be resolved. Management science may provide some guidance to the ordering and inventory solutions.

DEVELOP THE
FORMAT OF
REPORTS TO
MANAGERS

The output forms are what the managers see, and so these forms should be designed so that key information and variances are easily discernible. A periodic report form should be a summary form that is keyed to a hierarchy of increasingly detailed forms. Managers may then pursue specific questions easily by calling for the underlying details.

DEVELOP THE FILES

The specifications for the files and the file structure have been developed in the detailed design stage. In the implementation stage, the actual data must be obtained and recorded for the initial testing and operation of the system. This requires a checklist of data, format of data, storage form and format, and remarks to indicate when the data have been stored. The implementation also requires the development of a procedure for updating each piece of the data and for updating entire sections of the file as required. This collection of data used in routine operations is often called the *master file*.

COLLECT THE DATA
FOR THE FILES AND
STORE THEM ON
TAPES, CARDS, IN
FOLDERS, OR
WHATEVER

When data are obtained from the environment—as are economic, competitive, and financial data, or vendor sources—a procedure for obtaining the data may be developed along with the initial acquisition. Responsibility for file maintenance for each file item should also be assigned. For internal data, the generating source or the compiling source (such as marketing) is usually assigned responsibility for file items. The structure of such information is more generalized than that of the master file. This file is often called the *data base*, although in practice the master file and data base elements are usually stored together.

In the detailed design phase, each item of data for the files is specified and the retrieval methods (indices) are developed. In the implementation stage, forms must be designed so that the data may be analyzed by the programmers and coders for storage in the computer. Thus, the file name, maximum number of characters required to record each data element, frequency of access, volume of operations on the element, retention characteristics, and updating frequency are examples of relevant information required to translate a specification into a file element. A sample form, not to be taken as ideal or generalized, for recording a file element is shown in Figure 9-4. Although separate forms are often used

DATA ELEMENT DESCRIPTION

File Name _____

File Number _____   Date _____

Data Element _____

Field Element _____   Group Label _____

Form _____   Source _____

Maximum Length (Characters/Item Group) _____

Storage Medium _____

Retention Characteristics _____

_____

Update-Procedure _____

_____

_____

Initial Value _____

Units _____

Figure 9-4   File form.

for recording data before they are stored. Figure 9-4 includes a space for initial values.

The development of files or data bases belongs in the conceptual realm of information systems designers and storage and retrieval experts. The translation of specifications for files into computer programs is a function of computer specialists. For our purposes, only an insight into the relation of these specialists' problems to management decision systems is needed.

TEST THE SYSTEM

As each part of the total system is installed, tests should be performed in accordance with the test specifications and procedures described in Chapter 8. Tests of the installation stage consist of component tests, subsystem tests, and total system acceptance tests. Components may consist of

1. Equipment, old or new.
2. New forms.
3. New software programs.
4. New data collection methods.
5. New work procedures.
6. New reporting formats.

Components may be tested relatively independently of the system to which they belong. Tests for accuracy, range of inputs, frequency of inputs, usually operating conditions, "human factor" characteristics, and reliability are all of concern. We do not require vast amounts of input data for this but rather representative elements of data and limiting or unusual data. During component testing, employees are further familiarized with the system before the organization switches over to complete dependence on it. Difficulties occurring during component tests may lead to design changes that will bring large benefits when systems tests and operations are carried out.

One point difficult to cover in a general discussion of testing, but a very important and *practical* one, is, How are the new pieces of equipment, new forms, new procedures, and so on being tested in an organization where daily operations must be maintained? This is particularly relevant where substitution of components cannot be made, but the entire new system must be installed, operated in parallel, and then cut in on a given day. It is a test of the ingenuity of the MIS project manager in preventing utter chaos. One possible approach is to plan for new equipment to be in different locations from old equipment and available areas. Sometimes it is possible to have operating personnel, using a few files and tables fitted into the room, handle both old procedures and testing of the new components from their regular work stations. In other cases, adjacent available office space may be utilized for testing, and the physical substitution of the new for the old system may take place in overtime on the night before cutover. The fact that partitions may have to be removed may permit temporary, crowded, side-by-side arrangements until the acceptance testing is complete.

Does Each
Subsystem Provide
Reliable and
Accurate
Information
on Time?

As more components are installed, subsystems may be tested. There is a considerable difference between the testing of a component and the testing of a system. System tests require verification of multiple inputs, complex logic systems, interaction of humans and widely varied equipment, interfacing of systems, and timing aspects of the many parts. If, for example, the programming for the computer fails to work in the system test, costly delays may take place. Often, minor difficulties cropping up require redesign of forms, procedures, work flow, or organizational changes. The training program itself is being tested, because, if the supervisors and operators lose confidence in the system at this point, they may resist further implementation of the new system in subtle ways.

Although complete parallel testing before a target day cutover is perhaps the most difficult to implement, it is sometimes necessary. Consider a bank that must collect and process millions of dollars in checks before shipment to various points in the country for collection. A delay of a day, or even of several hours, can be very expensive in terms of interest foregone. Order processing, payroll operations, project management control, retail operations management, and airline reservation service are other examples in which a break in system operation is extremely undesirable.

CUTOVER

CUT OUT THE OLD, BRING ON THE NEW MIS

Cutover is the point at which the new component replaces the old component or the new system replaces the old system. This usually involves a good deal of last-minute physical transfer of files, rearrangement of office furniture, and movement of work stations and people. Old forms, old files, and old equipment are suddenly retired.

Despite component and system testing, there are still likely to be "bugs" in the system. One of the chief causes of problems is inadequate training of operating personnel. These people are suddenly thrown into a new situation with new equipment, procedures, and co-workers. If the training has been superficial, mass confusion may result. Having extra supervisory help, with the systems designers on hand, is one way of preventing first-day cutover panic. Design analysts should also be present to iron out "bugs" of all kinds that may arise.

The systems designer may observe the cutover and the smoothing out of system operations over a few weeks with some gratification. If he is naive, he will depart believing that his system is installed. The more experienced designer will make a few informal return calls later on; he knows that often employees go through the motions of adopting the new system while maintaining secret files in their desks and performing old procedures in parallel with the new. This resistance to change, belief that the old methods were best, or lack of confidence in the new system must be detected and overcome. The systems designer may detect such activities, and he should report them to the supervisor for corrective action. The supervisor should recognize that improper handling of such cases may make it more difficult to ferret out future instances.

The debugging process associated with the cutover to the new system may extend for several months. Programs may require improvement, forms may need to be changed for more efficient operation, or employees may desire transfer to different jobs within the system. In particular, the operational testing of the system over a period of several months exposes it to a volume and variability of data and conditions that could not be practically achieved in preacceptance testing. Production records such as productive time and nonproductive time give indications of future maintenance requirements and idle-time costs.

DOCUMENT THE SYSTEM

Documentation of the MIS means preparation of written descriptions of the scope, purpose, information flow components, and operating procedures of the system. Documentation is not a frill; it is a necessity—for troubleshooting, for replacement of subsystems, for interfacing with other systems, and for training new operating personnel and also for evaluating and upgrading the system.

If the system is properly documented,

1. A new team of operators could be brought in and could learn to operate the MIS on the basis of the documentation available.
2. Designers not familiar with the organization or MIS could, from the documentation, reconstruct the system.
3. A common reference design is available for managers, designers, and programmers concerned with system maintenance.
4. The information systems analyst will have a valuable data source for developing new MISs, schedules, manpower plans, and costs.

Documenting a Manual MIS

The documentation of a manual information system may consist of the following documents:

1. A system summary of scope, interfaces with other systems, types of outputs and users, assumptions and constraints for design, and name of design project leader.
2. Old and new organization charts and comparison of number and kinds of people before and after the new system is installed.
3. Flow charts and layout charts.
4. Desk equipment.
5. Forms.

6. Output reports and formats.
7. Manual data processing procedures.
8. Methods for controlling and revising the system—that is, specification of faulty operation and organizational procedures for initiating changes.

Documenting a Computer-Based MIS

Documentation of a computer-based MIS is similar to that of a manual system except that all software development, programs, files, input/output formats, and codes should be documented. Of particular importance is the documentation of the master file and the means for entering, processing, and retrieving data.

EVALUATE THE MIS

After the MIS has been operating smoothly for a short period of time, an evaluation of each step in the design and of the final system performance should be made. There is always the pressure to go on to new jobs, but the feedback principle should apply to the work of the MIS as well as to the product. Thousands of dollars are invested in an MIS, and it is good business to measure the value of the results.

Evaluation should not be delayed beyond the time when the systems analysts have completed most of the debugging. The longer the delay, the more difficult it will be for the designer to remember important details.

MANAGERS ARE
RESPONSIBLE FOR
MEASURING; THIS
INCLUDES
EVALUATING THE
DESIGN AND
PERFORMANCE OF
THE MIS

The evaluation should be made by the customer as well as by the designers. For each step we have covered in this and the last three chapters, the question should be asked, "If we were to start all over again, knowing what we now know, what would we do differently?" The customer may ask, "How does the system now perform and how would we like it to perform?" In addition, though it is less important than the previous evaluations, the financial specialists should evaluate the project in terms of planned cost versus actual cost of design, implementation, and operation. They should also attempt to identify cost savings and increased profits directly attributable to the MIS.

A clear-cut method for measuring the costs and benefits of a new MIS has not yet been found. We present here a structure which, when adapted to a specific company, will permit partial evaluations.

Structure

The measurement of costs or benefits of an MIS is the measurement of a change or difference between the old and the new. The measurement of change must be related to the basic goals of the MIS, the principal activities that further these goals, or the many minor activities that further these goals. In other words, we may measure the change in the total output of the system or measure the many changes accomplished throughout the system. The former is obviously the most desirable.

What we have is a hierarchy of levels at which we consider measuring costs and benefits. Figure 9-5 shows this hierarchy. For a particular

Figure 9-5 Measurement hierarchy.

Hierarchy in the MIS	*Change that is Measured*
Level 1 Company Profit, Return on Investment	Dollars
Level 2 Company Costs, Revenues	Dollars
Level 3 Planning	Specificity, quantification, degree to which plans are achieved, time required to produce plans, number of alternative plans made available for consideration, cost.
Control	Degree of control by exception, selection of activities to be controlled, fore-warning of activities going beyond acceptable limits, managerial time required for control, automation of control of repetitive situations, cost.
Level 4 Decisions	Quality of decisions, frequency of reversal of decisions by superiors in the organization, number of alternatives examined in arriving at decisions, sophistication of "what if . . . ?" questions permitted, time required for decisions, automation of repetitive decision situations, cost.
Level 5 Information	Validity, accuracy, clarity, distribution, frequency, appropriateness of detail for each level of management, timeliness, format, availability on demand, selectivity of content, disposition method, retention time, cost.
Level 6 System characteristics	Number of people required, equipment and facilities, response time, frequency of breakdowns, inputs, outputs, number of forms, number of operations, number of storages, sizes and quality of data bank, size and quality of model bank, flexibility, simplicity, degree of automation, scope of business components that are related by the MIS, user satisfaction, error rates, persistent problem areas, ease of maintenance and modification, unplanned-for impact on company performance, savings, cost, etc.

MIS, the designer may select the level at which measurement is to take place based on specific objectives of the MIS. It is probably rare that a measurement of the total system is attempted at the system level. At the system level, judgment of broad concepts might be employed, such as

System integrity. How well are the subsystems integrated into the total system without redundancy? How flexible is the system? How easily may the system be expanded?

Areas for Measurement

Operating integrity. How skilled are the people operating the system? What backup is there to prevent system breakdown in the event of loss of key personnel or equipment failure?

Procedural integrity. How good is the documentation of the system and procedures? Are procedures such that employees are motivated to follow them? How well are procedures followed in practice? What controls ensure that procedures are followed?

Internal integrity. How well does the system do what it is supposed to do? How valid are system outputs? How secure is the system against human error, manipulation, sabotage, or theft?

A 17-year-old youth tapped into the Pacific Telephone & Telegraph Co. computer via an unprotected remote terminal. He typed out orders for switchboards and telephone sets and stole over $800,000 worth of equipment over a four-year period.

To impress his employer with the need for additional security, a programmer designed an undetectable program to automatically write payroll checks for several of his relatives, including a two-year-old girl. He ran the system for three months, keeping the checks in their unopened envelopes; then he dropped the entire collection of 30 checks on the security director's desk. He is now in charge of DP security.

"Computer Security . . . The Imperative Nuisance," *Infosystems*, Feb. 1974, p. 27.

Formulation of the Measurement

Once the variables of interest have been identified, a table should be set up to formalize the measurement. Figure 9-5 illustrates how this might be done. Figure 9-6 indicates how the computer hardware might be evaluated.

CONTROL AND MAINTAIN THE SYSTEM

Control and maintenance of the system are the responsibilities of the line managers. Control of the system means the operation of the system as it was designed to operate. Sometimes operators will develop their

		PAGE _____
		DATE _____
MIS PROJECT NAME _____		NO. _____

Initial Costs	1974	1975	1976	TOTAL
1. Project planning	$5,000			$ 5,000
2. Gross design	1,000	$ 2,000		3,000
3. Detailed design		10,000	$ 23,000	33,000
4. Implementation			7,000	7,000
5. Testing			4,800	4,800
6. Special			600	600
TOTAL INITIAL COSTS	$6,000	$12,000	$ 35,400	$ 53,400
Capital Costs				
7. Computer center hardware		$10,300	$ 33,000	$ 43,300
8. Facilities		5,000	13,000	18,000
TOTAL CAPITAL COSTS		$15,300	$ 46,000	$ 61,300
Annual Operating Costs				
9. Computer and equipment lease		$ 5,000	$ 24,000	$ 29,000
10. Personnel		47,000	200,000	247,000
11. Overhead and supplies		10,000	20,000	30,000
TOTAL ANNUAL OPERATING COSTS		$62,000	$244,000	$306,000
Benefits				
12. Reduced salary and labor costs			$ 2,000	$ 2,000
13. Reduced inventory costs			97,000	97,000
14. Better strategic decisions (estimated impact)		$50,000	320,000	370,000
15. Freeing up of managerial time (estimated)		5,000	60,000	65,000
TOTAL BENEFITS		$55,000	$479,000	$534,000

Figure 9-6 MIS evaluation form.

CHECK ON HOW WELL THE MIS IS WORKING AT REGULAR INTERVALS —IS IT BECOMING OBSOLETE?

own private procedures or will short-circuit procedures designed to provide checks. Often well-intentioned people make unauthorized changes to improve the system, changes that are not approved or documented. Managers themselves may not be factoring into decisions information supplied by the system, such as sales forecast or inventory information, and may be relying on intuition. It is up to management at each level in the organization to provide periodic spot checks of the system for control purposes.

Maintenance is closely related to control. There are times when the need for improvements to the system will be discovered. Formal methods for changing and *documenting* changes must be provided. There are times when failure to change the system will cause confusion and error. Changes in the tax rate, in price of the firm's products, or in assumptions about competitors, among many possibilities, must be entered into the system by means of a formal maintenance program.

SUMMARY

The implementation of the MIS is the culmination of the design process. We have pointed out the close pre- and postimplementation relationships between design and implementation. We have discussed three major approaches to implementation from the design time standpoint. Finally, we have given a step-by-step procedure for implementation. As we pointed out in the chapters on design, such a procedure is only an approximation of the timing, because there may exist a parallel execution of some steps. Thus, it seems logical to document the system after it has been debugged and is in final form. In practice, however, it is necessary to document the system as installation takes place, so that there will be an up-to-date reference design during the design phase. The final documentation should be a complete, formal, accurate version of the MIS as it exists in operation.

We have given the major implementation steps as

1. Plan the implementation.
2. Acquire the floor space and plan space layouts.
3. Organize for implementation.
4. Develop procedures for implementation.
5. Train the operation personnel.
6. Develop the software; acquire the hardware.
7. Develop the necessary forms for data collection and information dissemination.
8. Develop the files.
9. Test the system.
10. Cut over to put the new system on line.
11. Document the system.
12. Evaluate the MIS.
13. Control and maintain the system.

In conclusion, we point out that many practitioners believe that the design and implementation of an MIS is always an evolutionary process. There are, however, many advantages to a complete redesign of the MIS despite the difficulties of installing a new system while an old one is in operation. The "big-step" approach permits complete rethinking of the entire system and encourages innovative ideas. Indeed, it *is* the systems approach.

QUESTIONS AND PROBLEMS

1. **Case study: An information problem**

   To: J. Berkman, Manager, Systems Planning
   From: J. Manley, Executive Vice-President
   Re: Repairs

   Our policies and systems for handling goods returned for repair and orders for repair parts should be reviewed. Our customers and our operating personnel are dissatisfied.

   With respect to customers, my attention has been directed to numerous complaints, in the following areas in particular:
   1. Delays occasioned by correspondence.
   2. Requests for payment of nominal amounts before repairs are undertaken by us. In some instances, I understand, customers were industrial firms having established accounts with us. Further, payment requests have been made in instances where items are still under warranty.
   3. Where items have been repaired within the last year and are returned for a second time, customers believe a new warranty period was established at the date of this first repair and that no further charges should be made. The two repairs may or may not be related. Admittedly, our policies are vague in this area.

   With respect to our internal deficiencies, I am aware of the following problems:
   1. Customer service requires two men and four clerks to match receiving reports, customer correspondence, and repair cost estimates from the Repair Department, and then to carry on the necessary correspondence with customers.
   2. As I understand it, over eight different forms are involved in our handlings, some with five copies. This does not include individually dictated letters to customers. Included are receiving reports, item identification, tags, cost estimate forms, work orders and material requisitions. There may be others.
   3. The Repair Department claims they are not informed of the exact nature of customer complaints and must therefore conduct a text search to ascertain malfunctions.
   4. As I understand it, warranty cards are not now being used. Repairs are being made based on serial numbers of items. This causes difficulties because of item layover in our warehouse, distributors' warehouses, and retailers' shelves. Thus, a customer may be entitled to service under warranty but we refuse him, basing our decision on elapsed time from date of manufacture.
   5. Engineering and Product Development inform me there is no formal means of channeling data to them on the nature and causes of malfunctions.

6. The Sales Department believes analysis of warranty cards returned could provide the basis for sales forecasting by product, distributor area, etc. Since much of our distribution is from our warehouse—to distributors, to dealers and, finally, to consumers—demand can actually be strong at consumer levels and we might not know of it for weeks or months. Sales also has some ideas about using the warranty names and addresses for direct mail promotions to support national advertising.

These observations are not meant to be exhaustive but rather to indicate some of the areas that need to be explored.

I shall appreciate your comments.

[Author's suggestion: As a point of departure, read Warren W. Menke, "Determination of Warranty Reserves," *Management Science*, June 1969, pp. B542–B549; or "Call Out the Reserves—Warranty, That Is," *Management Services*, Jan.–Feb. 1970, pp. 47–54.]

a. Sketch a flow chart and describe a system, information system, and an MIS to solve the problems of the case.

b. Describe how you would implement your systems.

2. Relate the items listed below to MIS implementation activities by placing the correct numbers in each block of activities.

(1) Identify implementation tasks
(2) Multiply number of people by square feet required per person
(3) Assign responsibilities for implementation tasks
(4) Cut out the old and install the new MIS
(5) Initial installation
(6) Establish relationships among tasks
(7) Detailed procedures for converting files
(8) Give seminars to orient personnel in the MIS
(9) Give many people a part in implementation
(10) Test the system as a whole
(11) Develop forms for data collection
(12) Lay out office and equipment positions
(13) Prepare the software program
(14) Cut over to the new MIS by segments
(15) Evaluation of the system
(16) Establish a time schedule
(17) Procedure for selecting hardware
(18) Install the hardware
(19) Test the computer programs
(20) Develop MIS output forms
(21) Relate the time schedule to cost and performance
(22) Gather data to be stored in files
(23) Prepare operating procedures to test the new MIS
(24) Operate in parallel and then cut over
(25) Implement the system as the design progresses
(26) Establish a reporting and control system
(27) Give formal training programs for technical specialists

E

Organize for implementation

A

How to implement the MIS

B

Phases of implementation

F

Develop procedure for implementation

C

Plan the implementation

G

Train the operating personnel

D

Acquire floor space

H

Develop forms

I

Develop software, acquire hardware

appendix

Systems Design Techniques

DATA GATHERING

The gathering of facts must be carried out with some goal, direction, intuitive feeling, or structure as a guide. Without such, data gathering becomes a random scanning. The MIS designer will have a good knowledge of the business world and his company to guide his fact gathering; otherwise he would be unlikely to have responsibility for systems design.

What Guides Should Be Considered?

We recall that managers make strategic decisions, tactical decisions, and implementation decisions. Under these headings we would seek data that would assist managers in

1. Identifying opportunities for the company in the marketplace.
2. Describing the long-range goals and strategies of the company.
3. Evaluating goals and strategies.
4. Developing marketing systems, manufacturing systems, and financial and other systems within the company that are related to the total operational system of the company.
5. Developing standards of performance, methods of measurement, and methods of control over long-range and operational activities.
6. Achieving greater effectiveness (reaching goals) and greater efficiency (decreasing costs).
7. Preventing disasters.

Methods of Data Gathering

We knowingly limit the scope of this discussion. In particular, operations analysis analogous to the work of the industrial engineer is not covered.[1] Our emphasis here is on managerial problems of the strategic, tactical, or major operating problem level. On this basis, we suggest methods for looking at all types of data but oriented toward these managerial problems:

1. *Search* for and examine records such as organization charts, files, reports and report forms, flow charts, system descriptions, position guides of managers, and records of major decisions. Plans and problems reported with implementation of plans should be sought, as should correspondence that indicates customer complaints, vendor complaints, or other indicators of company problems.

2. Utilize *questionnaires* to obtain from managers their ideas of their information needs. The questionnaires may be loosely structured by asking broad questions (see Figure A-1) with regard to problems, types of information they would like to receive, frequency, and detail. On the other hand, the systems designer, *in a particular company and organizational situation*, may elect to develop more detailed questionnaires tailored to each individual manager (see Figure A-2, for example).

POSITION TITLE: DATE:

1. What are the major problems you anticipate facing over the next two years?
2. What information would you like to have to help you solve such problems that is not available to you under present circumstances?
3. What repetitive problems do you face that you feel could be resolved by the development of a set of rules (decision table) or model (mathematical relationship) to yield the "best" answer?
4. What reports do you receive that you don't have time to read at all?
5. What reports do you receive so frequently that you read one only once in a while?
6. What reports do you receive that are much more detailed than you need?
7. If you had more time, what operations or systems for which you are responsible do you feel could be significantly improved?

Figure A-1 General questionnaire.

[1] See, for example, Gerald Nadler, *Work Design: A Systems Concept*, Homewood, Ill.: Richard D. Irwin, 1970; or Delmar W. Karger and Franklin H. Bayha, *Engineered Work Measurement*, New York Industrial Press, 1966.

POSITION TITLE: MARKETING MANAGER   DATE:

1. What information would you like to have to help you estimate market potential and forecast sales?
2. Would you like information on structural change of our industry such as mergers, new competitors, etc., besides what you are now getting?
3. What information would help you with pricing decisions?
4. What additional information about customers do you desire?
5. What additional information would help you to find, evaluate, and select new products for your company?
6. What additional information do you need to make product decisions on mix, lines of products, warranties, price/quality combination, etc.?
7. What additional information do you need to control sales operations?
8. What type of information would help you in making major promotional decisions?
9. Are you obtaining adequate information on new technological developments? Government and legal actions?
10. Do you need more information on channels of distribution? Physical distribution?

Figure A-2   Structured questionnaire.

3. *Interview* managers and key personnel.
4. *Sample* inputs, outputs, or status. For example, take a sample of sales orders, customers complaints, inspection reports, and employee grievances to determine where problems may be occurring. Sample machine down time, records of ages of machines, computer center log, back orders, or even scrap containers. In particular, sample opinions of operating employees. *Statistical* sampling allows fairly rigorous conclusions to be drawn in many cases concerning needs or problems.
5. *Estimate* cost savings or revenue gains due to changes in the present MIS and concurrent changes in operations. Such estimates are, of course, extremely crude at the information-gathering stage but may suggest priority of emphasis in gathering further information.

Elaboration of Interview Techniques[2]

[2] For supplementary ideas, the reader is referred to Martin L. Rubin, *Introduction to the System Life Cycle*, Princeton, N.J.: Brandon/Systems Press, 1970, pp. 62–65. Also see W. Hartman, H. Matthes, and A. Proeme, *Management Information Systems Handbook*, New York: McGraw-Hill Book Company, 1968, Section 6.3. An additional reference is Frank J. Clark, Ronald Gole, and Robert Gray, *Business Systems and Data Processing Procedures*, Englewood Cliffs, N.J.: Prentice-Hall, Inc., 1972, Chap. 10, "Information Gathering."

Either initially or eventually, the MIS designer will need to interview the managers-users. If other techniques are employed first, he will be able to communicate more easily and gain better rapport. Top management is usually interviewed first, then middle management, supervisors, and finally operating personnel.

SCHEDULE

The interviewer should establish a schedule for his interviews. No interviews should be scheduled just before lunch or late in the afternoon (or on Friday afternoon, if possible), because interviewees are apt to be tired or anxious to get away from the office. The systems analyst should remind the manager several days in advance of the forthcoming interview.

APPROVAL

The systems designer should not enter a department for any interview without obtaining permission from the department manager.

SELLING A SERVICE

Outside investigators coming into a department are usually viewed with suspicion and distrust. In the initial interview, the systems analyst must gain the trust and confidence of the respondent. To do this, he must present his role as a *service* to the respondent. He must not come on strong as an efficiency expert. An informal manner and a sincere desire to uncover problems he can help with through the MIS are important. The first interview should be short; the objectives of the study and the involvement of all personnel in the study should be brought out. Broad questions may be raised so that both parties will think about their elaboration before subsequent meetings.

CONDUCTING THE INTERVIEW

The systems analyst should try to obtain a location where there will be no distractions. He should attempt to keep the interview on the subject to make the most of the time the manager has allocated to him. Questions that can be answered "yes" or "no" should be avoided because they may elicit snap judgments or easy agreements. In fact, the interviewer should encourage "thinking time" before answers.

The systems analyst is at the interview to learn. He should avoid any intimation of criticism. Rather he should encourage the idea that every healthy organization constantly seeks new ideas and ways to improve.

The systems analyst must be interested and show interest in what the respondent is saying at all times. He should never contradict or express disagreement with the interviewee; he is there to *get* information, not give it or stifle it.

Note-taking may slow down the interview and make it difficult for the systems analyst to probe more deeply into problems. If possible, a tape recorder should be used. This requires agreement with the interviewee in advance as to how tape will be used.

Interviews should be brought to a close when the respondent shows signs of fatigue or restlessness. The interview should not be terminated abruptly, however. A review of key ideas, followed by a brief interval or pause, may cause an important idea to surface at this time.

INVESTIGATION QUESTIONS

Investigation questions for managers may deal with such topics as suggested below or as appropriate for the problem at hand. Possible questions are

1. What are your principal responsibilities, goals, and problems, as *you* see them?
2. What programs are you now administering?
3. What are your sources of information?
   a. What reports or documents do you receive—how frequently, and how timely?
   b. What action do you take with the documents?
   c. What information do you find it necessary to request because it is not supplied to you routinely?
   d. What other information do you receive periodically or by request through other modes (telecommunications, video, staff meetings, etc.)?
   e. What documents or formal transmittals of information do you prepare and to whom do these go?
4. What information do you receive that is unnecessary for your job?
5. What information would you like to receive to aid you with planning, implementing, and controlling?
6. What files do you maintain in your office?
7. What information in your files is also stored in other files?
8. What suggestions do you have for rearranging responsibilities, relationships, and work systems to form an integrated system for your department and all components to which your department relates?
9. Describe how you feel toward the computer center as providing a systems type of service for the company.
10. How do you feel about using a computer terminal in your office to ask "What if . . . ?" questions for planning?
11. How do you feel about all managers becoming familiar with the use of computer terminals through short workshop programs?

DECISION TABLES

A decision table (DT) is a visual means for showing how a rule (or set of rules) applies to repetitive situations. Figure A-3 demonstrates a simple example of a rule. An order for the company's product is received by a clerk. She examines the order and finds that the order comes from someone with whom the company has never done business. She therefore sends the order to the credit department. (If the order had come from a regular customer, she would have sent it to the shipping department.) The decision table shows the two possible conditions as statements. The two columns on the right each represent a rule. A rule says "If conditions A, B, C, . . . exist, then take action 1." In essence, the rule when applied to a specific case yields a *decision* on action to be taken.

One purpose of the MIS is to relieve managers from routine decision making. Quite complex decision rules may be structured by the use of decision tables. *If a decision table can be formulated, the decision can be programmed for the computer to make.*

Figure A-3   Decision rule.

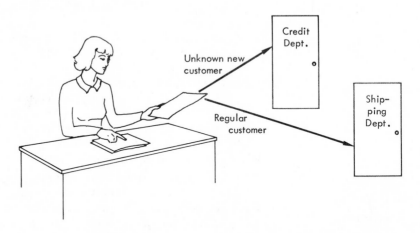

Conditions	Rules	
	1	2
Order from new customer	Yes	No
Order from regular customer	No	Yes
Action: Send to Credit Dept.	Yes	–
Action: Send to Shipping Dept.	–	Yes

Another purpose of the DT is to force the decision maker to clarify the basis of his decisions on objective rather than subjective grounds. Once this has been done, *consistency* of decision making will result, even though several different people deal with the repetitive situations. In fact, if it is economical, the decision making may again be turned over to the computer.

A further use of the DT is to facilitate communication between the manager and the systems analyst or programmer. The logic flow chart of the programmer can be converted to DTs for the manager. On the other hand, the manager can represent his decision process through DTs to the systems analyst in a form that can be readily converted to flow diagrams for computer programming.

Finally, the DT is a method of documentation in MISs that is easily prepared, changed, and updated.

Definitions

Decision tables are visual representations of a decision situation consisting of

1. *Conditions:* factors to consider in making a decision.
2. *Actions:* steps to be taken when a certain combination of conditions exists.
3. *Rules:* specific combinations of conditions and the actions to be taken under these conditions.

We refer now to Table A-1. In this table, C1 refers to condition 1, and A1 refers to action 1; Y and N stand for yes or no, the condition exists or it does not; X indicates the action to be taken. Rule 2, indicated as R2, says that C1 exists but C2 does not, so the credit should be approved.

Table A-1   Simple example of limited entry decision table.

Credit Order Approval Procedure

		R1	R2	R3
C1	Pay experience favorable	—	Y	N
C2	Order is within credit limit	Y	N	N
A1	Approve credit	×	×	—
A2	Return the order to sales	—	—	×

Note: Check to see that latest credit information is used.

The parts that make up this table are shown in Table A-2. The description of each part is

1. *Condition statements:* statements that introduce one or more conditions.
2. *Condition entries:* entries that complete the condition statements.
3. *Action statements:* statements that introduce one or more conditions.
4. *Action entries:* entries that complete the action statements.
5. *Rules:* unique combinations of conditions and the actions to be taken under those conditions.
6. *Header:* a title and/or code identifying the table.
7. *Rule identifiers:* codes uniquely identifying each rule within a table.
8. *Condition identifiers:* codes uniquely identifying each condition statement/entry.
9. *Action identifiers:* codes uniquely identifying each action statement/entry.
10. *Notes:* comments concerning the contents of the tables. Notes are not required but might be used to clarify some items recorded in the table.

Types of Decision Tables

There are three types of decision tables: limited entry, extended entry, and mixed entry. Table A-1 is a limited entry table because the entries give simple "yes" and "no" answers to condition and action statements.

In an extended entry table, the wording of all statements carry over into the condition and action entries. Table A-3 gives us an example. The third type of table, mixed entry, is one in which there are some limited entries and some extended entries.

Table A-2   Components of a decision table.

Header		
		Rule identifiers
Action condition identifiers	Condition Statements	Condition entries
	Action statements	Action entries
Notes		

Table A-3   Extended entry decision table.

Policy Coverage				
C1	Miles driven per year	<8000	<15,000	≧15,000
C2	Age of youngest driver	>24	>24	≦24
C3	Driving record	Good	Good	Fair
C4	Major use	Pleasure	Pleasure	Business
A1	Type of policy	A	D	J
A2	Policy limit	100/300	75/50	25/50

Open tables are tables wherein the last action of each rule tells you to go to another table and gives the name and number of this next table.

Closed tables are those which do not tell you where to go when the table is completed. Control remains with the original table, which sends you to a closed table. When the closed table has been executed, you return to the original table.

Guidelines for Constructing a DT

When beginners start to make decision tables, they tend to make them too large. Often several small tables are better than one large table because the decision may be made in the first table or, at worst, by the use of two small tables. The size that best facilitates communication should be sought.

In constructing tables, keep the following points in mind:

1. All possible rules must be presented.
2. Every rule must have an action entry associated with it. That is, a rule must state the action to be taken under a given set of conditions.
3. Tables can be more action tables consisting of a single rule; i.e., the only condition satisfied is that the table is entered. Such a table is illustrated in Table A-4. The condition "enter" implies that a decision maker/reader has entered the table from somewhere outside the table. That being the case, the indicated actions are then taken.
4. Rules are unique and independent—they do not duplicate or contradict one another. Therefore, only one rule will apply in any given situation.
5. The sequence of rules is immaterial, because only one rule can satisfy the conditions in a given situation.
6. Within a rule an "and" relationship exists among applicable conditions and actions. That is, for a rule to be satisfied, the first applicable condition *and* the second applicable condition *and* the third must exist. Likewise, all of the applicable actions must be taken.

Table A-4 Single-rule action table.

Morning Routine

		R1
C1	Enter	Y
A1	Check sales report	×
A2	Call shipping on delayed sales	×
A3	Make scheduled sales calls	×

7. Within a rule an "if–then" relationship exists between conditions and actions. That is, a rule implies that *if* certain conditions exist *then* certain actions are to be taken.

Some rules for constructing a DT are

Rule 1: Define specific boundaries for the decision problem.
    a. Define the objective. For example, a firm may have the option of answering a sales inquiry by personal telephone call, sending out a salesman, writing a letter, or ignoring it. The objective of the decision table would be to provide a decision for the order-inquiry dispatcher.
    b. Identify the variables. In our example, customer characteristics, size of order, and timing might be the variables that affect the decision.
    c. Set limits and ranges on the variables. Thus, orders between $2000 and $5000 might be a range that would influence the decision heavily toward making a personal telephone call. Orders over $500 might be the limit set to trigger off sending a salesman, *provided* some other condition statements such as credit rating were favorable.

Rule 2: Enumerate individual elementary decisions. Rarely are real-world decisions simply "yes" or "no." Often, decisions call for further steps and decisions.

Rule 3: Define all alternative outcomes.

Rule 4: Develop the set of value states (conditions) that yield each outcome.

Rule 5: Assign a decision to each outcome.

SUMMARY

This introduction to DTs plus common sense will carry the novice through most practical situations. Those desiring to master more intricate aspects of DTs may refer to such texts as the following: •

GILDERSLEEVE, THOMAS R., *Decision Tables and Their Practical Application in Data Processing,* Englewood Cliffs, N.J.: Prentice-Hall, Inc., 1970.

HUGHES, MARION L., RICHARD M. SHANK, AND ELINOR S. STEIN, *Decision Tables,* Wayne, Pa.: Information Industries, Inc., 1968.

McDANIEL, HERMAN, ed., *Applications of Decision Tables,* Princeton, N.J.: Brandon/Systems Press, Inc., 1970.

FLOW CHARTING

Flow charts are diagrams representing sequencing of operations and flow of information. Elements or concepts are represented by standardized symbols and relationships by connecting lines. Flow charts are used in all phases of MIS design. They are referred to alternatively as block diagrams or logic diagrams.

Basic Purposes

Flow charts assist the problem solver by giving a simpler visual expression of complex system relationships. They may be used to check the logic of the system relationships. Flow charts facilitate communication between managers and between manager and specialist. They are used to document total system operations and procedures of human operators; flow charts are often incorporated in procedures by being referenced.

Levels of Flow Charts

The novice systems designer should recognize that differences in flow charts occur because of the level of detail (see Figure A-4).

> *Level 4:* system flow chart (alternatively called *run diagram, procedure chart, flow chart*). This chart links together aggregates such as systems or subsystems. They are useful in the first-step conceptualization of a total system. The system flow chart emphasizes *what* is involved in the system.
>
> *Level 3:* program flow chart (alternatively called a *flow chart, logic diagram, block diagram*). The program flow chart traces the flow of information and shows the structure of the system in terms of sequence of transactions. It amplifies on the level 4 diagram. This chart bridges the gap between manager and technician.
>
> *Level 2:* computer program flow chart (alternatively called *detailed program flow chart*). This chart shows the computer logic and represents an amplification of level 3. It is of primary interest to computer programmers and computer coders.

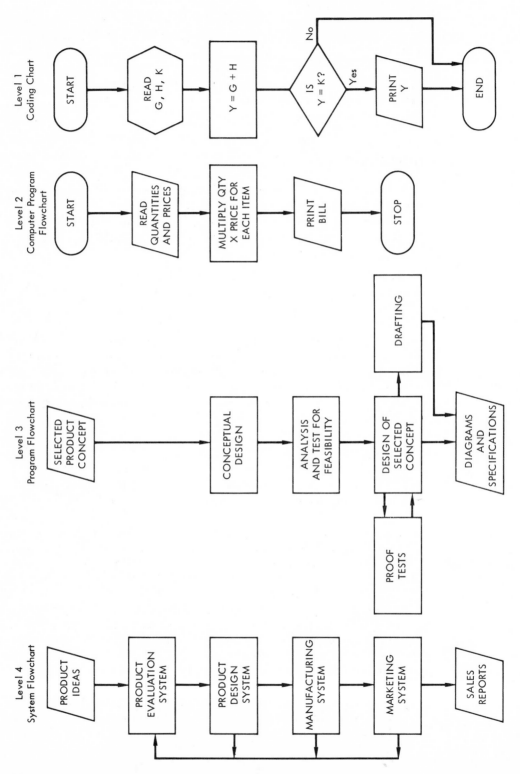

Figure A-4 Levels of flow charts.

Level 1: coding charts. These show the sequence of instructions that make up a computer program.

Types of Flow Charts

In essence, flow charts show activities, transactions, document flow, information flow, and/or organizations or managers involved.

An activity is usually understood to be an organizational task such as marketing, quality control, purchasing, consumer loan service, hospital admissions, warehousing, or building maintenance. A transaction is an elemental step such as editing, completing a form, accepting a payment, checking out supplies, or batching sales reports. A document may be a business form, report, book, manual, letter, memo, minutes of a meeting, or other written copy, and is often referred to as *hard copy.*

Flow charts appear to be commonly prepared according to these types:

1. Process flow charts to show the basic steps of operation, transportation, inspection, delay, and storage of both documents and materials (Figure A-5).
2. Activity flow charts, which show the sequencing and interrelationships of activities or subsystems (Figure A-6).
3. Data and document flow charts, which show the processing and transformation of data to different forms and formats (Figure A-7).
4. Information flow charts, which show managers and information they receive (and use) and the source of the information (Figure A-8).
5. Combinations of the above charts 2 through 4 (Figure A-9).
6. Computer programming (macro) charts (Figure A-10).
7. Computer coding (micro) charts (Figure A-11).

For the MIS designer concerned with the manager side of MIS, chart types 2, 3, 4, and 5, and particularly 4, are the most useful.

Flow-Chart Symbols

The reader should be warned that there is a lack of uniformity in the use of flow-chart symbols at each level. Often this is because the designer has failed to distinguish the level at which he wishes to diagram. In addition, special cases arise such as general purpose systems simulation (GPSS) wherein the symbols have complex or high-level significance yet are directly related to entry on the computer. GPSS flow charts actually overlap levels 3 and 2.

The International Standards Organization and the American National Standards Institute (ANSI) have established flow-chart symbol standards.[3]

[3]ANSI, *Standard Flowchart Symbols and Their Use in Information Processing,* X3.5, New York: American National Standards Institute, 1971.

FLOW PROCESS CHART

No. 765B

Page 1 of 1

	Present		Proposed		Difference	
	No	Time	No	Time	No	Time
Operations	4		2		2	
Transportations	4		2		2	
Inspections	2		1		1	
Delays	6		3		3	
Storages	0		0		0	
Distance Travelled	1560'		1525'		35'	

Job Complete Expense Acct.

Man ☐ Mat'l ☒ Form

Chart begins _____

Chart ends _____

Charted by _____ B. Davis

Date _____ 7/27

	OPER TRANS STORE INSP DELAY	Dist.	Time	~~(PRESENT)~~ Details of (PROPOSED) Method
1	○⇨△☐D			Expense account form written (4 copies) by employee
2	○⇨△☐D			In basket awaiting interoffice mail pickup
3	○⇨△☐D	1500'		To accounting office
4	○⇨△☐D			Waiting on accounting officer's desk
5	○⇨△☐D			Examined by accounting officer
6	○⇨△☐D			Approved by accounting officer
7	○⇨△☐D	25'		To accounting clerk's desk
8	○⇨△☐D			On desk waiting for preparation of check
9	○⇨△☐D			
10	○⇨△☐D			
11	○⇨△☐D			
12	○⇨△☐D			
13	○⇨△☐D			
14	○⇨△☐D			
15	○⇨△☐D			
16	○⇨△☐D			
17	○⇨△☐D			
18	○⇨△☐D			

COMMENTS:

Source: Arthur C. Laufer, *Operations Management*, Cincinnati, Ohio: South-Western Publishing Company, 1975, p. 306.

Figure A-5 Flow process chart for completing an expense account form.

The basic system flow chart and program flow-chart symbols are depicted in the figure at the top of page 263. Two additional symbols, which permit connecting a flow chart from one page to the next, are shown at the bottom of page 263. Additional and specialized symbols were

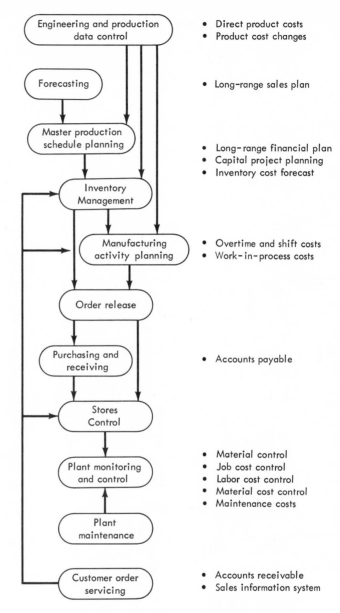

Source: *Communications Oriented Production Information System*, Vol. I, IBM, White Plains, N.Y., 1972, p. 68.

Figure A-6 Relationship of manufacturing systems to cost planning and control.

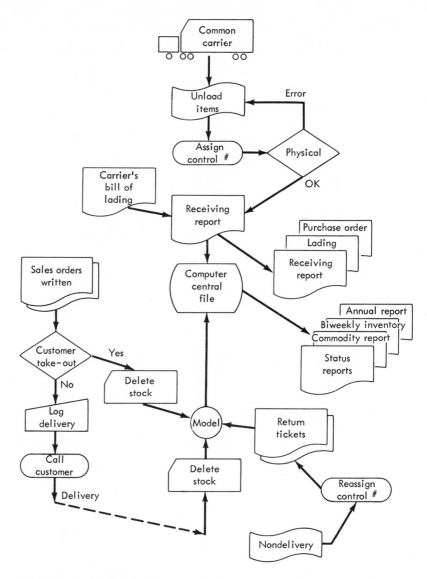

Figure A-7   Simplified work and paper flow.

shown earlier in Figure 7-9, flow-chart symbols.[4] These are adequate for the MIS designer. The important point is that *standardization within the company is essential.*

Guidelines to Flow Charting

The expert systems analyst will develop his own approach to creating flow charts. Flow charting is indeed a creative problem-solving

[4]For an extensive treatment of symbol definitions, see also Marilyn Bohl, *Flowcharting Techniques*, Chicago: Science Research Associates, 1971.

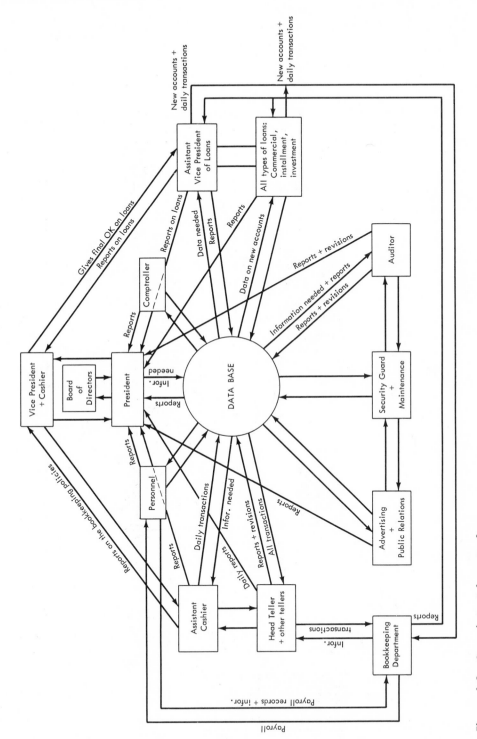

Figure A-8 Gross design information flow.

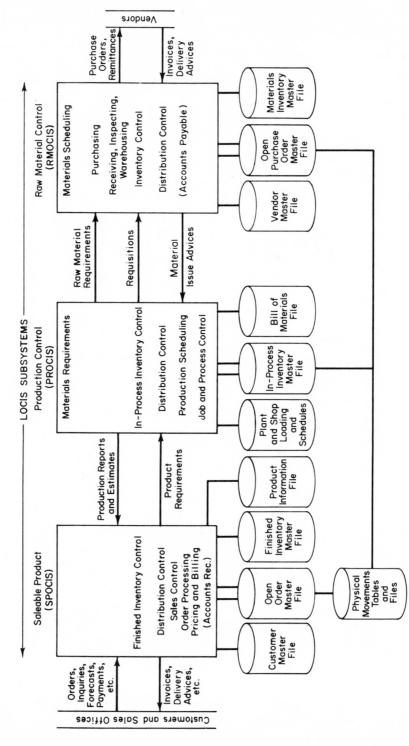

Source: Sherman C. Blumenthal, *Management Information Systems: A Framework for Planning and Development*, © 1969, p. 76. Reprinted by permission of Prentice-Hall, Inc., Englewood Cliffs, N.J.

Figure A-9 Logistics Operations Control Information System (LOCIS) (overall view).

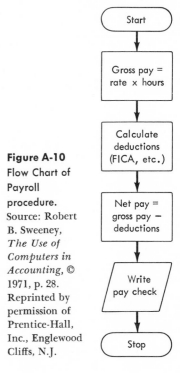

Figure A-10
Flow Chart of
Payroll
procedure.
Source: Robert
B. Sweeney,
*The Use of
Computers in
Accounting*, ©
1971, p. 28.
Reprinted by
permission of
Prentice-Hall,
Inc., Englewood
Cliffs, N.J.

process, so that no method can be completely prescribed. Some guidelines that may help the novice are

1. Establish the level at which you are going to flow-chart.
2. If a completely new system is being developed, start with a high level of aggregation and block out major subsystems.
3. Proceed from the known to the unknown. That is, identify subsystems that you know must appear and develop the subsystems that must relate to them.
4. Use standardized symbols and a template, plastic device with symbols cut out. Templates are available from computer vendors or office equipment stores.
5. Chart the main line of data flow in the system or program first.
6. Begin flow charting at the top of each page. The charts should run from top to bottom or left to right.
7. Each page should have a heading or caption that clearly identifies the project, the chart, the date (of revision, if any), the author, and the page number.
8. Write within the symbols, using as few words as possible. Use the annotation symbol to describe data more fully.
9. Collect incoming flows so that the flow lines shown actually entering a symbol are kept to a minimum—and similarly for outgoing flow lines.

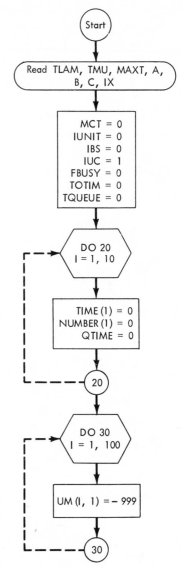

Figure A-11 Micro flow chart.
Source: Reproduced with permission from J. W. Schmidt and R. E. Taylor, *Simulation and Analysis of Industrial Systems*, Homewood, Ill.: Richard D. Irwin, Inc., 1970, jp. 381.

10. Leave blank space around major nonconvergent flows.
11. For many flow lines on complex charts, use connectors to reduce their number.
12. Avoid intersecting (crossover) flow lines.
13. Be neat. Put yourself in the place of the reader and ask if the diagram can be quickly and clearly read.

DATA BASE DEVELOPMENT AND MANAGEMENT

A true data base is a data storage and retrieval system that is efficient, rapid, capable of managing more data sets than conceivable for its

Input/Output	Process	Flowline	Annotation

application, and performs on an integrated nonredundant basis. The data base may be subdivided into levels as follows:

Data base: aggregate of files to meet MIS requirements.

File: related records or blocks.

Block: two or more records retained in a particular storage medium such as a file cabinet or computer tape.

Record: a collection of data elements related to a common identifier such as a person, machine, place, or operation.

Group: two or more data elements that are logically related and must appear together to form a complete unit of meaning (street number and name, first and last name of a person).

Data element: sometimes called *words, fields,* or *data items,* is the lowest level of the data structure and the only one with which a specific value may be associated. For example, age, part number, or department number are data elements, as are names or descriptions.

General Procedure for Data Base Development

Although it might appear logical to work down the data base hierarchy by first asking managers what information they need, the practical approach is somewhat different. We first study the data currently being gathered and then construct management's needs. Management's needs are thus determined by finding out what information they *think* they need and examining their use of information as presently available. Following this investigation, the systems analyst will then work with management to determine needed changes.

The first step in the investigation is to survey current files and record their characteristics. "Unofficial" files in individuals' desks or elsewhere should be sought. The analyst should design a form appropriate to his needs, but Figure A-12 illustrates the nature of such a form.

Connectors

Exit   Entrance

```
                        FILE DESCRIPTION SHEET


    System:_____        File Name: _____     File Number:_____


    Dept: _____        Storage Medium & Mode: _____
    _____

    Record Type _____     Maximum Length _____


    Block _____         Maximum Size _____
    _____

    No. of copies: _____      Usage/day: Average _____  Peek _____


    Reporting delay: _____     Labels: Header _____


                                                  Trailer _____


    Retention file: Period _____     Sequence _____
    _____

    Record volume estimates: Current _____ Projected _____


    Remarks: _____

             _____

    _____


                        SECURITY CLASSIFICATION

                        _____


                              Prepared by: _____ Date:_____
```

Figure A-12 File description sheet.

Once the files have been identified, described, and listed on a summary sheet, duplication of files may be determined. Standard nomenclature should be developed in records and data elements so that the data base may be developed without redundancy. The data elements must be identified and described, of course, on a suitable form for the particular company. Figure A-13 is suggestive of such a form.

File Characteristics

The design of the data base depends on characteristics of its files, some of which may not appear on the file description forms. Some of these characteristics are

Volatility: high rate of additions or deletions indicates a volatile file, and a low rate indicates a static file.

Activity: the number of records processed or updated during a single run through the file.

Permanence: master files are considered permanent files, while a transportation file (hours worked, orders completed, etc.) is a temporary file.

File size and record length: may be variable or fixed.

Inputs and outputs: type of source documents that supply inputs and type of outputs (media and form).

Response time: retrieval time.

Figure A-13   Data element description sheet.

```
                        DATA ELEMENT DESCRIPTION


System: _____   File Name:_____   File Number _____

Departments using data element: _____

Data Element: _____

Field Element: _____   Group Label: _____

Form: _____   Source: _____

Maximum Length (characters/Item Group) _____

Storage Medium _____

Update Frequency (approximately) _____

Update Procedure _____

_____

_____

Initial Value _____      Units _____



                        Prepared by: _____ Date: _____
```

Table A-5 File characteristics of a consulting firm, AD & B, Inc.

	Characteristic					
File	*Storage: Disc or File Cabinet*	*Input: Card or Manual*	*Update*	*Retention Rule*	*Disposal Method*	*Accessibility*
Job master	D	C	Weekly	Duration of job	Purge	Principals & managers
Payroll	D	C	Weekly	12 months	Purge	Principals
Accts payable	F	M	Monthly	Continuing	—	Principals & managers
Accts receivable	F	M	Monthly	Continuing	—	Principals & managers
Contracts	F	M	As required	Duration of job	Shred	All
Client pay file	F	M	Monthly	Duration of job	Shred	Principals & managers
Purchases	F	M	Monthly	Duration of job	Shred	Principals & managers
General accounting	F	M	Weekly	7 years	Shred	Principals & managers
Design	F	M	As needed	15 years	Shred	All
Shop drawings	F	M	As needed	15 years	Shred	All
Inspection	F	M	As needed	15 years	Shred	All

Currency: time between origination of event or data and its storage in the file.

Physical nature of the file: file cabinets, microfiche, magnetic tape, drum, card file, etc.

Cost and space

Methods of organization: sequential, partitioned, indexed sequential, direct or random, and list.

In the design of an MIS for a consulting engineering company, the file characteristics were expressed in the form of Table A-5.

SUMMARY

The problems of developing indices for large files have been complex and difficult in the past. The computer has changed the nature of the problems because it may conduct searches that were almost out of the question previously. At the same time, characteristics of the computer and related storage devices have introduced different problems. Although we have not discussed any of these problems, we have given a brief discussion of considerations for data base development and file organization that will extend the knowledge of the manager.

For the novice MIS analyst, the following references are suggested:

BINGHAM, J. E., AND G. W. P. DAVIES, *A Handbook of Systems Analysis,* New York: John Wiley & Sons, Inc., 1972.

CLARK, FRANK J., RONALD GALE, AND ROBERT GRAY, *Business Systems and Data Processing Procedures,* Englewood Cliffs, N.J.: Prentice-Hall, Inc., 1972.

HARTMAN, W., H. MATTHES, AND A. PROEME, *Management Information Systems Handbook,* New York: McGraw-Hill Book Company, 1968.

HARVISON, C. W., AND K. J. RADFORD, "Creating a Common Data Base," *Journal of Systems Management,* June 1970.

KINDRED, ALTON R., *Data Systems and Management,* Englewood Cliffs, N.J.: Prentice-Hall, Inc., 1973.

SALTON, GERARD, *Automatic Information Organization and Retrieval,* New York: McGraw-Hill Book Company, 1969.

DOCUMENTATION

Documentation is one of the most important steps in MIS design and is the one most inadequately performed. Documentation is the physical record, generally in written or printed form, describing the structure of, operation of, method for testing, and method for revising the MIS. It provides descriptions of the system from the most general nature down to the finest detail, if it is carried out properly. *The MIS has not been completely designed until the documentation has been completed.*

Purposes of Documentation

Documentation of the MIS may save a company hundreds of thousands of dollars. Some companies have depended on a key individual who has kept the information flows and programs in his head only to have him leave the company. The only choice of the company was then to restudy the entire system and document it or design a new system. Some of the reasons, then, that *good* documentation is important are

1. Turnover of key personnel. If the MIS designer failed to document the system or did an inadequate or piecemeal job, his successor must restudy the system to solve problems or make modifications.
2. The MIS will require modification, either for improvement or because of changing conditions. Even if there is no personnel turnover, it is very unlikely that systems analysts can retain all details of the MIS in their heads over a period of time.

3. The increasing complexity of the fourth- and fifth-generation computer systems and data transmission systems will require documentation so that the original systems designers will not have to keep refamiliarizing themselves with equipment as the MIS design progresses.

4. Equipment conversion will require new flow charts and new programs. Good documentation will make this much easier to carry out.

5. Documentation will reveal poor design features and lack of standards so that corrective action may be taken.

Specification, Standardization, Presentation, and Preservation

The four components of good documentation are specification, standardization, presentation, and preservation.

SPECIFICATION

Specification means a clear, sufficiently detailed description. At the beginning of the MIS design process, *performance* specifications are prepared that describe objectives of the system. During the detailed design process, *design* specifications should be prepared that describe the systems. Then *operating* specifications should be prepared that describe the functions and activities of personnel who run the system. Finally, *test* specifications describe the tests and their conduct for checking out the system.

STANDARDIZATION

The use of standardized procedures and standardized documentation provides a basis for clear, rapid communication, for less costly training of analysts, for reduced filing costs, and for assessing performance of the analysts and the MIS.

Standardization means that standard symbols are used in all flow charts, that procedures manuals are prepared to prescribe standardized MIS and operating procedures, and that standardized forms are used for documentation.

Sources of standards are

1. American National Standards Institute (ANSI) and International Standards Organization (ISO).

2. Industry users.

3. Manufacturers.

4. Published articles and books.

5. Internal company staff organizations.

Maintenance of standards is achieved by publication of a manual of standards and proper training and control.

Documentation

Documentation of the MIS should be combined into a *documentation manual*. Table A-6 suggests the possible contents of such a manual.

Table A-6 Documentation manual.

Topic	Purpose	Forms	Tables	Diagrams	Narrative
I. Total MIS					
A. System objectives	Defines what the system is supposed to achieve				X
B. Performance specifications	States each requirement of the system, preferably in quantitative terms		X		X
C. Conceptualization	Describes the gross design or arrangement of subsystems			X	X
D. System flow chart	Shows flow of information through the MIS as well as relationships with the operating systems			X	
E. Data base					
1. File organization	Describes the file organization and retrieval method	X			
2. Data element descriptions	Defines and describes data elements	X			
3. File interrelationships			X		
F. Model base description	Lists models, applications, and presents the models in detail		X		X
G. Output description	Describes the medium, the format, the frequency, and the uses of each MIS output	X	X	X	X
II. System operation					
A. Work flow chart	Shows the sequence of operations of the operating system and the forms that accompany the work from station to station			X	
B. Processing instructions	Gives step-by-step procedures for processing data before it goes into the computer, during, and after	X	X	X	X
C. Other instructions	Defines special actions required for MIS operations				X
III. Computer programs					
A. Identification	Shows program number and subsystem identification	X	X	X	

Topic	Purpose	Forms	Tables	Diagrams	Narrative
B. Input definition	Defines the medium (cards, tapes, optical reader, etc.) and formats of input	×	×		
C. Processing	Describes the computer logic for the MIS programs		×	×	
D. Output definition	Defines the medium and format of output reports and displays	×			×
IV. User's manual					
A. System description	Defines the objectives of the system, the arrangement of subsystems, and the general flow of work and information			×	×
B. Data preparation	Gives instructions on how to prepare and edit data entering the MIS		×		×
C. Error correction procedures	Explains how to correct errors made in operating the MIS that yield error messages			×	
D. Linear responsibility chart	Specifies the specific tasks and roles of each person in the MIS (in matrix form)			×	
E. Glossary of terms	Defines terms and abbreviations used in the MIS			×	

Table A-6 Documentation manual (cont'd)

The reasons for poor documentation stem from the attitude of management. When management constantly presses for new developments and new jobs, documentation receives a low priority. Documentation is a tedious detailed job at best, and systems designers are only too glad to turn to new, more exciting work. If management wants good documentation, it must rate the documentation manual as the completion event of design. Until the manual has been published, the MIS project manager must retain responsibility for an unfinished project.

Some suggested readings relating to documentation are

BINGHAM, J. E., AND G. W. P. DAVIES, *A Handbook of Systems Analysis*, New York: John Wiley & Sons, Inc., 1972.

MENKUS, BELDEN, "Defining Adequate Systems Documentation," *Journal of Systems Management*, Dec. 1970, pp. 16–21.

MILLER, FLOYD G., "Managing Forms," *Journal of Systems Management*, Aug. 1972, pp. 27–29.

MURDICK, ROBERT G., JOEL E. ROSS, AND JACK E. WESTMORELAND, "Linear Organization Chart Clears Away Confusion," *Journal of Systems Management*, Aug. 1971, pp. 23–25.

RUBIN, MARTIN L., *Introduction to the System Life Cycle*, Princeton, N.J.: Brandon/Systems Press, 1970.

SIMULATION

Simulation means to "make like" the real system in process, in the context of MIS. Simulation will not provide optimization except by trial and error. It will provide comparisons of alternative systems or show how a particular system works under specified conditions. It requires a representation of the system and/or a representation of the inputs to the system. Thus we can

1. Use the actual MIS and introduce the kind of job mixes and timings that we think will occur in actual practice. Representative job mixes are called *bench marks*.
2. Use the actual job mixes and timings and run them through a simplified version of the system, a portion of the system, or a computerized model of the system.
3. Use the kind of job mixes and timings we think will occur and run them through a computerized model.
4. Use extreme values of the job mix and run them through a computerized model.

In real life, we find that work (input) usually arrives in a random fashion. For example, invoices reach a clerk's desk or customer orders by the day. (An exception, of course, is the paced mass production line.) When it arrives at a desk or work station it must wait its turn in line to be serviced. Also, the length of time it takes a person or "work station" to service a work unit (such as preparing a customer's order or a purchase order, assembling a component, starting a computer run, or preparing a report) varies randomly. The complexity of many random arrivals and random transactions (servicings) in a system and the complex relationships with the system can be handled economically only with a computer.

Components of Simulation

Simulation depends on four basic concepts: probability distributions of arrivals of units to be serviced, probability of service times, a model that represents the flow of work and/or information, and a computer.

EXAMPLE

Now that we have told you how complex it is to simulate a system, we shall show you several simulations of a very simple system as done with pencil and paper. In practice, the computer may perform hundreds or thousands of simulations to obtain probability distributions of the output rate.

Probability for Number of Arrivals in a Time Period

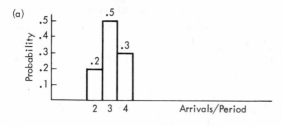

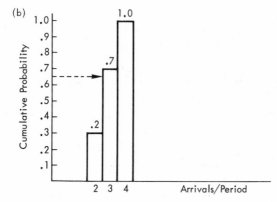

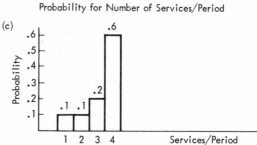

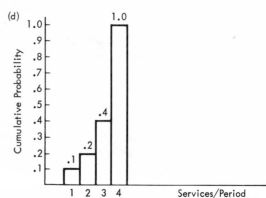

Figure A-14

Figure A-14(a) and (c) in our case are based on historical relative frequencies or estimates by the system designer. Figure A-14(b) and (d) are the corresponding cumulative probability distributions.

In our example, we assume that nothing happens in the first period as the employee sets up his work. The simulation procedure is as follows:

1. Set up table headings to represent the time and position characteristics of each item in the system as in Figure A-15.
2. Obtain a table of random numbers (found in most statistic texts or math tables). A portion of a table of such unrelated numbers is shown in Figure A-16.
3. Select a row and column, *and then* proceed to the RN table. We selected the first and second column to start and decided to read *down*. Enter the RN in the table representing the system. The number was 0.63 for the second column and 0.17 for the fourth column.
4. Go to the first cumulative probability chart (b); find 0.63 on the vertical scale. Draw a horizontal line to the bar it first meets. This is the three arrivals per period bar. Enter 3 in the table in the appropriate column.
5. Go to the second cumulative probability chart and find 0.17 on the vertical scale. Draw a horizontal line to the bar it first meets. This is the two units serviced per period bar. Enter 2 in the appropriate column in the table.
6. Units arriving minus units serviced in the period gives a surplus of one waiting to be serviced in the next period.
7. Repeat steps 3 through 5, keeping track of units left over to be serviced in each following period, *if any*.

Note that no matter how complex the system may be, simulation consists of examining the inputs, waiting lines, services, and output at one particular time period. Then the "clock" is moved up one time period, and the system is examined again. After hundreds of simulations, breakdowns in the system may be noted or average waiting periods or

Figure A-15 Simulation of customer order processing for three weeks.

Period	RN	Units Arriving During the Period	RN	Units Serviced During the Period*	Units in Line Waiting to be Serviced at End of Period
1	—	0	—	0	0
2	.63	3	.17	2	1
3	.87	4	.03	1	4
4	.11	2	.42	3	3

*These would proceed to the next station

5497	(6317)	5736	9468
0234	8703	2454	6094
9821	1142	6650	2749
9681	5613	9971	0081

Figure A-16   Portion of a table of random numbers.

average total service times through many different transactions may be found, or idle times may be noted.

Besides statistically varying inputs, systems designers like to know how the system will respond to sudden surges in the quantity of inputs (step functions), steady and more gradual increases in input (ramp functions), or oscillating inputs. Simulation may provide answers in all cases.

When inputs consist of representative job mixes, the simulation is called *bench-mark simulation.*

Advantages and Disadvantages

The advantages of simulation are

1. When a model has been constructed, it may be used over and over to analyze all kinds of different situations.
2. Simulation allows modeling of systems whose solutions are too complex to express by one or several grand mathematical relationships.
3. Simulation requires a much lower level of mathematical skill than do analytical (mathematical) models.
4. Simulation is usually cheaper than building the actual system and testing it in operation.

The distadvantages of simulation are

1. Simulation models may be very costly to construct and program for the computer.
2. Running a simulation program often requires hundreds of simulations and consequently much computer time. This may be very costly.
3. Because it is so easy to carry out the steps of developing a simulation model, people tend to employ simulation when analytic (mathematical modeling) techniques are better and more economical.

Simulation Languages

If a simulation of a system were to be programmed in FORTRAN, a great deal of effort would be required to include all the detail, much of the effort being repetitive in nature. Therefore, simulation languages have been developed that allow the system designer to write down *characteristics* of the system components so that the built-in computer program will take over from this description. Programming of elemental time steps is not required.

We present here only enough to give the reader the flavor of two of these languages. To know that they exist is enough to know to seek your local computer programmer.

GPSS

In GPSS (general purpose systems simulation), a system is described by terms of four types of entities:

1. Dynamic.
2. Statistical.
3. Equipment.
4. Operational.

Each entity is described by its own standard numerical attributes (SNA). For example, suppose a series of invoices arrive at the accounting department for processing and payment. These *dynamic* entities are described by *transit time* (accumulated time in the system waiting and being processed) and priority relative to others in the system. The accounting department is an *equipment* entity and is called a *facility*.

A simple queueing system is represented by the block diagram in Figure A-17. The first block indicates that the computer program will generate the arrival of invoices according to a uniform (equal) probability distribution with mean of 12 time periods and range of 12 ± 4 periods. Equally spaced arrival times or other probability functions may be specified in GPSS. In the second block, the invoice is told to enter waiting line 1. Block 3 tells the invoice to attempt to be serviced in FACILITY 1. When FACILITY 1 is available, the invoice departs from the waiting line as instructed by Block 4 and enters the FACILITY. Block 5, ADVANCE, provides the random time interval for servicing the invoice. Block 6 releases the FACILITY for further processing. Block 7 says to tabulate certain information that the user of the simulation desires and has previously specified on card 70. Finally, the transaction (invoice) is TERMINATED and leaves the system.

This example shows only a few of 43 specific block types available in GPSS.

SIMSCRIPT II

Simscript II is a language that is divided into essentially five levels. Level 1 is a very basic programming language for teaching programming concepts. The highest, level 5, introduces the simulation features such

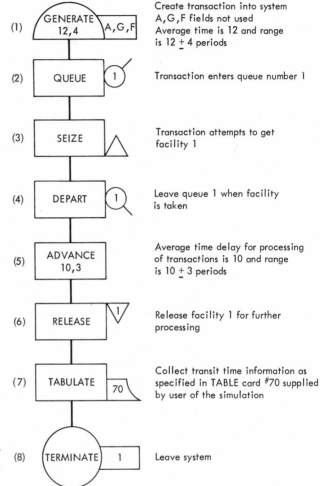

Figure A-17 GPSS flow chart of the system for processing an invoice.

as time-advance routines, event and activity processing, process generation, and accumulation and analysis of statistical information.

The concepts used in Simscript are

Entities: things that exist in the simulated world
  Temporary: such as a job that passes through for processing and then leaves the system
  Permanent: receipt times of a service facility, types of machines, types of personnel, etc.
Attributes: characteristics of entities such as number of each type of machine, age of each type of machine, number of each type of personnel
Sets: sets to which entities belong or are made up of

Events $\begin{cases} \textit{Exogenous} \text{ events that arise from outside the simulation process such as the addition of new machines into the system} \\ \textit{Endogenous} \text{ events, which are caused by prior occurrences in the simulation} \end{cases}$

A good introductory text on simulation is Geoffrey Gordon's *System Simulation* (Englewood Cliffs, N.J.: Prentice-Hall, Inc., 1969). More advanced texts are

KIVIAT P. J., R. VILLANUEVA, AND H. M. MARKOWITZ, *The Simscript II Programming Language*, Englewood Cliffs, N.J.: Prentice-Hall, Inc., 1969.

SCHMIDT, J. W., AND R. E. TAYLOR, *Simulation and Analysis of Industrial Systems*, Homewood, Ill.: Richard D. Irwin, 1970.

GPSS/360 *Introductory User's Manual*, IBM Corp., White Plains, N.Y.

GPSS/360 *User's Manual*, IBM Corp., White Plains, N.Y.

International
Medical
Instruments, Inc.

In late 1973, Robert F. Dobrynski, M.D., president of International Medical Instruments, Inc., called an emergency meeting of the executive committee. He was furious over the cancellation of a $60,000 order from a large soon-to-be-opened municipal hospital in Chicago. Among those reasons that were given for cancellation were late delivery dates, the large number of substitutions, and the fact that over 30% of the items had been marked "back-ordered" or "out of stock."

Dr. Dobrynski termed the loss of the order a "fiasco" and blamed it on a breakdown in the order processing system. He stated that the majority of the items were either in stock or expected shortly from production or outside suppliers.

After cooling down somewhat, Dr. Dobrynski concluded the meeting with the comment, "Some heads are going to roll if this happens again. We've got to clean up the order processing system and those others related to it, even if we have to get rid of that new computer and return to our old card system. Incidentally, I want full cooperation from everyone in helping Frank Bemis [the controller] install management information systems throughout the company."

The normal output from an executive committee meeting was an updated quarterly sales plan. The committee met monthly and was composed of

R. F. Dobrynski, M.D., president and treasurer

James Blackwell, Ph.D., director of research and engineering

Frank Bemis, C.P.A., controller

Solomon Katz, vice president, marketing

John Rogers, vice president, manufacturing

Robert Dobrynski

After Robert Dobrynski was graduated from medical school in 1946, his interests quickly turned to research and medical administration rather than medical practice. He founded the company in 1949 to provide a source of high-quality, dependable, medically related research and diagnostic equipment. Over the intervening years he maintained that same basic product strategy but became more businessman than medical doctor. He was particularly frustrated that increasing sales accompanied by increasing size and complexity had made the management of the firm so difficult and time-consuming.

Dr. Dobrynski saw his problems as threefold. First, he felt that he was unable to set a long-term course of action because of outside events (customers, markets, technology, economy, etc.) over which he had no control. Second, he could not get his directors and vice presidents to act as a team. "Synergism" was his favorite managerial expression, but he was unable to achieve integration between people and operations. Third, he felt that the work force was unwilling to perform because of lack of motivation. He was particularly annoyed that policies and plans were not always adhered to.

Dr. Dobrynski had attended a three-day manufacturer's seminar on computers in late 1972 and had returned with enthusiasm for MISs. For about a month he took an active hand in planning for the design and installation of management information systems, but more pressing matters had diverted his attention. Shortly thereafter he delegated the entire operation to Frank Bemis. Although Dr. Dobrynski retained the title of president and treasurer, the majority of the work in the treasurer's department was supervised by Bemis.

Frank Bemis

Frank Bemis was first employed by the company in 1949 as a bookkeeper. Through attendance at evening college classes he passed the C.P.A. examination in 1958. After an abortive effort to begin his own accounting firm he returned to the company in 1962 and in 1970 was appointed controller. Frank was a walking encyclopedia of company financial information, and he was familiar with every facet of operations. He frequently stated that accounting information was the backbone of the company and that his procedures were to be strictly followed at all costs. His primary concern was the cost variance report, and he tended to view the preparation of this report as his objective rather than the utilization of the report to reduce costs. Because he was so quick to produce financial data, other department heads tended to be slack in this regard.

Jim Blackwell

Jim Blackwell was co-founder of the company along with Dr. Dobrynski. He received his Ph.D. from M.I.T. in 1947 and shortly thereafter began the association that led to the company's founding. Blackwell, an introvert and by nature quiet and withdrawn, was interested solely in the more esoteric aspects of his engineering task. Consequently, much of the success of the company could be attributed to his excellent design talent.

Sol Katz

Sol Katz had been the number one district sales manager and before that the number one salesman. He was sometimes described as a "born salesman." Although Katz did have an excellent talent for the sales management function, he admitted to deficiencies in the headquarters functions of research, advertising, and the duties associated with warehousing and inventory.

Katz had very recently taken over the job of vice president in marketing, having been promoted from head of the New York district. He therefore felt that the loss of the $60,000 order and the performance of the order processing system was not entirely his fault. Moreover, in view of his short tenure at Stoughton headquarters, he felt he could be somewhat more critical of company operations than other executives.

John Rogers

John Rogers was an industrial engineer who had come with the company upon graduation from college in 1965. He was promoted to vice president in 1970. Hard work was his most noticeable attribute. He could be found either on the shop floor or in his office overlooking the shop floor from 7:00 A.M. to 7:00 P.M. It was a common practice for Rogers to join a production crew in order to demonstrate an unfamiliar method or procedure.

COMPANY BACKGROUND

International Medical Instruments (IMI) had been founded in 1949 in Stoughton, Massachusetts, by a small group of physicians and engineers. These men had a great deal of interest in the research and development of hospital and laboratory equipment and enjoyed a personal relationship dating back to college and medical school days. Except for

Dr. Dobrynski and Mr. Blackwell, the original founders had retired but remained stockholders. The original objective of the firm was to develop research and laboratory equipment, to produce the most modern microscopes available, and in general to improve significantly the quality of the laboratory research devices available to clinics, laboratories, hospitals, and universities.

During the first decade of its existence, the company enjoyed growth and prosperity, owing in large measure to the uniqueness of its products and the absence of significant competition. However, beginning in the early 1960s, competition grew as additional firms entered the industry. Among these were Beckman Optical Equipment Corporation, Littman Medical Supply Company, Perkins and Elmer Laboratory Equipment Company, and Bausch & Lomb Optical Company.

In 1969 the company acquired (through an exchange of stock) the Medical Science Instrument Corporation of Stoughton, Massachusetts, whose principal products were disposable laboratory and hospital supplies.

The operations of that company were subsequently merged into those of the parent company, and the combined operation utilized the same manufacturing facility, sales force, and other resources. The acquisition of this company also gave IMI additional product lines as well as additional engineering and research capability.

Growth in sales continued on an upward trend throughout the history of the company and by 1974 had reached a level of over $17 million. Despite this sales growth, there was not a corresponding growth in profits. Indeed, earnings after taxes had declined from a level of over $1 million ($2.50 to $3.00 per share) in the late 1960s to about $600,000 by 1973 ($1.00 per share after "dilution" by stock dividends). This decline was termed "alarming" by Dr. Dobrynski, who blamed declining profits on the inability to control costs. Profit planning existed in the company, but it was a major source of frustration for Dr. Dobrynski. Sales forecasts were made annually and updated monthly. Generally, these forecasts were met. However, it was in the area of cost control that the need for improvement was evident. When costs exceeded plan, as they often did, it was practically impossible to trace the variance to specific products or departments. Inventory control was a constant headache.

The company had four basic sources of revenue:

1. The established line of electron microscopes and standard inventory products such as electroencephalographs, blood reagent equipment, and flame photometers. This was the basic product line that the company emphasized, and it yielded the majority of revenue.
2. The high-volume laboratory supplies that have a high demand owing to their disposable features (syringes, laboratory glasswares, specimen containers, etc.). This was the basic product line of the acquired Medical Science Instrument Corporation. Since the acquisition of that company this basic product line, laboratory supplier, had suffered significantly in sales and profits. Two reasons were

given for this. First, sales volume was not large enough to offset the cost of small production runs, the proliferation of unprofitable products, the ready availability of the products elsewhere, and the fact that this type of product was foreign to the market strategy of IMI. Slowly but perceptibly the company began to purchase these items from outside vendors for resale rather than manufacture them. It was almost impossible to make a profit under these circumstances. In 1974 the line was viewed as a convenience to customers rather than a major product line.

3. The sale of spare and replacement parts to existing customers. This market will continue to grow in proportion to the sale of major equipment.

4. The design and manufacture of specially engineered products in response to requests from customers. This source had been rising at a rate of approximately 20% annually in recent years. Profits realized on these units are presumed to be substantially lower than on production-line products and spare or replacement parts; therefore, marketing efforts are not concentrated on products of this type. Replacement parts are expected to be profitable despite the difficulty of forecasting any level of sales. Unfortunately, adequate records of prior sales of parent equipment were not maintained.

Although no formal organization chart or position descriptions existed, the general organizational and reporting relationships are as shown in Exhibit 1.

DATA PROCESSING DEPARTMENT

This group had only recently been formed. Prior to 1972 it had been called the Accounting Machines Group. The new name presumably was granted to indicate a higher degree of status and responsibility upon the recent installation of an IBM System/3 Model 6 Card System with 8K internal storage. Prior to that time the department had made the usual progression from unit record equipment to electronic accounting machine systems. Configuration of the new equipment included

3 IBM 5496 Keypunches
3 IBM 5496 Verifiers
1 IBM 5486 Sorter
2 IBM 5424 Multifunction Card Units
1 IBM 5406 CPU with Console Keyboard
1 IBM 5444 Disc Storage Drive (Model 2)
1 IBM 5213 Printer (Model 2)

Although for organizational purposes the department was assigned to Frank Bemis, the controller, he was largely unconcerned with the

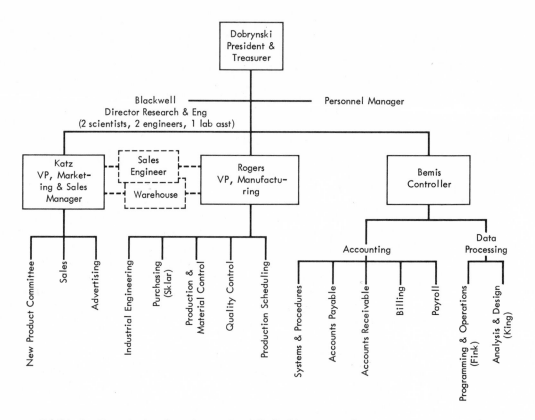

Exhibit 1   Organization chart—International Medical Instruments, Inc.

operation of the computer center except for the accounting applications of the accounts payable, general ledger, and accounts receivable. Indeed, except for one or two abortive attempts at sophisticated inventory control and sales analysis systems, the accounting applications made up the overwhelming usage of the old and the new computer hardware.

Immediately after the executive committee meeting when the president threatened that "some heads might roll," Frank Bemis felt that he was in a dilemma. On the one hand, he could feel the increasing operational pressures that demanded better information systems; on the other, he was uncomfortable in the knowledge that neither he nor Otto Fink (data processing manager) had the requisite background to oversee the design of these systems. Otto Fink had earned his job and title through diligent programming and operating efforts, but he knew little of the managerial decision-making needs of the company.

Bemis solved his problem, at least in the short run, by reorganizing the Data Processing Department. He placed himself at the head of the department and split the operation into two sections: programming and operating, and analysis and design.

As head of the analysis and design section, Bemis chose Bill King, a recently recruited young man who had just received his M.B.A. degree from a local Boston university. Although Bill King had no previous computer experience of an operational nature, he had taken several computer courses in college and had attended a short course on the IBM System/3. Moreover, Bemis concluded that King's general management background and his exposure to the company through his financial analysis experience would qualify him to take charge of companywide management information systems. Accordingly, Bemis transferred King to the job with instructions to "come up with a master plan in about five or six weeks."

King's Preliminary Study

King had already organized in his mind a tentative plan for the design and implementation of high-priority systems. He decided that he needed more operational details, so he scheduled appointments with various department heads and supervisors throughout the company. In preparation for these interviews he planned to observe operations and carefully review the documentation of systems and procedures in each department. After commencing his review, he was shocked to discover that documentation was either nonexistent or badly out of date. Procedures manuals were not updated, and system descriptions and flow charts did not exist for most systems.

Of particular concern to King was the fact that forms for initiating action were generally nonexistent, not used, or obsolete. Communications were often made by phone and followed up by handwritten memos without copies to all interested parties. Rarely were tickler files or follow-up files maintained on these memos or on other informal communications.

Personnel

Dr. Jerry Boffo, 48, was personnel manager and an administrative assistant to Dobrynski. Boffo was former dean of a small obscure school of business. His undergraduate training had been in accounting, although his terminal degree was Doctor of Education. He had intuitively felt that IMI should be reorganized and was glad that Bill King had taken the initiative on this.

He told Bill King, "We've got a great management team here. It's just that some of us seem to be going off in different directions. Also, I'd like to see an information system that would provide me with background information on all employees so that I could work up a training program."

Marketing

Marketing was organized into three departments: sales, advertising, and market research. The latter department was not really staffed but consisted of an interdepartmental "new products" committee whose job it was to discover and evaluate new product opportunities and follow up on design and sales. The sales department was also responsible for customer order processing. This function operated against the finished goods warehouse inventory, the special order section of manufacturing (for special customer's orders), and the resale warehouse inventory stocked from outside purchases. Sales also maintained a credit check activity and finished goods inventory records in order that the sales force could keep fully advised on product availability and relay product demand shifts quickly to the manufacturing department. Warehousing was a department reporting to sales manager for standard inventory (manufactured) items and to purchasing for disposable laboratory supplies and resale items.

Sol Katz was the vice president of marketing and also the general sales manager. The sales force was comprised of 68 salaried salesmen in the sales districts at Miami, St. Louis, San Francisco, New Orleans, and New York. The company also uses its research and development center at Stoughton, Massachusetts, and the main manufacturing plant to good advantage in the sales effort. Prospective customers visiting these locations gain a better appreciation of the products and are better able to verify for themselves their quality. Very often, purchasing agents, pathologists, clinical laboratory technicians, and pharmacologists visit the factory and the R&D center for the purpose of investigating innovative technology in the field of medical or medically related research devices. Moreover, ideas for new products are frequently obtained from these visitors.

Since its founding, the company had maintained a policy of building superior products. Stringent quality controls were maintained and this aspect was widely advertised in trade and professional journals. Although a substantial advertising budget (3% of gross sales) was utilized, the effectiveness of this advertising was open to question.

Sales of replacement parts, a growing source of revenue, were normally handled by a telephone call or on a mail-out basis as the customer needed the part. This portion of total sales was beginning to increase as the age and number of units in use increased. The company generally viewed this source of sales as a convenience to customers rather than as a primary profit item. Because there was no catalog or standardized inventory listing of these replacement parts, sales of these items caused considerable inconvenience and cost in terms of time necessary to process and locate the order. The number of parts stocked was about 1200.

Another growing segment of sales was that of custom-designed units, manufactured to meet the particular needs and specifications of research institutions and other customers needing one-of-a-kind products. The company had not generally been able to ascertain development and production costs on items of this nature and as a result did not devote active sales effort to their marketing. Distribution of such units was handled by the sales engineer from the production plant at Stoughton. It was believed by some managers that custom-designed units could represent a significant portion of total revenue, but the absence of development and design costs, in particular, made this a difficult fact to prove.

Growth patterns in sales, inventory, orders, and type of customers can be summarized as shown in the accompanying table.

Sales to hospitals, universities, and independent laboratories and clinics were made at list price less the usual time discount. Sales to supply warehouses and wholesale firms were made at list price less 40% on laboratory supplies. There were few occasions to sell standard inventory products through this outlet, and it was not the policy of the company to do so.

KING'S INVESTIGATION

Bill King decided to start his investigation by having an informal discussion with Katz. He made no formal appointment, nor did he prepare a structured plan for an interview.

After King introduced himself to Katz and explained the purpose of his visit, Katz, without further prompting, launched into his analysis:

"Listen kid, I'm all for you and Frank Bemis and your problems with the computer. And I don't blame Dobrynski for losing his cool

Historical and estimated growth.

	1960	1970	1973	1978
Sales ($mil.)	1.2	9.7	17.8	35.0
Suppliers	84	198	250	350
Purchase orders	185	560	920	1700
(average monthly)				
Customers				
Hospitals			1232	2000
Schools & universities			437	500
Supply warehouses & wholesale			86	100
Independent labs			427	1600
Government (federal and other)			26	40
Items (sale)				
Standard inventory products 34		46	68	100
Laboratory supplies		962	852	500
Replacement parts			Unknown	
Custom-engineered		540	620	2000
Sales breakdown ($mil.)				
Standard inventory products			11.6	
Laboratory supplies			4.7	
Replacement parts			0.3	
Custom-engineered			1.2	

about the lost order. How can we improve sales and profits with information systems that perform like our order-processing did? Some system!

"You ask me about my problems and what information needs I have for solving them. Well, some of my problems can't be helped by the computer and some can. It can't get me a higher advertising budget, it can't get me a better sales training program, and it can't get my sales force off the dime so they can uncover more customers. On the other hand, let me tell you how it can help.

"First, you can give me a sales analysis system so I can find out who our customers are, where they are located, and which ones are profitable. This applies likewise to inventory analysis. How many items are moving? Which are profitable? Which items and lines should be dropped and which should be given sales effort? I think we should stop selling to wholesalers or raise the price to them. I'm not sure that pricing at 40% off list is making us a dime. Besides, why can't we get those customers for ourselves?

"And what about our inventory control system? I think we could cut our inventory and at the same time improve customer service with proper inventory management. Let me add also that improvement of that system would also give us a catalogue we could trust. You won't believe this but I had to "borrow"—physically borrow—stock from two of our good customers this month to satisfy a high-priority sales demand that the warehouse said was out of stock. And while we're on warehousing, let me put in a complaint about that operation. It's in my area of responsibility, but their performance is getting embarrassing to our selling effort because of delays. The order pickers sometimes have to go to two or more locations to find stock, and then it sits around the warehouse waiting for the necessary paper work.

"Incidentally, before you do any final implementation of any management information systems, you might want to check back with me. I am now engaged in a rather comprehensive research effort to determine both the size and composition of our future sales. We aren't getting our share of industry sales in a growth industry. I think both our product mix and our customer mix is not only going to grow but it is going to change. These changes might affect the nature of your computer systems.

"Another comment. When you get around to investigating production control, I wish you could help the sales department get some information on a customer's order. From what we know of production, once a customer's order enters the manufacturing stream it's lost as far as identification and progress reporting is concerned. What do I say to a customer who wants a progress report? Or how do I find an item that gets set aside halfway through production and is forgotten?

"O.K. This will give you an idea of our problems. If I were you I would begin with order processing. This is our major bottleneck, and there's no excuse for the paper-work delays we are having. I know that order processing is my responsibility, but we've been putting out so many brushfires lately and answering so many customer complaints that the marketing department hasn't had time to revise the system."

Following this conversation with Sol Katz, Bill King began his investigation of the order processing subsystem. In his view this system was a logical starting point because it was not only causing immediate problems but it also interacted with so many additional subsystems in the company.

His initial step in the analysis of the order processing system was to try to unravel the "fiasco" on the $60,000 order from the Chicago hospital. After a day or two he was able to piece together the causes. He reviewed these in his mind:

1. The system was not organized to handle a large, out-of-the-ordinary "crash" order. The total paper-work time devoted to the Chicago order was 18 working days. This appeared to be their normal processing time, and the emergency nature of this large order did not give it any special attention.

2. The order had arrived in standard purchasing order form, and the order-entry clerk had made a substantial number of errors in transcribing the information to the sales order form. Numerous stock numbers and descriptions required clarification on the order, but subsequent editing did not correct the mistakes.

3. The errors on the sales order form that was prepared by the order-entry group were not subsequently checked by the warehouse. Any discrepancies or unclear items were marked "back-ordered," "not in stock," whereas later checks showed that many were in stock. Additionally, storage in the warehouse was in disarray, and some items could not be located even though they were in stock.

4. The customer was a municipal hospital and therefore entitled to the government discount. Not only was the discount not computed, but the order processing system wasted four days getting credit approval because no credit file was available. To make matters worse, the items were shipped to the downtown city office that prepared the purchase order and not to the hospital.

5. In terms of dollar value, about one-third of the items on the order were in production, but there was no procedure to inform a customer of delivery estimates on items that were not in finished goods inventory.

6. A number of the out-of-stock items were filled with acceptable substitutes, but prices were not changed on the customer's invoice.

It took Bill King two weeks to complete his preliminary study. After two weeks he was able to write the following descriptions:

Order Processing System (Marketing Responsibility)

Orders are received by mail and phone at the Stoughton plant (90,000 per year) by the *order-entry group*. Both salesmen and customers initiate orders by telephone, telegram, or mail. Orders are sometimes delivered by customers and salesmen at the plant. Regardless of the source, the order-entry group prepares a sales order form from the information received. Each order received is stamped with the time of receipt and entered in the sales order log. The purpose of this log is to determine the elapsed time between order receipt and shipment. A similar shipment log is maintained in shipping so that elapsed time can be determined at any time on any order or combination of orders.

After preparation, a number of editing operations are performed on the sales order form. First, it is given a credit check, utilizing the customer credit file. Second, the order is edited for clarification of product description, quantities, price, and customer code. For this purpose the order is compared against the company catalog, price list, and customer list. A third check involves the billing and shipping addresses. These are verified by comparing them with the master customer file.

Because so many delays and errors in order processing had been traced to the edit procedure, the marketing department had taken the trouble to write a detailed procedure (Exhibit 2) for that operation. An additional purpose of the procedure was to test it for the proposed automation of order processing. In conjunction with the proposed procedure, a new product/customer code system had been devised. The format for these codes was constructed as shown in Exhibit 3.

After editing, the sales order form is forwarded to the warehouse. Here the order is passed to the inventory clerk, who reduces the perpetual inventory record balance. If an item is out of stock, the ordered item is marked "BO" (for back-ordered, on the sales order form). The sales order form then goes to the data processing department, where a copy of it is made. This copy is sent back to the warehouse, where it is filed in the warehouse sales order file pending return of the sales order from data processing (following key punching and processing).

The data processing department keypunches detail cards and merges them with the customer master record cards to produce the six-part customer's invoice. This is done by sorting, collating, listing, and tabulating on the System/3. Upon completion of the six-part customer's invoice (shipping order) it is distributed—the original is sent to the accounting department. The first copy is for the salesman; the second copy is for the customer; and the third copy is for the order follow-up section. The fourth copy serves as a delivery receipt and the fifth copy as a shipping label. The format of the customer's invoice (shipping order) is shown in Exhibit 4. Copies 2, 3, 4, and 5 are sent to the "order picker" at the warehouse.

The warehouse order picker selects the item(s) ordered and delivers the items and the shipping order to the shipping department. The top invoice copy (the second copy of the original set) is detached and placed in an envelope marked "invoices inside," and the envelope is stapled be-

Sales Dept, Order-Entry Group	June 13, 1973	Copy to: Warehouse, Purchasing
SUBJECT: Order Processing Procedure (Edit Procedure)		

Purpose:	Detail the procedure to be followed in editing a Sales Order prior to submission to the warehouse.
Scope:	This procedure applies to all sections and departs involved in the order processing, warehousing, EDP, billing, and accounts receivable functions.
Form:	Sales Order Form (IMI S-23-73)
Responsibility:	ACTION
Sales Order Edit Clerk	1. Receive all orders from the Order-Entry Group

2. Edit all orders for presence, completeness, and organization the following entries:

    1. Credit--compare credit against Customer Credit File for:

        (a) Credit limitation compared with total value of order.

        (b) Credit limitation compared with total value of order and accounts receivable outstanding.

3. If credit limitation is exceeded or questionable, refer the sales order to the Sales Department.

4.   etc.   etc.   etc.   etc.

Exhibit 2 Procedure for order processing.

hind the invoice set. The date, time, and routing are stamped on the shipping label (the fifth copy), and a bill of lading is typed. The third copy of the shipping order is sent to "order follow-up." The price is blanked out on this copy.

Exhibit 3 Organization of product/customer codes.

CODE	*Product Code*	*REQUIREMENT*
99	Manufacturer	00 is assigned to the item if manufactured by International Medical Instruments, Inc. Other codes 01–99 are assigned to manufacturers (vendors) of resale items.
999	Product class (and location	Codes 00–50 assigned to IMI product lines manufactured by company. Codes 51-99 assigned to resale items. The third digit of the code indicates one of nine storage locations in the warehouse.
1234 . . . 90	Manufacturer's description and stock number	This ten-digit number is assigned by the manufacturer. For IMI products the assignment is: ×××× (IMICO), ×× (Product Class), and ××× (stock number of the item within the product class).
9	Special code	For product line.
999	Product number	Number assigned to product within the product line 001–999.
9		This last digit is reserved for future classification use.
	Customer Code	
××××	First four letters of customer's name abbreviated	Example: General Hospital Supply (GHSU).
××	Chronological customer number with first letter of name	Example: GHSU76 identify General Hospital Supply as the 76th Customer in the G's.
×	Customer Code	Nine classes of customers ranging from 0 (hospitals) to 9 (government).
×××××××	Customer number	First five numbers identifies zip code. Sixth number is "sold to" or "bill to" code and seventh number of "ship to" code.
×	Reserved	Presently unused but reserved for future classification and use.

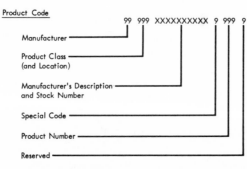

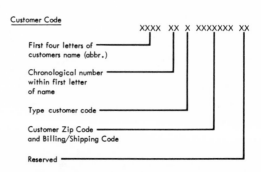

INTERNATIONAL MEDICAL INSTRUMENTS, INC.

68 Broad Street

Stoughton, Massachusetts   Tel: (202) 624-7564

Customer No.————————————

Date————————————

Invoice No.————————————

Salesman————————————

Quantity		Description	Unit Price	Total	Shipping Costs	Total
B/O	Ship'd					

SHIP TO:

IMI S-23-73   CUSTOMER COPY

Exhibit 4   Customer's invoice & shipping order.

In the order follow-up section the invoices are separated into two batches: (1) completed orders, which are filed in the closed-order file, and (2) incomplete orders, which are filed sequentially by order number in the open-order file (OOF).

As back-ordered goods are received, they are sent to the warehouse (from the receiving department if inside the company as a result of the back order purchase request or from the manufacturing department if manufactured in the company's manufacturing facilities as a result of the back order production request). When merchandise arrives from either source it is checked against purchase orders, purchase requests, and manufacturing requests, and the warehouse receiving clerk notifies the order follow-up section. The open-order file is then searched for back-ordered items by a follow-up clerk, and a new sales order is prepared for those items now available. This sales order is sent to the data processing department and is processed the same as a new, completely edited sales order.

In addition to preparing a new order for the back-ordered items, the old back order is placed in the closed-order file if the items completely fill the back order. If not, the open-order file copy is appropriately annotated with information concerning receipt of the partial order and is refiled.

The data processing department is also responsible for preparing two daily reports: (1) the back order production request for items to be produced in manufacturing, and (2) the back order purchase request for items to be purchased. The former goes to the production control department and the latter to the purchasing department. Copies of both go to the warehouse and to the order follow-up group.

Standard computer center controls have existed for some time for the engineering and materials operations. Otto Fink has made no plans for additional controls for the forthcoming conversion of manual systems and design of new ones.

Purchasing System (Manufacturing Responsibility)

Requisitions are received in the purchasing department from four sources. The first of these is the warehouse where stock records and inventory control of "stock" or "outside purchased" material is maintained. The second source is from manufacturing and materials control, where stock records and inventory control of raw materials for manufactured items are maintained. Third, R&D and engineering may order equipment, instruments, and supplies. Fourth, each department places orders for office supplies.

Requisitions are received in purchasing by a clerk, who arranges them by general category of buyer specialization and distributes them to the buyers. After editing the requisitions for correctness and completeness, the buyers refer to a manual vendor's historical file that is maintained by part number, price, and vendor information. If the last purchase for a specific item was more than six months ago, the buyer contacts one or more suppliers to verify price and delivery date. In most cases the delivery date agreed upon is within the safety stock level (30 days) of raw materials and stock items for resale. If the item exceeds $1000, three bids are obtained. After the buyer selects a vendor he indicates the necessary information on the requisition, which is then passed to a typist for the creation of a purchase order. In general, there is one purchase order prepared for each requisition. After the buyer edits and signs the purchase order, copies go to a clerk for mailing to the vendor, filing of a copy with the requisition in an open-order file for follow-up, a copy to the warehouse, and a copy to materials control in manufacturing.

Upon receipt of the material by receiving, the material is inspected and sent to manufacturing and materials control or the warehouse, depending on the nature of the items (for manufacturing or for stock resale). Receiving prepares a receiving report, attaches the vendor shipping documents, and sends copies of these forms to purchasing for closing of the open-order file and to accounts payable for payment. Purchasing also uses this form to update the vendor performance history. The basic system is shown in Exhibit 5.

Bill King's preliminary analysis of the purchasing function indicated a number of potentially dangerous problems. First, materials were coming in late. A quick review of three months' prior receipts (taken from the monthly materials inspection report) indicated that of 1920 requisitions, 20% had been received late, 12% had either shortages or overages, and 4% of shipments had to be rejected in whole or in part because of quality inspections. Moreover, there was a constant backlog of requisitions that had not yet been converted to purchase orders. The average time between the receipt of a requisition and the preparation of a purchase order was 13 days.

A quick survey of purchasing operations for the previous month yielded the following statistics:

1. 724 requisitions resulted in 832 purchase orders valued at $560 thousand.
2. Over half of the purchase orders were valued at less than $50.
3. More than 15% of the items were ordered more than once per month, and about half of these were ordered weekly.

Al Sklar, the purchasing manager, attributed his problem to "understaffing." He constantly reminded Bill King that "we can't get the work out with the people we've got." He also concluded that his work would be made much easier if requisitions were better prepared before they reached purchasing and if people would stop requesting emergency purchases that interrupted the routine of his department.

Sklar's annual budget was $65,000, of which $61,000 went to pay the salaries of himself, three buyers, and three clerical personnel.

Al Sklar reported to John Rogers, vice president of manufacturing and operations. In a brief interview with Rogers, Bill King elicited the following summary about the problems in purchasing:

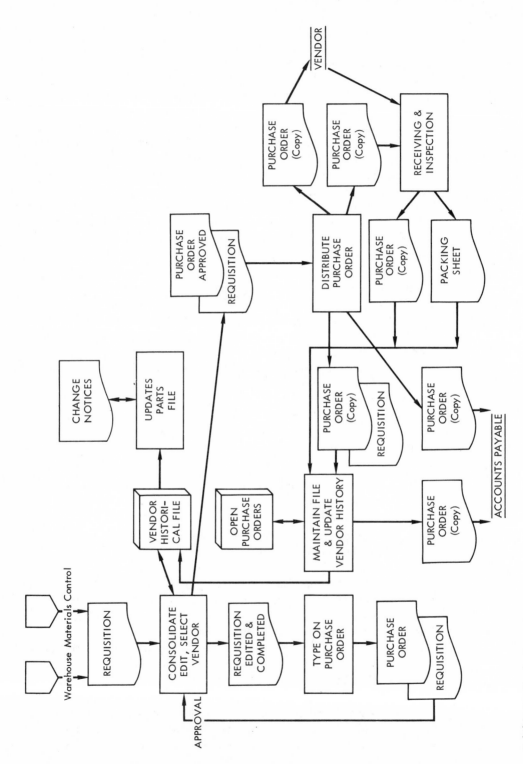

Exhibit 5 Purchasing system.

"Of course, they have problems in purchasing. But it's not all their fault. We've got to get after the fundamental causes, and I see these as three.

"First, we have lousy inventory control. If we could set good inventory levels and order quantities, we wouldn't be preparing the nickel and dime requisitions so frequently, and requisitions could be consolidated.

"Next, there's the engineering bill of materials. In a complex business such as ours with constantly changing products and technical specifications, it's almost impossible to establish adequate materials forecasting and control. This results in a lot of nonroutine and emergency requisitioning.

"Then there's the way we are organized. I'm in charge of manufacturing and naturally am in the best position to manage the raw materials inventory. But what do I know about the stock items that we purchase for resale? Maybe we should give that to marketing for forming a separate operation of some kind.

"Finally, the main problem as I see it is that those purchasing guys are so busy in the nit-picking paper work of order preparation and follow-up that they don't have time to do their sourcing job of seeking competitive bids, researching new materials, and seeking new sources."

The record descriptions of requisition, buyer's historical file, and purchase order are shown in Exhibit 6.

Despite what Sklar and Rogers had said, Bill King had a different view of the problems in purchasing. In a memorandum documenting what he had learned of the system he summarized his feelings on the objectives of any redesigned purchasing system:

Exhibit 6   Record descriptions: purchasing inputs/files/outputs.

Requisition	*Buyer's Historical File*	*Purchase Order*
1. Date	1. Part/assembly number	1. Date
2. Part number/assembly	2. Part description	2. Ship to
3. Part description	3. ID number of vendor	3. Terms of payment
4. Quantity desired	Name	4. Date delivery
5. Date required	Address	desired
6. Manufacturing or	4. Last price and	5. Quantity
stock	date of last price	6. Description
	5. Quantity discounts	7. Price
	6. Delivery time	8. Traffic routing
	7. Dates ordered	
	Items 3 through 7	
	are repeated for	
	second vendor.	
	Items 3 through 7	
	are repeated for	
	third vendor.	

1. Maintenance of an easily referenced vendor history file.
2. Evaluation of both vendors and buyers.
3. Reduction of clerical effort.
4. Ability to handle a variety of types of purchase orders.

Manufacturing and Material Control

The revised quarterly sales plan, received each month from the executive committee, provides the basic input from which the manufacturing and material control department plan and schedule the production portion of International Medical Supply, Inc. Manufacturing and material control work closely with marketing and the warehouse in monitoring the level of finished goods inventory. They work together with research and engineering in maintaining files of product specifications and the engineering bill of materials system. The major job in this department is translating the revised quarterly sales plan into a production schedule and determining what raw materials must be brought into inventories in order to support this schedule. Some 1860 components and parts make up the 68 items of equipment produced. Of these 1860 parts about 80% are purchased for direct assembly, while the remaining components are manufactured from raw materials at the Stoughton plant. Additionally, the company manufactures about 250 items of disposable laboratory supplies and purchases for resale another 250 to 300. Manufacturing is not concerned with the resale items.

The company has one manufacturing plant. This facility, at Stoughton, where all products are manufactured and assembled, is a modern production plant of 185,000 square feet. It could readily be increased to 225,000 square feet if demand for products created the need for additional capacity. A three-line capacity was built into the plant in anticipation of future manufacturing requirements, but only one line has been equipped and used.

The process of producing a piece of laboratory equipment is primarily a job-shop-type process. Parts are produced in three manufacturing shops and sent to shop stores in the assembly shop where purchased material is sent. There the assembly of the equipment takes place. Because of the sophisticated nature of the equipment and the large number of parts involved, there is a scheduling difficulty involved in assuring that the right number of parts are ready for assembly at the same time.

Except for custom-designed units, almost all the company's products are manufactured for inventory. The procedure of manufacturing for inventory has been the subject of constant debate between marketing and manufacturing personnel. Because of the high cost of the items and the inability to forecast sales accurately, the manufacturing group hesitated to produce for finished goods inventory that might never sell, but the sales force wanted the full line of products on hand for immediate delivery to customers.

Inventory was categorized as follows:

1. Shop stores: parts that had been purchased for production of standard products.
2. Work-in-process inventory: material and labor already expended against preplanned and project stock.
3. Finished goods inventory: completed standard products ready for sale or in fulfillment of customer orders.
   Note: General and administrative expenses were recorded and applied to inventory production costs.

Costs of producing standard products were recorded on a material-cost card and a payroll report. Each of these forms was prepared daily; i.e., materials drawn from stock and the transactions were recorded by the stock clerk on a material-cost card. Labor-hours were recorded on the payroll report by the accounting department as the time cards were collected each day.

When a particular unit or lot of units was completed, the total costs were computed and then compared with historical cost data that had been collected in the past for the production of the same units.

Production problems and production cost data problems arose when custom-designed units entered into the production process. The manufacture of custom-designed units specially produced rather than produced for inventory, caused production and assembly difficulties because their utilization of engineering, supervisory, and production personnel talents interrupted the producing-for-inventory process. Not only did these custom-designed and manufactured products require the services of various personnel normally involved in the standard production process, but they also caused an interruption of the use of production-line equipment, machinery, and materials. Quite often the costs of producing the custom units were in part unrecorded or charged against products manufactured for inventory. Basically, cost data were to be recorded in the same manner as standard inventory products, but because of the uncertainty and inaccuracy of machine time, personnel hours, and material allocation, it was difficult to determine the accuracy of the production costs of special or custom units under the current system.

In discussing the problems of manufacturing and material control with John Rogers, it appeared to Bill King that the difficulties lay not in production scheduling and control but in the materials subsystems. Both of these (engineering bill of materials and material status system) were being increasingly questioned. It was felt that a major redesign might be necessary because neither system was adequately doing the job. Problems were attributed to increasing product complexity. This, in turn, increased purchasing lead time. Moreover, the system was beginning to stagger under an increasing manufacturing volume. Accordingly, Bill King decided to place his initial emphasis on the material subsystems.

Both were punched card systems that had not been converted to the new IBM System/3.

Engineering Bill of Materials System

The original system had been designed in 1967 by Jim Blackwell, director of research and engineering, and his department controlled its operation. The design and operation was largely unchanged from the EAM "batch" system of 1967.

When a new product is developed or an existing one changed significantly, the material parts requirements are exploded into "engineering bills of materials." These are entered into the system by key punching the list of parts, assemblies, and raw materials that make up the item to be produced. The format of the list shows what items, subassemblies, and components are assembled together to create the next higher level of product assembly, as shown below:

Item Number	Item Name	Item Number of Next Higher Level
Subitem number	Subitem name	Quantity required
" "	" "	" "
" "	" "	" "
etc.	etc.	etc
etc.	etc.	etc.

Modifications are entered through an engineering change notice (ECN). This document is used to make changes on some item in the bill of materials master file. These are also keypunched and used as input to a computer file maintenance run, which updates that master file and also prints a detailed listing of the ECN list—a list of items entered through the ECN process. Updating is accomplished approximately once a month except when a new product or major modification is introduced.

The major purpose of the bill of materials master file is to provide manufacturing with the parts requirements for any production run or for any product engineering change. Therefore, parts requirements listings are initiated by two sources:

1. A sales plan (schedule of items being ordered for production):

Item Name	Item Number	Quantity Desired	Date Desired

2. Product engineering change:

Item Name	Item Number	Revision Code

The output of the system is the parts requirements list—those parts needed to produce the sales plan. The output is generated from the master bill of materials file by selecting those items to be produced and multiplying the unit parts requirements by the quantities of items on the sales plan. Hence,

Part Number	Part Name	Source Assembly Number	Quantity
"	"	"	"
"	"	"	"
etc.	etc.	etc.	etc.

A flow chart of the system is shown in Exhibit 7.

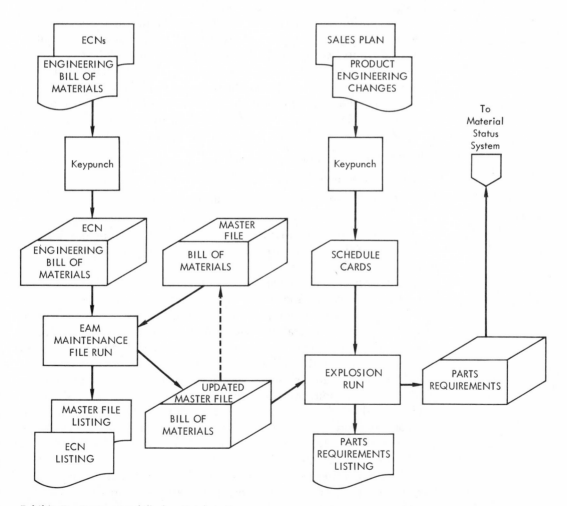

Exhibit 7 Engineering bill of materials system.

Material Status System

The two main purposes of this system are to generate an unordered requirements listing for input to the purchasing system and to provide a materials status and history report for use as follow-up and status information.

Each week, and more frequently in pressing situations, a computer parts requirement run is made to develop the new or changed parts requirements that have developed from the bill of materials system. This run uses the parts requirements file of the bill of materials system and material status file to create a purchase requirements list. This list is then used by the material ordering section to prepare requisitions for purchasing.

In addition to the requisitions for purchasing, material ordering personnel also manually prepare a material order card that is subsequently keypunched for purposes of preparing material status cards. These are used as input to the daily computer material status run. This run merges the status cards with the materials status file to produce the updated material status file and the materials status and history report. The file, and hence the report, is also changed from these events:

1. Release of purchase order to vendor.
2. Receipt of materials in receiving.
3. Material passed into the stockroom from inspection.

The computer requirements run is made weekly to develop the new or changed parts requirements that have been developed from the bill of materials system.

A flow chart of the system is shown in Exhibit 8.

After completing the initial survey of the material status system, Bill King made an appointment to see John Rogers, vice president of manufacturing and operations. He wanted to get the views of Rogers concerning any problems that existed in the materials status system. As usual, Rogers was candid and somewhat blunt.

"Sure, we've got problems, and I can tell you that most of them result from operations over in engineering. How the hell can I keep any kind of production line going when those guys change their minds so often on engineering specifications? Remember that an engineering change has a multiplier effect—on parts requirements, on purchasing, and on production. I say keep the changes down.

"I'm not trying to duck the blame, either. In materials control we have been remiss in not setting order quantities—or to put it another way, we don't always have the material on the production floor when

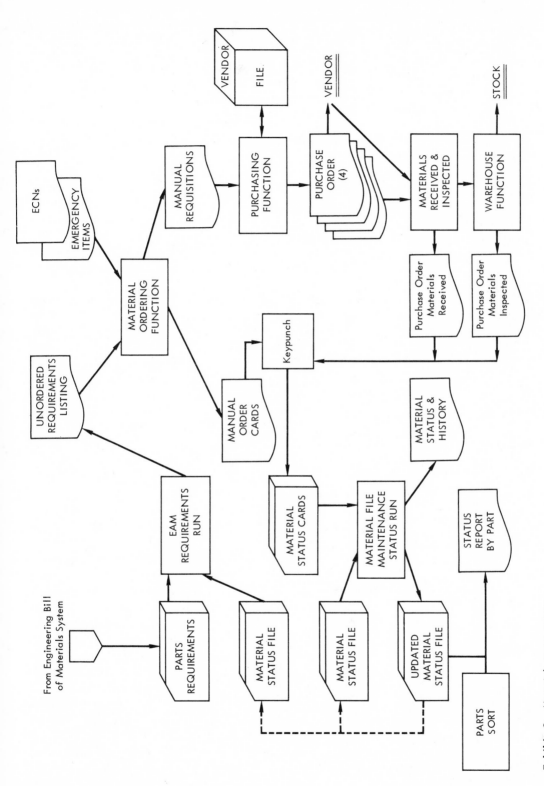

Exhibit 8 Materials status system.

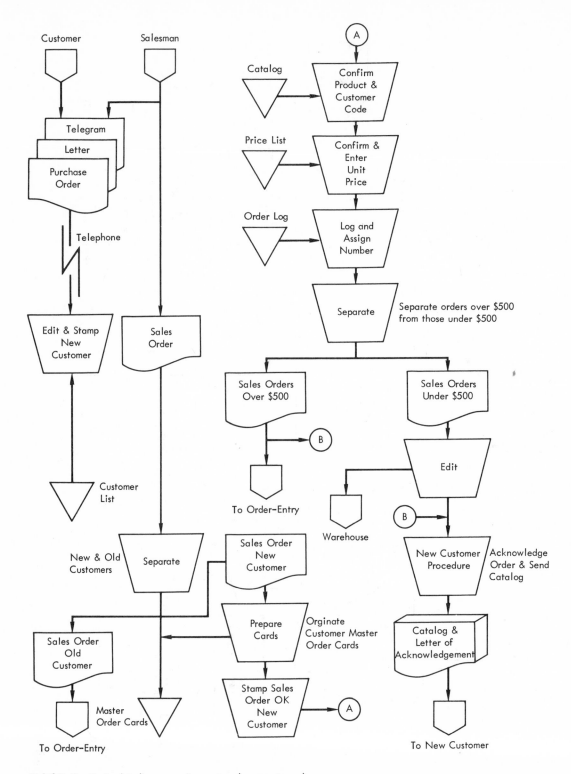

Exhibit 9 Revised order-processing system (new customer).

it's needed. Did you ever see a line close down for lack of a two-dollar part? I say let's invest in more raw materials inventory so the materials tail won't be wagging the production dog."

Bill King thanked Rogers and promised to investigate his suggestions. However, he did not agree with Rogers that the entire problem lay with engineering and materials control. Instead of identifying the specific problem and its causes, he decided to start with objectives and work from there. He therefore wrote down the following objectives for the materials status system:

1. Identify and order long lead-time items in the early stages of requirements determination.
2. Reduce the existing clerical work load by paper-work automation to the extent practicable.
3. Provide a system of quick, accurate follow-up and status reporting.
4. Provide whatever controls are needed to ensure that all required items are ordered; conversely, ensure that items are not duplicated.

BILL KING'S APPROACH

After conducting the foregoing interviews and performing his preliminary analysis, Bill King was at a loss on how to proceed with Bemis' instruction to "come up with a master plan in four or five weeks." He was not only becoming more confused by the day but was beginning to be overwhelmed by the magnitude of the tasks involved.

King's conviction, as he had been taught in business school, was that management information systems should be designed for decision making. Yet everyone in International Medical Instruments, Inc., seemed to focus their attention on the clerical nature of data processing—keeping the records. Moreover, there seemed to be little concern with production planning and control, a function that absorbed over half of the sales dollar.

King concluded that for the immediate future he should concentrate on three aspects of the overall problem:

1. *Order processing.* Because this system had been the one that was blamed for the loss of the $60,000 order, and because Dobrynski had ordered a review of it, the obvious first choice for redesign was this system. Frank Bemis was unwilling, or unable, to give King any guidance. His concluding comment was, "You've got the ball, now run with it. Don't bother me with details."

King decided that because the entire problem had been precipitated by new-customer orders he should concentrate on the processing of orders for new customers. A second consideration would be the dollar amount of the orders. He decided on his own authority that the credit check of new customers would be eliminated or minimized for orders less than $500. In addition, *all* new customers should receive a letter of acknowledgment accompanied by a company catalog.

For purposes of discussion and review he constructed the flow chart shown in Exhibit 9.

2. *Master plan.* No attempt had been made to design according to any master plan. Consequently, the company had a number of unrelated mechanized subsystems, which had "grown up" over the years. Privately, King labeled these a "patchwork" approach or "islands of mechanization." He began work on the master plan with misgivings. He suspected that the implementation of such a plan would take years, and he doubted that the company would want to allocate the resources to it. Nevertheless, he prepared an outline of a master plan (Exhibit 10) and an integrating information chart (Exhibit 11) for presentation to Frank Bemis.

Exhibit 10   Master plan of overall information flow.

Major Application	Responsible Department	Other Systems Inputs	Outputs to Other Systems
Order entry	Sales	Customer orders	Open orders
Open orders	Sales	Order entry Customer file Finished goods inventory	Marketing analysis Shipping & invoicing Finished goods inventory Customer file
Customer file	Sales	Open orders Accounts receivable	Open orders Shipping & invoicing
Sales analysis	Sales	Open orders Shipping & invoicing	Sales analysis reports Demand forecast Production scheduling
Shipping and invoicing	Sales	Customer file Open orders Finished goods inventory	Accounts receivable Sales analysis Customer invoice

Major Application	Responsible Department	Other Systems Inputs	Outputs to Other Systems
Finished goods inventory	Sales Controller Manufacturing	Open orders Transactions Accounts payable Production schedule & inventory status	Open orders Shipping and invoicing Production schedule & inventory status
Engineering bill of materials	Manufacturing	Parts list Shop floor control Production schedule & inventory status	Shop floor control Production schedule & inventory status
Production schedule & inventory status	Manufacturing	Production schedule Finished goods inventory Bill of materials Shop floor control Purchasing & receiving	Production schedule Finished goods inventory Bill of materials Shop floor control Purchasing & receiving
Purchasing & receiving	Manufacturing	Production schedule & inventory status	Production schedule & inventory status Accounts payable
Shop floor control	Manufacturing	Bill of materials Production schedule Shop paper	Personnel & payroll Shop paper
Accounts payable	Controller	Purchasing & receiving	General ledger Finished goods inventory

Note: This plan does not show information reports or inputs and outputs to systems but rather the information flow between systems.

3. *Files and data base.* Lack of records and historical data made analysis of sales by customer, location, and profitability impossible. Further, if IMI had complete records of sales of original equipment, then projections and analysis of sales of spare parts could be carried out.

A central data base would make it possible for management to track key orders and keep customers informed of the status of their orders. Orders could be related to the purchase of materials, engineering work, and production planning if a central data base were established.

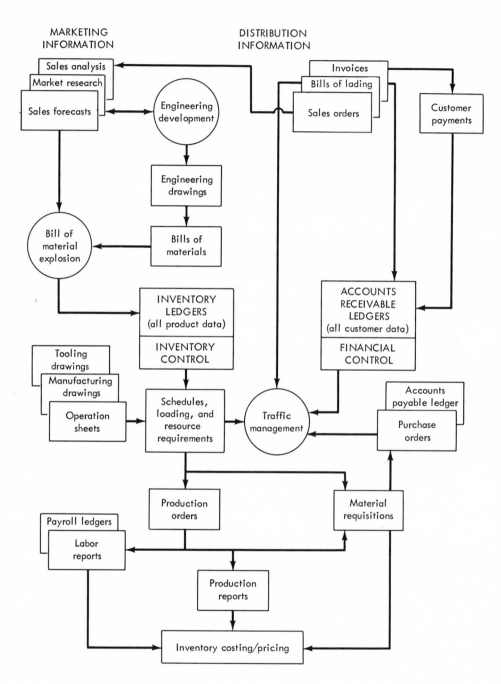

Exhibit 11   Integrating information flow chart.

QUESTIONS AND PROBLEMS

Chapter 1

1. Redesign the organization of IMI relating to MIS and its associated actitvities to give the MIS function a greater impact on IMI's operations.

2. Set up a table with headings across the top of System, Basic Goals, Elements, Inputs, and Outputs. Under the column, Systems, list Order Processing, Purchasing, Production Control, Engineering. Complete the table for these systems.

3. List each manager in the case, his position in the company, and his likely attitude towards a companywide MIS. Indicate one possible reason each manager might resist an MIS using the number associated with reason:

   1. Threat to status or ego

   2. Economic threat—fear of loss of job or downgrading of the job

   3. Dislike of changed personal relationships, breaking up of old work groups

   4. Fear of being unable to handle new complexity and dislike of further training

   5. Would have no reason to resist the MIS.

		Would Favor MIS		Possible Reason for
Manager	*Position*	*Yes*	*No*	*Resistance*

Chapter 2

1. Based upon Exhibit 10 of the IMI case and the coding below, complete the table below to show inputs and outputs of the systems.

   a. Accounts payable

   b. Accounts receivable

   c. Bill of materials and parts list

   d. Customer file

   e. Customer invoices

   f. Customer orders

   g. Demand forecast

   h. Finished goods inventory status

   i. Open orders

   j. Order entry

   k. Personnel and payroll records

   l. Production schedule and work-in-progress status

   m. Purchasing and receiving status

   n. Sales analysis reports

   o. Sales transactions

   p. Shipping and invoice documents

   q. Shop floor control

OUTPUTS FROM: \ INPUTS TO:	Sales Analysis	Order Processing	Finished Goods Inventory Control	Production and Scheduling	Billing	Purchasing and Receiving	
Sales Analysis	X						
Order Processing		X					
Finished Goods Inventory Control			X				
Production Scheduling				X			
Billing					X		
Purchasing and Receiving						X	

2. The systems approach requires identification of the needs of the users of the system. Relate the needs of the following managers for information from the systems listed by writing the numbers identifying the appropriate managers next to the systems.

   1. Dobrynski   a. Order processing _____
   2. Blackwell   b. Shipping _____
   3. Bemis   c. Strategic planning _____
   4. Katz   d. Engineering _____
   5. Rogers   e. Operations control _____
   6. King

3. Identify as part of (a) strategic plan, (b) operations plan, or (c) operating system.

   _____ Development of a new product by 1980
   _____ Order processing
   _____ Annual marketing budget
   _____ Flow of information for purchasing
   _____ King's proposal for the design of a total MIS, to be completed 5 years hence
   _____ Proposed procedure for improving the order processing
   _____ Opening of 5 new sales districts by Katz over the next six years
   _____ Shift of more resources to sales of replacement parts over the next five years
   _____ Production planning and control.

Chapter 3

1. Complete the following table:
   (a) IMI is organized on a (traditional) (systems) basis

   (b) The basis for departmentation at IMI is _____

   (c) Give span of management for
       Dobrynski _____
       Katz _____
       Rogers _____
       Bemis _____
       Blackwell _____

   (d) The number of levels of management at IMI is _____

   (e) IMI is a (tightly) (loosely) controlled company _____

   (f) A control device that Marketing introduced to reduce
       errors in processing orders is _____

2. For IMI, give a quantitative standard for control for each of the Key Performance Areas. If a specific standard is not mentioned in the case, propose one.

   KPA   *One Possible Control Standard*
   1. Profitability
   2. Market standing
   3. Productivity
   4. Innovation and product leadership
   5. Employee attitudes
   6. Public responsibility
   7. Use of resources
   8. Balance between short-range and
      long-range objectives

   (While specific standards such as dollars of income, ROI, or net income/sales are possible for KPA-1 above, the student may need to suggest an index and value of the index for items such as KPA-5, 6, 7, 8.)

3. a. Describe the feedback of information to management for the old order processing system. Explain why this did not work.
   b. Explain the feedback of information to management for the new system and why it *will* work.

Chapter 4

1. Give the objective, two inputs, and two possible outputs (reports) going to *management* for the following systems in IMI.

			Two Management
System	*Objective*	*Two Inputs*	*Reports as Outputs*
a. New product development			
b. Sales			
c. Purchasing			
d. Order processing			
e. Raw material control			
f. Production control			
g. Quality control			

    h. Billing

    i. Systems and procedures

    j. Data process programming and operations

2. In a well-managed company, the search for, and selection of new products to be introduced by the company involves people from several different functional areas within the company.

    Suppose that in IMI, both marketing or engineering personnel suggest new products. The suggestions are reviewed by the New Product Committee as the first screening. Those surviving are sent to Katz and Blackwell with a request for a preliminary market analysis and further engineering development.

    When these "quick and cheap" studies have been completed, the New Product Committee reviews them. Those that look promising are sent to a team of an industrial engineer and cost accountant to determine the cost of making such a product assuming normal engineering design and manufacturing improvements. If the cost appears good relative to the price assumptions made by marketing, the product is approved for final development and launching. Just before the product is launched on the market, it is reviewed once again.

    Draw a flow chart of this system. (You may show files required and possible computer participation if you wish to make this a major project.)

Chapter 5

1. Specific applications of the computer to improving profits in each of IMI's four basic sources of revenue are listed below. Match the application that appears to offer the greatest improvement in profit to each revenue source.

REVENUE SOURCE

_____ (1) Established line of electron microscopes and standard inventory products

_____ (2) High volume laboratory supplies

_____ (3) Sales of spare and replacement parts

_____ (4) Design and manufacture of specially engineered products

POSSIBLE APPLICATIONS OF THE COMPUTER

    a. Monthly sales forecasts

    b. Inventory control and demand forecasts

    c. Analysis of vendor prices to permit purchase of widely differing items at lowest cost

    d. Recording of sales, life of parts of products, and forecasting of spare parts demand

    e. Engineering and manufacturing cost analyses of products

2. For each major application of the computer that Bill King has listed in his Master Plan (Exhibit 10), describe briefly a possible report of information useful to a manager

in making, planning, organizing, or controlling decisions. Also identify the manager (or his title) who would use this report.

3. Give the function of each piece of computer hardware that IMI uses.

    Hardware   *Purpose*

   a. Keypunch
   b. Verifier
   c. Sorter
   d. Multifunction card unit
   e. CPU
   f. Disc storage drive
   g. Printer

4. Develop an alternative computer equipment configuration (list of hardware) that might serve IMI as well or better. (You might consult with students majoring in Computer Science or a salesman for companies such as NCR, Sperry Rand, Honeywell, or Control Data Corporation.)

Chapter 6

Exhibit 10 of the IMI Case shows Bill King's first concept of the information flow. He subsequently drew the schematic in Exhibit 11 to help visualize the relationships among activities and the flow of information. He is now ready to propose a plan with a schedule to management.

With the aid of Figure 6-2, prepare a simple list of tasks and subtasks (about 15-20) and completion dates if the start date is assumed to be January 2. (Dates will, of course, be very rough estimates because of the limited information in the case.)

Chapter 7

1. Bill King collaborated with Dobrynski to propose the reorganization of IMI as shown below.

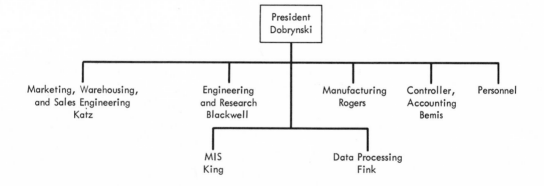

King wishes to identify the major subsystems in IMI, to determine who has responsibility for each, and to determine who participates in the operation of each. In order to do this, he sets up a table (matrix) as follows and checks off the responsibilities as:

✓   Responsible manager

X   Organization component participates in operation of the system

MANAGER / SYSTEM	President	Mgr. – Marketing	Mgr. – Engineering and Research	Mgr. – Manufacturing	Controller	Mgr. – Personnel	Mgr. – MIS	Mgr. – Data Processing
Order processing								
Raw materials inventory								
Finished goods inventory								
Production planning								
Capital budgeting								
Purchasing and receiving								
Shop floor schedule and control								
New product planning								
MIS								
Budgeting								
Cash flow								
Credit control								
Personal and nonpersonal product promotion								
Product research and design								
Quality assurance								
Strategic planning								

2. For the proposed IMI organization of Problem 1 above, check the problem areas associated with each manager as indicated by the Case.

Problem	President	Katz	Blackwell	Rogers	Bemis	Boffo	King	Fink
a. Lack of strategic planning								
b. Lack of unified sense of direction								
c. Failure to lead								
d. Failure to take a systems approach to his operation								
e. Narrow, limited, objectives								
f. Not qualified for job								
g. Failure to plan for better use of data processing								
h. Lacks understanding of MIS								
i. Failure to centralize common operations								
j. Cumbersome procedures. Lack of aggressive cooperation with other departments								
k. Poor inventory control								
l. Poor utilization of resources								

3.

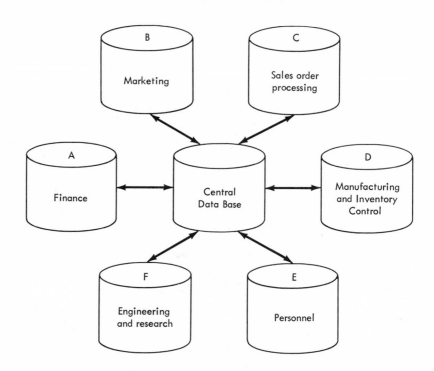

Indicate the files associated with each subsystem above.

1. Pricing	14. Production schedules	27. Financial plans
2. Billing	15. General ledger	28. Facility plans
3. Goods shipped	16. Design drawings	29. Cash flow
4. Budgets	17. Order entry	30. Material control
5. Quality control	18. Employee training	31. Customer service
6. Payroll	19. Shipping	32. Sales quotes
7. Receiving	20. Technical subcontracts	33. Wage & salary admin.
8. Purchasing	21. Capital assets	34. Promotional budgets
9. Employee benefits	22. Order filling	35. Cost accounting
10. Manpower inventory	23. Accounts payable	36. Parts lists
11. Sales forecasts	24. Accounts receivable	37. Drawing changes
12. Production plans	25. Back orders	38. Project plans
13. Sales analysis	26. Warehouse control	

A. _____ _____ _____ _____ _____ _____ _____ _____ _____

B. _____ _____ _____ _____ _____

C. _____ _____ _____ _____ _____ _____

D. _____ _____ _____ _____ _____ _____ _____ _____ _____

E. _____ _____ _____ _____

F. _____ _____ _____ _____ _____

Chapter 8

1. Check the sources of information which Bill King has utilized to develop his plan for an MIS.

   ( ) 1. Task force meetings
   ( ) 2. Personal interviews
   ( ) 3. Internal source documents
   ( ) 4. External source documents
   ( ) 5. Personal observation of operations and communications

2. Develop a form that IMI might use for:

   a. Purchase order
   b. Sales order
   c. Invoice and shipping form

3. For each of the following subsystems in IMI identify a possible specific report to management that is useful in managing the subsystem.

   Subsystem   *Possible Report*

   a. Resource subsystems
      (1) Human
      (2) Capital
      (3) Materials

   b. Phase subsystems
      (1) Forecasting
      (2) Processing of inputs
      (3) Financing
      (4) Costing
      (5) Human

4. Develop a detailed list of *periodic* reports that Dobrynski should receive and the frequency with which he should receive them.

Selected References

CHAPTER 1

BLUMENTHAL, SHERMAN C., *Management Information Systems*, Englewood Cliffs, N.J.: Prentice-Hall, Inc., 1969, Chap. 2, "An Information-Systems Perspective on the Corporation."

MURDICK, ROBERT G., AND JOEL E. ROSS, eds., *MIS in Action*, St. Paul: West Publishing Co., 1975, Part A, "The Scope of MIS."

PAYNE, EUGENE E., J. E. ROSS, AND R. G. MURDICK, *The Scope of Management Information Systems*, Norcross, Ga.: The American Institute of Industrial Engineers, 1975.

SCHREIBER, RALPH, "A Management Information System Overview," in Robert G. Murdick and Joel E. Ross, eds., *MIS in Action*, St. Paul: West Publishing Co., 1975.

SMALL, JOHN T., AND WILLIAM B. LEE, "In Search of an MIS," *MSU Business Topics*, Autumn 1975, pp. 47–55.

SMITH, AUGUST WILLIAM, "Towards a Systems Theory of the Firm," *Journal of Systems Management*, Feb. 1971, pp. 10–12.

SPIRO, BRUCE E., "What's a Management Information System?," *Data Management*, Sept. 1971, pp. 48–51.

WILKINSON, JOSEPH W., "Classifying Information Systems," *Journal of Systems Management*, April 1973, pp. 28–31.

CHAPTER 2

CLELAND, DAVID I., AND WILLIAM R. KING, "Competitive Business Intelligence Systems," *Business Horizons*, Dec. 1975, pp. 19–28.

HOFER, CHARLES W., "Emerging EDP Pattern," *Harvard Business Review*, March–April 1970, pp. 16–22, 26–31, 169–171.

KASHYAP, R. N., "Management Information Systems for Corporate Planning and Control," *Long Range Planning*, June 1972, pp. 25–31.

KING, WILLIAM R., AND DAVID I. CLELAND, "Decision and Information Systems for Strategic Planning," *Business Horizons*, April 1973, pp. 29–36.

MACE, MYLES L., ed., "Management Information Systems for Directors," *Harvard Business Review*, Nov.–Dec. 1975, pp. 14–18, 22–24, 166–167.

ZANI, WILLIAM M., "Blueprint for MIS," *Harvard Business Review*, Nov.–Dec. 1970, pp. 95–100.

CHAPTER 3

ADAMS, JAMES, "Understanding Adaptive Control," *Automation*, March 1970, pp. 108–13.

DRUCKER, PETER, "New Templates for Today's Organization," *Harvard Business Review*, Jan.–Feb. 1974, pp. 45–53.

FIELD, JOHN E., "Toward a Multi-level, Multi-goal Information System," *The Accounting Review*, July 1969, pp. 593–599.

KAST, FREMONT E., AND JAMES E. ROSENZWEIG, *Organization and Management: A Systems Approach*, McGraw-Hill Book Company, 1970.

MURDICK, ROBERT G., "Managerial Control: Concepts and Practice," *Advanced Management Journal*, Jan. 1970, pp. 48–52.

OPTNER, STANFORD L., *Systems Analysis for Business and Industrial Problem Solving*, Englewood Cliffs, N.J.: Prentice-Hall, Inc., 1965.

PELHAM, ROGER O., "Putting Information Systems into the Company Control Structure," *Data Processing Magazine*, July 1970, pp. 23–26.

CHAPTER 4

ANAUD, HARI, "A Computer-Based Hospital Information System," *Hospital Administration*, Sept. 1971.

Communications Oriented Production and Information Control System, Vols. I through VIII, IBM, Inc., 1972.

COMSTOCK, ROGER W., "MIS in Higher Education," *Management Controls* (Peat, Marwick, Mitchell & Co.), Sept. 1970.

Control System, Vols. I through VIII, IBM, Inc., 1972.

ERDMAN, ILARAE, AND ROBERT A. FLECK, JR., "Information: A Bank's Biggest Asset," *Data Management*, Jan. 1976, pp. 30–35.

HOLSTEIN, WILLIAM K., "Production Planning and Control Integrated," *Harvard Business Review*, May–June 1968, pp. 121–140.

Hospital Financial Management System Concepts, IBM, Inc., 1975.

MONTGOMERY, DAVID B., AND GLEN L. URBAN, "Marketing Decision-Information Systems: An Emerging View," *Journal of Marketing Research*, May 1970, pp. 226–234.

MURDICK, ROBERT G., AND JOEL E. ROSS, eds., *MIS in Action*, St. Paul: West Publishing Co., 1975.

NEEDLES, BELVERD, JR., "A Single Information Flow for Hospital Data Processing," *Management Services*, Sept.–Oct. 1969, pp. 27–37.

TOMESKI, EDWARD A., AND HAROLD LAZARUS, "The Computer and the Personnel Department," *Business Horizons*, June 1973, pp. 61–66.

CHAPTER 5

BURCH, JOHN G., JR., AND FELIX R. STRATER, JR., *Information Systems: Theory and Practice*, Santa Barbara, Cal.: (Div. of Wiley) Hamilton Publishing Company, 1974.

BURNETT, GERALD R., AND RICHARD L. NOLAN, "At Last, Major Roles for Minicomputers," *Harvard Business Review*, May–June 1975, pp. 148–156.

FORD, KENNETH W., "About Communications Processors," *Infosystems*, Feb. 1973, pp. 46, 47, 88, 89.

HAMMER, CARL, "Telecommunications," *Data Management*, April 1974, pp. 12–17.

JOSLIN, EDWARD O., "Management Roles in Computer Acquisition," *Data Management*, Sept. 1975, pp. 50–53.

KANTER, JEROME, *Management Guide to Computer Systems Selection and Use*, Englewood Cliffs, N.J.: Prentice-Hall, Inc., 1970.

KINDRED, ALTON R., *Data Systems and Management*, Englewood Cliffs, N.J.: Prentice-Hall, Inc., 1973.

"1975 Product Review," *Infosystems*, Dec. 1975, pp. 32–60.

CHAPTER 6

GUNDERMAN, JAMES R., AND FRANK W. McMURRY, "Making Project Management Effective," *Journal of Systems Management*, Feb. 1975, pp. 7–11.

METZGER, PHILIP W., *Managing a Programming Project*, Englewood Cliffs, N.J.: Prentice-Hall, Inc., 1973.

MURDICK, ROBERT G., "MIS Development Procedures," *Journal of Systems Management*, Dec. 1970, pp. 22–26.

PIERCE, RICHARD F., "Managing an Information Systems Activity," *Management Accounting*, Sept. 1968, pp. 23–28.

SELIG, GAD J., "Planning New Applications of Management Information Systems," *Industrial Engineering*, June 1972, pp. 19–23.

SIEGEL, PAUL, *Strategic Planning of Management Information Systems*, New York: Petrocelli Books, 1975.

SHAYS, E. MICHAEL, "The MSP: A Master Plan for Systems Design and Development," *Data Management*, Nov. 1971, pp. 17–23.

THOMPSON, LLOYD A., "Effective Planning and Control of the Systems Effort," *Journal of Systems Management,* July 1969, pp. 32–35.

WILLOUGHBY, THEODORE C., "Origins of Systems Projects," *Journal of Systems Management,* Oct. 1975, pp. 19–26.

CHAPTER 7

BERENSON, CONRAD, "Marketing Information Systems," *Journal of Marketing,* Oct. 1969, pp. 16–23.

BLUMENTHAL, SHERMAN C., *Management Information Systems: A Framework for Planning and Development,* Englewood Cliffs, N.J.: Prentice-Hall, Inc., 1969.

BURCH, JOHN G., JR., AND FELIX R. STRATER, JR., *Information Systems: Theory and Practice,* Santa Barbara, Cal.: Hamilton Publishing Company, 1974, Chaps. 10 and 11.

COLLARD, ALBERT F., "Sharpening Interviewing Techniques," *Journal of Systems Management,* Dec. 1975, pp. 6–10.

COUGER, J. DANIEL, AND LAWRENCE M. WERGIN, "Small Company MIS," *Infosystems,* Oct. 1974, pp. 30–33.

GLANS, THOMAS B., *et al., Management Systems,* New York: Holt, Rinehard and Winston, Inc., 1968.

TESTA, CHARLES J., AND SHELDON J. LAUBE, "How Do You Choose a Data Base Management System? Carefully!" *Infosystems,* Jan. 1975, pp. 36–39.

WILKENSON, JOSEPH W., "Specifying Management's Information Needs," *Cost and Management,* Sept.–Oct. 1974.

CHAPTER 8

BURCH, JOHN G., JR., AND FELIX R. STRATER, JR., *Information Systems: Theory and Practice,* Santa Barbara, Cal.: Hamilton Publishing Company, 1974.

CHOW, JOHN V., "What You Need to Know About DBMS," *Journal of Systems Management,* May (pp. 22–27) and June (pp. 28–35), 1975.

ENGBERG, ROBERT E., AND ROGER L. MOORE, "A Corporate Planning Model for a Construction Materials Producer," *Management Adviser,* Jan.–Feb. 1974, pp. 43–51.

HARTMAN, W., H. MATTHES, AND A. PROEME, *Management Information Systems Management,* May (pp. 22–27) and June (pp. 28–35), 1975.

JENNY, JOHN A., "The Crucial Element in Effective Computer Utilization Is Man-Machine Interaction," *Automation,* May 1973, pp. 72–76.

KINDRED, ALTON R., *Data Systems and Management,* Englewood Cliffs, N.J.: Prentice-Hall, Inc., 1973.

NOLAN, RICHARD L., "Computer Data Bases: The Future Is Now," *Harvard Business Review,* Sept.–Oct. 1973, pp. 98–114.

STULTS, FRED C., "Data, Information, and Decision Making," *Journal of Systems Management*, June 1971, pp. 22–27.

TURN, REIN, "Cost Implications of Privacy Protection in Data Bank Systems," *Data Base*, Spring 1975, pp. 3–9.

VOICH, DAN, JR., HOMER J. MOTTICE, AND WILLIAM A. SCHRODE, *Information Systems for Operations and Management*, Cincinnati: South-Western Publishing Co., 1975.

WEISSMAN, CLARK, "Trade-off Considerations in Security Design," *Data Management*, April 1972, pp. 14–19.

CHAPTER 9

BARNETT, JOSEPH I., "How To Install a Management Information and Control System," *Systems Procedures Journal*, Sept.–Oct. 1966.

BURCH, JOHN G., JR., AND FELIX R. STRATER, JR., *Information Systems: Theory and Practice*, Santa Barbara, Cal.: Hamilton Publishing Company, 1974.

CAMPANELLA, JOSEPH J., AND HAROLD E. FEARON, "An Integrated Computer Materials Management System," *Journal of Purchasing*, Aug. 1970, pp. 5–27.

DUFF, IAN, AND MALCOLM HENRY, "Computer-Aided Management: A Case Study," *Management Decision*, Winter 1971, pp. 204–12.

HARTMAN, W. H. MATTHES, AND A. PROEME, *Management Information Systems Handbook*, New York: McGraw-Hill Book Company, 1968.

JOSLIN, EDWARD O., "Costing the System Design Alternatives," *Data Management*, April 1971, pp. 23–27.

KINDRED, ALTON R., *Data Systems and Management*, Englewood Cliffs, N.J.: Prentice-Hall, Inc., 1973.

MURDICK, ROBERT G., AND JOEL E. ROSS, *Information Systems for Modern Management*, 2nd ed., Englewood Cliffs, N.J.: Prentice-Hall, Inc., 1975.

RAUSEO, MICHAEL J., "How to Develop a Master Plan for Systems Analyst Training," *Training and Development Journal*, March 1971, pp. 26–30.

THORNE, JACK F., "Critical Factors in the Implementation of a Real-Time System," *Data Management*, Jan. 1972, pp. 36–40.

VOICH, DAN, JR., HOMER J. MOTTICE, AND WILLIAM A. SCHRODE, *Information Systems for Operations and Management*, Cincinnati: South-Western Publishing Company, 1975.

Index